21 世纪国际商务教材教辅系列

编写委员会

21世纪国际商务教材教辅系列

中国商业联合会国际商务单证员
专业技能证书培训考评指定教材

总 主 编　余世明
副总主编　袁绍岐　张彬祥　何　静

Pre-service of International Business

国际商务岗前实训

余世明　冼燕华　编著

暨南大学出版社
JINAN UNIVERSITY PRESS
中国·广州

图书在版编目（CIP）数据

国际商务岗前实训/余世明，冼燕华编著. —广州：暨南大学出版社，2023.12
（21 世纪国际商务教材教辅系列）
ISBN 978-7-5668-3815-5

Ⅰ.①国…　Ⅱ.①余…②冼…　Ⅲ.①国际商务—岗前培训—教材　Ⅳ.①F740

中国国家版本馆 CIP 数据核字（2023）第 228711 号

国际商务岗前实训
GUOJI SHANGWU GANGQIAN SHIXUN
编著者：余世明　冼燕华

出 版 人：阳　翼
策划编辑：武艳飞
责任编辑：陈俞潼
责任校对：苏　洁　王燕丽
责任印制：周一丹　郑玉婷

出版发行：暨南大学出版社（511443）
电　　话：总编室（8620）37332601
营销部（8620）37332680　37332681　37332682　37332683
传　　真：（8620）37332660（办公室）　37332684（营销部）
网　　址：http：//www. jnupress. com
排　　版：广州市新晨文化发展有限公司
印　　刷：佛山市浩文彩色印刷有限公司
开　　本：787mm×1092mm　1/16
印　　张：14
字　　数：328 千
版　　次：2023 年 12 月第 1 版
印　　次：2023 年 12 月第 1 次
定　　价：46.00 元

目　录

编写说明

为了更好地适应现代职业教育的发展和要求，加强实践性教学，提高学生的专业操作技能，使国际商务专业的学生经过各门专业理论知识的学习和专业技能的训练后，能通过校内岗前实训，将国际商务专业各课程的理论知识和专业技能综合运用起来；同时，作为学生到企业上岗实习前的综合练兵，检验学生综合分析能力和操作能力的高低，毕业后能尽快地适应工作需要，编著者编写了这本《国际商务岗前实训》教材。

本实训教材是编著者根据多年的教学经验和公司的实践调研经验，以出口公司实际操作规程为准则，以国际商务专业的教材为基础，以完整的出口业务为内容，以学生直接参与业务当事人角色的方式编写而成。本书全部训练内容来自出口公司的实际案例，并对部分资料稍作修改，其内容全面完整，实际操作性强。

本书可作为国际商务专业和其他涉外经贸专业综合实训的教材，也可作为培训国际商务基础知识的教材以及有志于从事国际商务的人员的参考书。

国际商务专业依据出口公司实际案例编写的实训教材比较少，本书是编著者在校内多年使用的《对外贸易业务模拟实习指导书》《国际商务模拟实习教程》基础上编写而成的。在编写中，得到了很多外贸公司的支持和帮助，参考了大量的教材，引用了外贸公司的大量材料，特别是原广东省轻工家电公司业务部经理余镇强对本书的编写提供了很多实际案例，同时提出了很多宝贵意见，在此谨向有关作者和公司的经理、业务员和单证员表示衷心的感谢！由于水平有限，书中定有不少疏漏和不妥之处，诚恳欢迎老师和同学们提出批评意见。

编著者

2023 年 3 月

岗前实训背景材料

一、卖方和买方

（一）卖方

中文名称：广东中山威威照明有限公司
英文名称：GUANGDONG ZHONGSHAN WEIWEI LIGHTING CO.，LTD.
地址：中山翠华路52号（52，CUIHUA ROAD，ZHONGSHAN，CHINA）
业务员：张大同
电子邮箱：234 * * 56123@qq.com

（二）买方

中文名称：法国巴黎Le Vernet贸易有限公司
英文名称：Le Vernet TRADE COMPANY LIMITED，PARIS FRANCE
地址：法国巴黎福煦大街245号（245 Avenue Foch，PARIS FRANCE）
业务员：PIERRE先生
电子邮箱：567 * * 56789@qq.com

二、购销意图

广东中山威威照明有限公司主要从事家用照明设备的设计、生产和国内外销售业务。业务员张大同主要经营对欧美国家的灯具、灯饰出口。通过2021年中国进出口商品交易会，张大同认识了法国巴黎Le Vernet贸易有限公司的PIERRE先生，从此建立了联系。PIERRE先生来函询问LED球泡灯的价格，张大同有意以此为突破口，拓展在巴黎的业务。

法国巴黎Le Vernet贸易有限公司是法国家用电器经销商，拥有比较广泛的营销网络，PIERRE先生通过交易会了解到，广东中山威威照明有限公司的家用电器物美价廉，有意发展中国电器产品在法国巴黎的业务。特别是威威牌节能灯，从款式、质量和价格来看，在法国巴黎都比较有竞争力，于是主动联系广东中山威威照明有限公司的张大同先生。

三、商品介绍

商品介绍表

商品裸装图片	商品销售包装图片	商品运输包装图片

货名：威威牌 LED 球泡灯（Weiwei Brand LED Bulb）

规格及收购价（包含 17% 增值税）：

LY－5W－A50　110V 5W　E27/B22　￥2.00/只

LY－5W－A60　110V 7W　E27/B22　￥2.50/只

商品编码：94054090

纸箱规格：63 厘米×32 厘米×24 厘米

净重：每箱 2.4 千克

毛重：每箱 4.5 千克

包装：每 100 只装 1 纸箱，每 1 个 20 英尺集装箱可装 580 纸箱，每 1 个 40 英尺集装箱可装 1 400 纸箱

四、其他

（一）运杂费（拖车费、报关费、码头费）

拖车费、报关费、码头费合计表

工厂所在地	规格	
	40′柜	20′柜
广州	￥1 800	￥1 550
顺德	￥2 200	￥1 750
中山	￥3 200	￥2 500
佛山	￥2 800	￥2 000

注：(1) 以上费用为工厂所在地拖至广州黄埔港装运的费用。

(2) 以上规格的集装箱是指普通集装箱。

（二）公司办公费用

按外汇净收入中每 1 美元扣 0.30 元人民币计算

（三）汇率

100 美元 =687.78 ~689.88 元人民币

（四）保险费率

货物海洋运输保险费表

<table>
<tr><th rowspan="2">洲别</th><th rowspan="2">目的地</th><th colspan="3">险别</th></tr>
<tr><th>平安险
F. P. A</th><th>水渍险
W. A</th><th>一切险
A. R</th></tr>
<tr><td rowspan="6">亚洲</td><td>中国香港、中国澳门、日本</td><td>0.18</td><td>0.22</td><td>0.33</td></tr>
<tr><td>新加坡、马来西亚、约旦、巴基斯坦、菲律宾、巴林、阿拉伯联合酋长国</td><td rowspan="5">0.25</td><td rowspan="5">0.30</td><td>1.00</td></tr>
<tr><td>印度</td><td>1.50</td></tr>
<tr><td>尼泊尔、阿富汗</td><td>2.50</td></tr>
<tr><td>南、北也门</td><td>3.50</td></tr>
<tr><td>其他</td><td>0.60</td></tr>
<tr><td rowspan="2">欧洲、美洲、大洋洲</td><td>法国、英国、意大利、葡萄牙、法国巴黎</td><td rowspan="2">0.25</td><td rowspan="2">0.30</td><td>1.60</td></tr>
<tr><td>美国、加拿大、大洋洲、欧洲</td><td>1.50</td></tr>
<tr><td colspan="2">中 、南美洲</td><td>0.25</td><td>0.35</td><td>2.50</td></tr>
<tr><td rowspan="3">非洲</td><td>刚果、毛里求斯、贝宁、安哥拉、卢旺达</td><td rowspan="3">0.30</td><td rowspan="3">0.40</td><td>3.50</td></tr>
<tr><td>尼日利亚、利比里亚、乌干达</td><td>5.00</td></tr>
<tr><td>其他</td><td>2.00</td></tr>
</table>

（五）运价表

运价表

（单位：美元）

航线	港口	中译名	国家/地区	20′柜	40′柜
欧洲	LE HAVRE	勒阿弗尔	法国	2 688	3 850
	AMSIERDAM	阿姆斯特丹	荷兰	2 350	3 400
	STOCKHOLM	斯德哥尔摩	瑞典	2 350	3 530
	LIVERPOOL	利物浦	英国	2 550	3 640
	MANCHESTER	曼彻斯特	英国	2 550	3 640
	OSLO	奥斯陆	挪威	2 380	3 600
	ISTANBUL	伊斯坦布尔	土耳其	2 650	4 150
	GOTHENBURG	哥德堡	瑞典	2 250	3 300
	LONDON	伦敦	英国	2 500	3 520
	DUBLIN	都柏林	爱尔兰	2 770	4 000
	HAMBURG	汉堡	德国	2 160	3 200
	ROTTERDAM	鹿特丹	荷兰	2 160	3 200
地中海	LA SPEZIA	拉斯佩齐亚	意大利	2 280	3 400
	PORT SAID	塞得港	埃及	2 650	4 150
	THESSALONIKI	塞色勒狄克	希腊	2 680	4 180
	LATTAKIA	拉塔基亚	叙利亚	2 650	4 150
	CEUTA	休达	西班牙	4 100	6 050
日本	YOKOHAMA	横滨	日本	880	1 280
	TOKYO	东京	日本	880	1 280
	OSAKA	大阪	日本	880	1 280
	NAGASAKI	长崎	日本	880	1 280
	MOJI	门司	日本	880	1 280
东南亚	SINGAPORE	新加坡	新加坡	750	1 300
	MANILA	马尼拉	菲律宾	750	1 300
	KOTA KINABALU	亚庇	马来西亚	2 400	3 480
中国台湾	JILONG	基隆	中国台湾	630	1 050
波斯湾	SHARJAH	沙加	阿联酋	2 280	3 350
	DUBAI	迪拜	阿联酋	2 070	3 020
	KUWAIT	科威特	科威特	2 280	3 350

（续上表）

航线	港口	中译名	国家/地区	20′柜	40′柜
韩国	BUSAN	釜山	韩国	750	1 280
美国	LOS ANGELES	洛杉矶	美国	2 200	2 850
	NEW YORK	纽约	美国	2 660	2 980
加拿大	VANCOUVER	温哥华	加拿大	2 220	2 500
	TORONTO	多伦多	加拿大	2 780	4 480
	MONTREAL	蒙特利尔	加拿大	2 780	4 480
澳大利亚	SYDNEY	悉尼	澳大利亚	1 880	2 850

注：该运价属 CY 价，不包括码头费及拖柜去仓库、工厂的费用。

（六）银行国际结算业务收费

银行国际结算业务收费费率表

（单位：元人民币）

业务项目		费率/费额	最低	最高	备注
一、跟单信用证					
1. 通知/转递费		200			
2. 修改/预通知/注销费		100			
3. 议付费/验单费		0.125%	200		
4. 保兑费		0.2%	300		每三个月收取一次，不足三个月按三个月计算，不另收通知费
5. 转让费	信用证条款不变	300			
	信用证条款改变	0.1%	300	1 000	
6. 付款费		0.15%	200		付款信用证
二、跟单托收					
1. 跟单托收手续费		0.1%	100	2 000	
2. 免付款交单手续费		100			
3. 退单费		100			
三、光票托收					
1. 手续费		0.1%	20	1 000	
2. 退票费		50			
3. 收益人退汇/转汇		0.1%	50	1 000	按汇出汇款业务收费

实训模块一　函电往来

一、实训目的

通过本模块的实训，使学生掌握交易磋商中函电往来中各基本环节（如建立业务关系、报盘、还盘、接受等）的英文信函表达。学生能根据提供的资料，采用正确的信函格式拟出英文信函，并通过电子邮件发送。

二、实训任务

（1）掌握撰写商务英文信函的格式、步骤和技巧。

（2）根据提供的资料译写信函，要求清楚、准确，并符合英文用法和外贸习惯。

三、实训提示

在交易磋商中的英文函电一般包括建立业务关系、询盘、报盘、还盘、成交等环节，在书写过程中要遵循“清楚、简洁、礼貌”等基本要点。

（一）建立业务关系（ESTABLISHING BUSINESS RELATIONS）

1. 写信要点

（1）信息来源：从何处得悉公司名称、地址和经营范围等。

（2）写信目的：建立业务关系等。

（3）自我介绍：公司经营范围等。

（4）要求寄送有关资料。

（5）表达愿望。

2. 常用句型

句型 1　信息来源：我们从……处得知……

通过……我们了解到……

（1）We learn your company from the Internet that you are one of the leading manufacturers in this line.

我们从网上了解到你公司是这个行业的主要生产商之一。

（2）We own your name and address to the Commercial Counsellor's Office.

我们从商务参赞处得知你公司的名称和地址。

(3) Having obtained the name and address of your company through ABC Trading Company, we know that you deal in textiles.
通过 ABC 贸易公司的介绍，我们得知你公司的名称和地址，并获悉贵公司经营纺织品。

句型 2　写信目的：建立业务关系等

(1) We are writing you in the hope of entering into business relations with you.
我们今去函你方，希望与你方建立业务关系。

(2) We are writhing you and willing to open up business relations with you.
我们写信与你联系，以期与你方建立业务关系。

(3) We would like to take this opportunity to establish business relations with you.
我们愿借此机会与你公司建立业务关系。

句型 3　自我介绍：公司经营范围等

(1) We are an exporter handling textiles for many years. Our products have enjoyed a high reputation in the world for their good quality and reasonable price.
我公司作为纺织品出口商已有多年。我们的产品因质量好、价格合理，在世界上享有极高的声誉。

(2) We are writing to introduce ourselves as one of the important exporters of home appliances in United States. We have been exporting the commodity of high quality and have enjoyed more and more markets in the world.
我公司是美国主要家电产品出口商之一，我们出口的商品品质优越，并且在全世界拥有越来越多的市场。

(3) We are a state-owned enterprise specialized in handling the import of arts and crafts. We have our firms in many of the countries in Europe, and are keeping a close connection with many wholesalers and retailers there.
我公司是一家国有企业，专营工艺品的出口。我们在欧洲许多国家都有公司，并且与当地的许多批发商和零售商关系密切。

句型 4　要求寄送有关资料

(1) Please send us your catalogues and quotations.
请给我们寄你公司的商品目录和价目单。

(2) We shall appreciate your catalogues and quotations.
如能寄公司的商品目录和价目单，我方将十分感谢。

(3) We'll be pleased to have your catalogues and quotations.
如能收到你公司的商品目录和价目单，我们将非常高兴。

（二）询盘（INQUIRIES）

1. 写信要点

(1) 起首（自我介绍等）。

(2) 说明感兴趣的商品并请求提供有关资料。

(3) 要求报价。

(4) 其他要求：强调产品价格、数量等。

2. 常用句型

句型 1　对某产品感兴趣

(1) We take interest in various kinds of Men's Shirts.
我们对各种男式衬衫感兴趣。

(2) We are interested in the Energy Saving Electronic Lamps.
我们对节能灯感兴趣。

(3) Your textiles are of interest to us.
我们对你公司的纺织品有兴趣。

句型 2　要求寄送有关资料

(1) We shall be glad if you will send us your samples.
请给我们寄你公司样品。

(2) We shall appreciate it if you will send us your samples and brochure.
如能寄给我方你们的样品和宣传小册当十分感谢。

(3) It will be appreciated if you could send us your latest catalogues and samples.
请寄来最新的目录和样品，我方将十分感谢。

句型 3　要求报价

(1) We shall appreciate it if you could make us the best offer for your Children's Bicycles on CIF New York basis.
请报你公司童车的 CIF 纽约最低价。

(2) We will be pleased if you could quote us a price for Printed Shirting on the basis of CIF New York.
如能报印花细布的 CIF 纽约价当十分感谢。

(3) Please make us your lowest quotation for 500 tons of Walnuts.
请报我方 500 吨核桃的最低价。

句型 4　其他要求

(1) We have to point out that we intend to place a large order with you if your price is competitive.
请注意，如你方价格具有竞争性，我们将大量订购。

(2) If your prices are workable and the delivery date are acceptable, we intend to trade with you.
如你方价格合理，交货期合适，我们将与你方做贸易。

(3) If your prices are in line, we trust important business can materialize.
如你方价格可行，我们相信可以达成大笔交易。

(三) 报盘 (OFFERS)

1. 写信要点

(1) 感谢对方的来函。

(2) 报盘（商品、数量、价格、支付条款、装运、有效期）。

(3) 盼早答复。

2. 常用句型

句型 1　感谢对方的来函

(1) We've received your letter of May 2nd, and as requested, we are offering you the following subject to our final confirmation.
我们已收到你方 5 月 2 日来信，根据你方的要求我们发盘如下，以我方最后确认为准。

(2) We thank you for your inquiry of May 10th for 500 tons of Groundnuts.
感谢你方 5 月 10 日来函询购 500 吨花生。

(3) In reply to your inquiry for Walnuts, we offer you 500 tons of Walnuts as follows.
为答复你方对 500 吨核桃的询盘，我们现向你方发盘如下。

句型 2　报价

(1) We offer you 500 tons of Walnuts at USD 1 000 per ton CIF London.
我们向你们发盘，500 吨核桃，每吨 1 000 美元 CIF 伦敦。

(2) We are making you an offer for 500 dozen Men's Shirts at USD 80 per dozen CIFC 5% San Francisco for shipment in May.
我们现向你方发盘，500 打男式衬衫，每打 80 美元 CIF 旧金山，包括 5% 佣金，5 月装运。

(3) We offer, subject to your reply reaching here on or before May 5th, 500 pcs bicycles at USD 35 per set CIF New York for shipment in July.
我们发盘，500 辆自行车，每辆 35 美元 CIF 纽约，7 月装运。此发盘以你方 5 月 5 日前回复到为有效。

句型 3　支付条款

(1) Payment is to be made by irrevocable L/C at sight to be opened in our favour.
付款方式为不可撤销即期信用证，并以我方为受益人。

(2) We require payment by irrevocable L/C payable by draft at sight to be opened 30 days before the time of shipment.
我们要求以不可撤销信用证凭即期汇票支付，在装船前 30 天开证。
(3) Our terms of payment are by T/T.
我们的支付方式是电汇。

句型 4 装运
(1) Shipment is to be made in May.
五月装运。
(2) We will deliver the goods within 30 days after receipt of your L/C but specific time is to be fixed upon receipt of your official order.
我们将在收到你方信用证后 30 天内装运，但具体时间要在收到你方正式订单后再定。
(3) The goods will be shipped within 3 months upon receipt of your relative L/C.
货物将在收到你方相关信用证的 3 个月内装运。

句型 5 报盘有效期
(1) This offer is valid for 3 days.
本报盘有效期为 3 天。
(2) The offer is subject to our final confirmation.
本报盘以我方最后确认为准。
(3) The offer is subject to the reply reaching here before 23rd of May.
本报盘以你方 5 月 23 日复到为有效。

（四）还盘（COUNTER-OFFERS）

1. 写信要点
(1) 报盘信函收悉。
(2) 抱怨价格太高。
(3) 还盘建议。
(4) 结束。
2. 常用句型
句型 1 对价格的抱怨
(1) We regret to inform you that your price is rather on the high side though we appreciate the good quality of your products.
我们遗憾地告知你方，尽管我们很满意你方产品的质量，但我们认为你方价格偏高。
(2) We very much regret that your price is out of line with the prevailing market.
我们很遗憾你方的价格与现行市场不符。

（3）Although we are desirous of doing business with you, we regret to say that your price is unacceptable to us.
尽管我们渴望与你方成交，但我们遗憾地说，你方价格不可接受。

句型2　与其他供应商价格相比

（1）Indian makes have been sold here at a level about 10% lower than yours.
印度商品在此地出售的价格比你方的低10%。

（2）When comparing with the prices of other suppliers, your price is almost 10% higher than theirs.
与其他供应商的价格相比，你们的价格几乎比他们的高出10%。

（3）Your price compares much higher than that we can get from elsewhere.
你方的价格比我们从其他地方知悉的价格高多了。

句型3　还盘建议

（1）To step up trade, we counter-offer as follows: 500 tons of Walnuts at USD 900/ton CIF London.
为达成贸易，我方还盘如下：500吨核桃，每吨900美元CIF伦敦。

（2）As the market of Walnuts is declining, there is no possibility of business unless you can reduce your price by 5%.
由于核桃市价下跌，建议你方降价5%，否则无法成交。

（3）We don't deny the quality of your products is superior to that of Indian makes but the difference in price should in no case be as big as 10%. Let's set the price at USD 900 per ton CIF EMP.
我们并不否认你方产品的品质比印度商品略佳，但无论如何价格的差距不应大到10%。为了达成贸易，我方的还盘是每吨900美元CIF欧洲主要港口。

（五）成交（CONCLUSION OF BUSINESS）

1. 写信要点

（1）报盘/还盘信函收悉。

（2）报盘/还盘条件可接受。

（3）寄送订单/合同。

（4）其他要求（质量、装运等）。

2. 常用句型

句型1　寄送订单/合同，签退一份存档

（1）Enclosed please find our order No. 04 – 134 in duplicate, one of which please sign and return for our files.
随函附上我们第04 – 134号订单一式两份，请签退一份供我方存档。

（2）We enclose here with our S/C No. 123 in duplicate. Please sign and return one copy for our files.
随函附上我们第 123 号销售合同一式两份，请会签并退回一份以便我方存档。

（3）Our Sales Confirmation No. 123 was sent to you by EMS, please send back one copy duly countersigned.
今通过 EMS 寄去我方第 123 号销售确认书，请尽快签退一份给我方。

句型 2　其他要求（质量、装运等）

（1）As we are in urgent need of the goods, you are requested to effect shipment during May as promised in your offer.
由于我方急需此货，希望你方按订单所规定的 5 月装运。

（2）Please note that the goods are required to reach us regularly from May.
请注意此货应按要求从 5 月起定期运达我方。

（3）Please have the goods carefully examined, we rely on your special attention on this.
我们希望你方仔细检验货物。

四、实训内容

（一）询盘

法国巴黎 Le Vernet 贸易有限公司业务员 PIERRE 先生在 2021 年秋季广交会参观了广东中山威威照明有限公司的展品，对该公司的家电产品很感兴趣，与该公司的业务员张大同取得联系，考察了该公司在中山的生产基地并取得了有关产品资料。回国后，经过市场调查，PIERRE 先生于 2021 年 11 月 2 日向广东中山威威照明有限公司的业务员张大同发去询盘。请将下面信函翻译成为英文。

张大同先生：

在 2021 年秋季广交会上，获悉贵公司生产威威牌节能灯，我方对下述型号的产品感兴趣，请报 CIF 勒阿弗尔（LE HAVRE）。

货号（ARTICLE NOS.）	数量
LY－5W－A50　110V 5W　E27/B22	20 000 只
LY－7W－A60　110V 7W　E27/B22	20 000 只

我方渴望了解你公司最优惠的交易条件和有关的资信情况，我公司业务往来银行是法国巴黎商业银行。盼早复。

PIERRE　敬上

2021 年 11 月 2 日

（二）发盘

广东中山威威照明有限公司的业务员张大同收到法国巴黎 Le Vernet 贸易有限公司 PIERRE先生的电子邮件后，即于 2021 年 11 月 4 日发盘并建议增加订货数量拼成一个 20 英尺集装箱货柜。请将下面信函翻译成为英文。

PIERRE 先生：

很高兴收到你方 11 月 2 日询价，我公司经营威威牌节能灯已有二十多年的历史。该产品在欧洲深受欢迎。建议你方将每种产品数量增加至 58 000 只，以便我们装一个 20 英尺集装箱整柜。现报价如下：

1. 商品：威威牌节能灯
2. 包装：箱包装，每箱 100 只
3. 数量、型号及价格：

LY－5W－A50　110V 5W　E27/B22　29 000 只　每只 0.50 美元

LY－7W－A60　110V 7W　E27/B22　29 000 只　每只 0.60 美元

4. 价格术语：CIF 勒阿弗尔
5. 支付方式：不可撤销即期信用证，以我方为受益人
6. 装运：收到信用证后 30 天内装运

我公司业务往来银行为中国银行广州分行，有关我公司的资信情况，请向中国银行法国巴黎分行咨询。

盼早来首次订单。

张大同　敬上

2021 年 11 月 4 日

（三）还盘

PIERRE 先生收到张大同先生的电子邮件后，认为商品的报价太高，于 2021 年 11 月 8 日发邮件给张大同先生，说明该公司的经营优势，要求张大同先生降低价格。请将下面信函翻译成为英文。

张大同先生：

你方 11 月 4 日邮件已收到，谢谢。你方要求将数量增加到 58 000 只，我方没有异议。但价格偏高，我方难以接受。建议你方将价格降到与市场行情相符。

我方对本地区市场有充分的了解并在法国巴黎拥有广泛的销售组织，我们有信心推广贵公司的产品，请你方报最优惠价。

盼早复。

PIERRE　敬上

2021 年 11 月 8 日

（四）再还盘

业务员张大同收到对方的还盘电邮后，经与公司经理商议后同意降低报价，以便打开法国巴黎的市场。张大同于 2021 年 11 月 12 日给 PIERRE 先生发电子邮件。请将下面信函翻译成为英文。

PIERRE 先生：

你方 11 月 8 日邮件收悉，谢谢。

我方在欧洲销售该产品的价格均不低于原来报价。但考虑到贵公司首次与我方合作，并对我方产品有信心，我方愿降低价格，现报价如下：

1. 商品：威威牌节能灯
2. 包装：箱包装，每箱 100 只
3. 数量、型号及价格：

LY－5W－A50　110V 5W　E27/B22　29 000 只　每只 0. 45 美元

LY－7W－A60　110V 7W　E27/B22　29 000 只　每只 0. 55 美元

4. 价格术语：CIF 勒阿弗尔

同时，我方要求以不可撤销即期信用证支付，若你方能在本月底前下订单并开立信用证，我方可保证在 12 月底交货。

正如你方所看到的那样，我方产品在欧洲地区享有盛名。由于我方产品物美价廉，无疑将有助于你方开拓市场。

请贵方尽快答复。

张大同　敬上

2021 年 11 月 10 日

（五）接受

PIERRE 先生收到对方电子邮件后，认为广东中山威威照明有限公司的最新报价可以接受，马上去邮张大同表示接受 11 月 10 日电子邮件中所列的交易条件，同时要求张先生尽快寄送销售合同。请将下面信函翻译成为英文。

张大同先生：

你方 11 月 10 日邮件收悉。

我们很高兴接受你们在信中所列的价格和其他交易条款。

另：请在装船后两天内给我们发装船通知，告知包装件数、毛重、净重、船名、提单号码和日期、合同号码和货值。

请你方尽快给我方寄送销售合同。如果这次订货令人满意的话，我相信我方今后将大量订购。

PIERRE　敬上

2021 年 11 月 12 日

五、强化提高

强化提高一

基本资料：

买方：MIRACLE TRADING COMPANY

地址：98 HIGH STREET, SYDNEY, AUSTRALIA

卖方：广东纺织品进出口针织品有限公司

GUANGDONG TEXTILES IMPORT & EXPORT KNITWEARS COMPANY LIMITED

地址：广州小北路 168 号粤纺大厦 15 楼

15/F, GUANGDONG TEXTILES MANSION, 168 XIAOBEI ROAD, GUANGZHOU, CHINA

请将下列信函翻译成为英文。

（一）询盘

MIRACLE TRADING COMPANY 向广东纺织品进出口针织品有限公司发出询盘。

敬启者：

我们在网上了解到你们的名称和地址。

我们有意订购你们货号 GS01A 的棉质男士衬衫 1 000 打。希望寄你们衬衫的详细资料，包括颜色和价格，并给我们提供该型号不同颜色的棉衬衫样品，以便我们能对你方商品的质量和价格有所了解。

如果你们的价格和质量有吸引力，你们将得到我们的订单。

我们期盼尽早得到你们的答复。

MIRACLE TRADING COMPANY

2020 年 4 月 18 日

______

______

______

______

______

______

（二）发盘

广东纺织品进出口针织品有限公司接到 MIRACLE TRADING COMPANY 的信后，即复信如下：

敬启者：

根据你们 4 月 18 日来函要求，我们报实盘如下，以你们在本月底复到有效。1 000 打货号 GS01A 棉质男士衬衫，每打 CIF120 澳元悉尼价，要求以不可撤销的即期信用证支付，7 月一批装运。

由于我们的棉衬衫质量好、款式新，市场对我们棉衬衫的需求很大，我们希望你们立即接受这次报盘。

我们将另邮一些样品供你们参考。期望早日收到你们的订单，请放心，我方将给予仔细处理。

广东纺织品进出口针织品有限公司

2020 年 4 月 26 日

（三）还盘

MIRACLE TRADING COMPANY 收到报盘和样品后，来信要求广东纺织品进出口针织品有限公司降低价格。

敬启者：

谢谢你们 4 月 26 日报盘以及寄来的棉衬衫样品。

尽管我们很欣赏这些衬衫的优良品质，但我们遗憾地说，你们的价格似乎太高。如果接受你们的报价将使我们在销售中无利可图，因为在本地竞争非常激烈，其他供应商对同样品质的商品出价更低。

因此，我们还盘如下：

你方 4 月 26 日报盘无法接受，建议每打 CIF110 澳元悉尼价，其他条款不变。

我们期待着你们的确认。

MIRACLE TRADING COMPANY

2020 年 5 月 4 日

（四）接受

广东纺织品进出口针织品有限公司收到 MIRACLE TRADING COMPANY 的还盘后，决定接受对方的还盘，并将销售确认书一并寄去。

敬启者：

谢谢你们 5 月 4 日对棉衬衫的还盘，我们很高兴接受你方 5 月 4 日还盘。

但请注意，我们之所以特别接受你们的要求是因为我们希望以此获得你们未来的大量订单。

现寄去我们的销售确认书一式两份，请签退其中一份以供我方存档。

广东纺织品进出口针织品有限公司

2020 年 5 月 8 日

强化提高二

（一）买方信函练习

1. 建立贸易关系信函

假设你是美国 ABC 海外贸易公司的业务员 Andy Burns，你公司主要经营五金产品的进口。你在网上看到了深圳成明塑胶五金工艺厂的网页，拟与他们建立贸易关系。请给他们写一封拟与他们建立贸易关系的信。（写信时间为 2020 年 3 月 18 日）

To：master@ szchengming. com

Date：20200318

2. **询盘信函**

你收到了深圳成明塑胶五金工艺厂业务员 Sunny Zhang 给你方寄来的商品目录后，经过仔细研究，你方打算订购以下型号的手把（Handles）。请你就此向成明塑胶五金工艺厂的张小姐发去一封电子邮件。

货号（Article Nos.）	数量（Quantities）
XF25B/96 mm	10 000 pieces
XF33/96 mm	10 000 pieces
XF106/128 mm	10 000 pieces
XF107/96 mm	10 000 pieces

To：master@ szchengming. com
Date：21 March，2020 3：25 pm
Subject：Inquiry

Dear Ms. Zhang，

____

____

____

____

____

____

____

____

____

____

____

____

Best regards，
Andy Burns

3. **接受信函**

深圳成明塑胶五金工艺厂的张小姐向你方报盘如下，请根据他们的下述报盘回信，表明：①价格可以接受；②要求装运提前到5月。（回复邮件时间为2020年3月25日）

SHENZHEN CHENGMING HARDWARES TRADING CO., LTD.

Baoan Industrial Area, Baoan, Shenzhen

Tel: 86－0755－27916389　　Fax: 86－0755－27915550

E-mail: master@szchengming.com

March 23, 2020

Dear Mr. Burns,

We thank you for your e-mail of March 21 asking us to make you an offer for the following items. In reply, we are offering you as follows, subject to your reply reaching here not later than March 30.

货号（Article Nos.）	数量（Quantities）	单价（Unit Price）
XF25B/96 mm	10 000 pieces	USD 0.30/PC FOB Shenzhen
XF33/96 mm	10 000 pieces	USD 0.34/PC FOB Shenzhen
XF106 /128 mm	10 000 pieces	USD 0.68/PC FOB Shenzhen
XF107/96 mm	10 000 pieces	USD 0.62/PC FOB Shenzhen

Please note that we require payment by irrevocable L/C at sight and shipment will be made in June.

We trust the above offer will be acceptable to you and look forward to your early order.

Yours faithfully,

Sunny Zhang

4. 合同会签信函

深圳成明塑胶五金工艺厂同意提前到5月装运，并寄来了销售确认书一式两份，请你给他们发去传真一份，说明合同已经会签并请按时装运。

AMERICAN ABC OVERSEAS TRADING CO.

5325 Boul. St. , San Francisco, CA94112, USA

Tel: 001 - 415 - 587297　Fax: 001 - 415 - 587297

E-mail: abctrading@ msn. com

From: Andy Burns

To: Sunny Zhang

Date: March 27, 2020

best Regards

Andy Burns

enclosed

（二）卖方信函练习

1. 建立贸易关系信函

你是广州艺华贸易有限公司的业务员 Grace Li。你公司主要经营各种电动自行车。一位英国客户从网上了解到你公司情况并给你公司发去以下邮件，希望购买你公司的产品。请根据该邮件给你的客户回复，表示欢迎他们与你方建立关系，并寄送有关资料。请在提供的公司信笺上拟写信函。（回复邮件时间为 2021 年 10 月 4 日）邮件如下：

To：yihua@ 21cn. com
Date：October 3，2021 10：15 am
Subject：Hello
Dear Sirs,
Having obtained your name and address from the Internet. We are writing you in the hope of entering into trade relations with you.
We have been one of the leading importers of Bicycles in our country and enjoyed high reputation in European markets. At present, we are interested in your products and will appreciate it if you could send us your latest catalogues.
We are looking forward to your early reply.
Best regards,
Peter White

GUANGZHOU YIHUA TRADING CO. , LTD.
Rm. 1303 – 1305 Huaxin Mansion, Huanshi Road, Guangzhou, China
Tel：86 – 020 – 07654321　Fax：86 – 020 – 07654213
E-mail：yihua@ 21cn. com

2. **发盘信函**

你的英国客户 Peter White 先生在收到你寄来的信和目录后向你公司询盘，请你根据以下邮件进行发盘（发盘条件中的单价、付款方式、装船期限、发盘有效期等自行设定。如设定为每辆电动自行车 35 英镑 CIF 欧洲主要港口，不可撤销即期信用证，发盘有效期 5 天）。（回复邮件时间是 2021 年 10 月 8 日）

October 7，2021
Dear Ms. Grace Li，
Thank you for your catalogues forwarded to us and we find some items are of interest to us. We should appreciate it if you would give us the best quotation for the 1000 pcs Free Baby Brand Electric Bicycles Art. No. KH 145. If your prices are reasonable，we trust large business can be concluded.
We look forward to your early reply.
Yours faithfully，
Peter White

GUANGZHOU YIHUA TRADING CO.，LTD.
Rm. 1303 – 1305 Huaxin Mansion，Huanshi Road，Guangzhou，China
Tel：86 – 020 – 07654321　　Fax：86 – 020 – 07654213
E-mail：yihua@21cn. com

3. **拒绝降价信函**

Peter White 先生对你们公司产品的质量很满意，但认为你方的报价偏高，要求减价 5%。你方在收到该信后，经过研究，认为你方的报价与现行价格相符，因此拒绝他的还价。请你给他写一封邮件表明你方的观点。

To：Williams@ hotmail. com Date：October 9，2021 11：23 am Subject：Price

4. **接受信函**

Peter White 先生收到你的来信后，认为你方的产品质量好，决定按你方的报价订购 1 000辆型号 KH145 的电动自行车，希望你方能提前到 11 月中旬装运，以便赶上圣诞节的需求。请你给 Peter White 先生回信，表明：①很高兴能成交，可以提前到 11 月中旬装运；②请会签销售确认书，尽快开立信用证。请在下面提供的公司信笺上拟写信函并通过电子邮件发送。

GUANGZHOU YIHUA TRADING CO.，LTD. Rm. 1303 – 1305 Huaxin Mansion，Huanshi Road，Guangzhou，China Tel：86 – 020 – 07654321　　Fax：86 – 020 – 07654213 E-mail：yihua@ 21cn. com

强化提高三

请根据以下情境，按正确的信函格式（包括信头、封内地址和日期的排列）拟写英文信函。

（一）建立业务关系

写信人：Messrs. Anderson & Co.
地址：17 Mayfield Road, Copenhagen, Denmark
收信人：Tianhong Trading Co., Ltd.
地 址：Rm. 1201 Yinze Mansion, Huangpu Road, Guangzhou, China
写信日期：2022 年 6 月 3 日
要点：
（1）介绍本公司是哥本哈根的一家贸易公司，具有多年的经商经验。
（2）本公司与国内的许多百货商店有广泛联系。
（3）从商界朋友处得知公司名称和地址，对中国制造的茶具（TEA SETS）感兴趣。
（4）写信目的是建立业务关系，并希望得到目录和价目单。
（5）若价格合理将大量订购，盼早复。

（二）欢迎与我们建立贸易关系

写信人：Tianhong Trading Co. , Ltd.

地址：Rm. 1201 Yinze Mansion, Huangpu Road, Guangzhou, China

收信人：Messrs. Anderson & Co.

地址：17 Mayfield Road, Copenhagen, Denmark

写信日期：2022 年 6 月 5 日

要点：

（1）欢迎与我们建立贸易关系。

（2）按要求寄送商品目录和价目单。

（3）希望收到对方订单。

（三）主动发盘

写信人：Tianhong Trading Co. , Ltd.
地址：Rm. 1201 Yinze Mansion, Huangpu Road, Guangzhou, China
收信人：Messrs. Anderson & Co.
地址：17 Mayfield Road, Copenhagen, Denmark
写信日期：2022 年 6 月 8 日
要点：
（1）商品和数量：5 000 套粤花牌茶具。
（2）价格：每套 USD 45 CIF 哥本哈根。
（3）装运：2022 年 8 月到 9 月装运。
（4）支付：付款以不可撤销即期信用证。
（5）包装：每套一个纸箱，每 5 套一个运输包装箱。

（四）接受

写信人：Messrs. Anderson & Co.

地址：17 Mayfield Road, Copenhagen, Denmark

收信人：Tianhong Trading Co. , Ltd.

地址：Rm. 1201 Yinze Mansion, Huangpu Road, Guangzhou, China

写信日期：2022 年 6 月 10 日

要点：

（1）谢谢对方的报价和寄来的样品。

（2）认为对方的粤花牌茶具品质优良，价格合理。

（3）随信附寄 5 000 套茶具（货号：SM213）购买合同一式两份，会签后请归还一份以便存档。

（4）由于客户急需该货，希望尽快装运。

实训模块二　洽商谈判

第一部分　中文谈判

一、实训目的

通过本模块的实训，使学生了解商务谈判的一般原则，能拟订谈判计划，掌握商务谈判中报价还价阶段的策略，能灵活运用价格谈判中的让步技巧，能根据合同的主要条款如价格、数量、贸易术语等进行规范的外贸业务口语表达。

二、实训任务

（1）拟订商务谈判计划。
（2）根据提供的资料与外商洽商谈判。

三、实训提示

（一）商务谈判的一般原则

（1）客观性原则：尊重客观事实，实事求是，不感情用事。
（2）求同存异原则：寻求共同点，保留分歧，逐步解决。
（3）公平竞争原则：通过竞争，从对方承诺的行为中获得自己尽可能大的利益。
（4）妥协互补原则：相互妥协，相互让步，互有进退，互惠互利。
（5）合法原则：依法办事，守法经营，遵循国际法和国际惯例，尊重对方国家的风俗习惯和信仰。
（6）时效性原则：追求效率，降低成本，应对国际市场商品行情急剧变化的特点。
（7）最低目标原则：确定最低目标是谈判的底线，在此基础上争取更大的利益。

（二）谈判计划的主要内容

谈判计划的主要内容有：确定谈判目标、拟订议程、确定进度。

1．确定谈判目标

谈判目标即通过谈判要解决的问题。它具体分为三个层次：理想目标、可接受目标和最低目标。

2. 拟订议程

谈判议程即谈判的程序，包括所谈事项的次序和主要方法。如先谈什么问题后谈什么问题，每个问题大体谈多久，用什么方式谈，最后达到什么目的等。

3. 确定进度

谈判进度是对谈判所需时间的估计。这个时间的长短主要由谈判双方时间的充裕程度和具体内容来决定。一般说来，在确定谈判进度时，要本着效率与目的及具体谈判目标一致的原则，以及适当控制谈判进度的原则。

（三）商务谈判中报价还价阶段的策略

1. 报价策略

（1）何时报价。报价之前一定要先把商品的使用价值介绍清楚，待对方对其产品已有所了解之后，再提出价格。

（2）价格分割策略。报价方可利用对方的求廉心理，用较小的计价单位报价，造成需方心理上的便宜感。

（3）价格优惠策略。报价时可把价格与商品的优越性联系起来一块讲，或者把价格与达成协议的优惠条件联系起来一起报。

（4）价格比较策略。提出己方商品价格时，可联系另一种可比商品的价格进行比较，突出相同使用价值的不同价格，或突出相同价格的不同使用价值。

（5）价格差异策略。根据商品的流向、买方的需求急缓程度、购买次数、购买时间、付款方式的不同，可采取不同的价格。

2. 还价策略

（1）摸清真实价格策略。

（2）询问紧迫策略。该策略是指在还价中提出一些问题，或是变更一些条件，要求报价方答复，从而达到了解和掌握对方底数的目的。

（3）吹毛求疵策略。

（4）不开先例策略。

（5）最后通牒策略。

（四）价格谈判中的让步技巧

（1）在让步的最后阶段一步让出全部可让利益。

（2）一开始就拿出全部可让利益。

（3）等额地让出可让利益。

（4）让步先大后小，然后逐步提高。

（5）让步从大到小，然后微升。

（6）让步由大到小，渐次缩小。

（7）让步高开后大幅度递减，最后反弹。

（8）出让全部可让利益后赔利相让，然后再讨回赔利。

（五）谈判报价中使用的贸易术语

谈判报价中使用贸易术语一览表

<table>
<tr><th>组别</th><th>项目</th><th>中文含义</th><th>交货地点</th><th>风险划分界限</th><th>出口结关</th><th>进口结关</th></tr>
<tr><td rowspan="7">第一组：适用于任何运输方式</td><td>EXW</td><td>工厂交货</td><td>商品生产或储存地</td><td>商品生产或储存地</td><td colspan="2">买方</td></tr>
<tr><td>FCA</td><td>货交承运人</td><td rowspan="3">指定装运地点</td><td rowspan="3">货交承运人</td><td rowspan="3">卖方</td><td rowspan="3">买方</td></tr>
<tr><td>CPT</td><td>运费付至目的地</td></tr>
<tr><td>CIP</td><td>运费保险费付至目的地</td></tr>
<tr><td>DPU</td><td>目的地交货并卸货</td><td rowspan="3">指定目的地</td><td rowspan="3">指定目的地</td><td>卖方</td><td>买方</td></tr>
<tr><td>DAP</td><td>目的地交货</td><td>卖方</td><td>买方</td></tr>
<tr><td>DDP</td><td>完税后交货</td><td colspan="2">卖方</td></tr>
<tr><td rowspan="4">第二组：适用于水上运输方式</td><td>FAS</td><td>装运港船边交货</td><td>装运港船边</td><td>装运港船边</td><td>卖方</td><td>买方</td></tr>
<tr><td>FOB</td><td>装运港船上交货</td><td rowspan="3">装运港船上</td><td rowspan="3">装运港船上</td><td rowspan="3">卖方</td><td rowspan="3">买方</td></tr>
<tr><td>CFR</td><td>成本加运费</td></tr>
<tr><td>CIF</td><td>成本加运费保险费</td></tr>
</table>

四、实训内容

假设买方法国巴黎 Le Vernet 贸易有限公司 PIERRE 先生直接来到中山与广东中山威威照明有限公司的业务员张大同洽谈商品的价格、支付等问题，假如你是张大同，请你拟订谈判计划，两人一组，用中文进行谈判并做好谈判记录。

（一）拟订谈判计划

谈判计划	
谈判期限	
谈判地点	
谈判队伍	
谈判目标	
谈判策略	
谈判议程	

（二）谈判记录

谈判记录	
谈判时间	
谈判地点	
谈判人员	
谈判内容	

五、强化提高

强化提高一

（一）卖方：广州华威进出口公司

（二）买方：荷兰达明贸易公司

（三）产品：光管支架（HOLDER FOR FLUORESCENT LAMP）

（四）卖方产品规格及最低目标价格：

FOB 广州

ART NO. H－20　USD 1. 40/PC

ART NO. H－30　USD 2. 00/PC

ART NO. H－40　USD 2. 50/PC

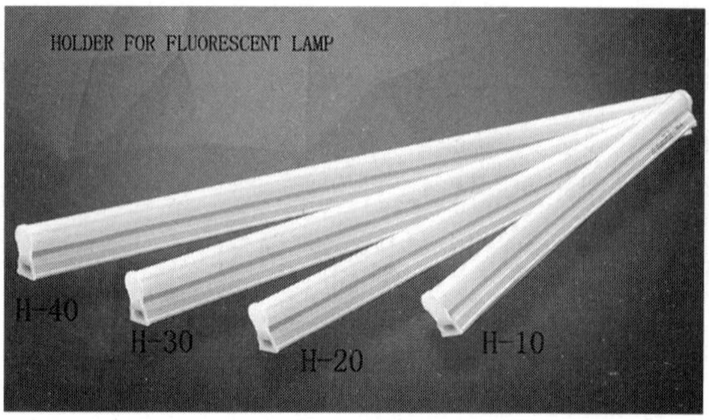

（五）买方目的地市场同类产品价格：

ART NO. H－20　USD 2. 40/PC

ART NO. H－30　USD 3. 00/PC

ART NO. H－40　USD 3. 50/PC

（六）其他参考条件：

1. 包装：12 PCS/CTN
2. 退税率：15%
3. 信用证通知/转递费：200 元人民币
4. 议付费：0. 125%
5. 托收手续费：0. 1%
6. 欧洲及北美地区邮费：20 美元
7. 运费：1×20’ FCL　3 560 美元
8. 运杂费（拖车费、报关费、码头费）：2 800 元人民币
9. 公司办公费用：按外汇净收入中每 1 美元扣 0. 30 元人民币计算
10. 保险费率：平安险（0. 25%），水渍险（0. 30%），一切险（1. 50%）
11. 国内购货价（含 17% 增值税）：

ART NO. H－20　8 元人民币/PC

ART NO. H－30　10 元人民币/PC

ART NO. H－40　12 元人民币/PC

12. 货物装箱情况：

型号	净重	毛重	尺码
ART NO. H－20	36 KGS/CTN	42 KGS/CTN	（45×35×40）CM/CTN
ART NO. H－30	48 KGS/CTN	54 KGS/CTN	（120×35×40）CM/CTN
ART NO. H－40	60 KGS/CTN	66 KGS/CTN	（150×35×40）CM/CTN

要求：拟订谈判计划，以价格为主要内容展开谈判并做好谈判记录，做到互利互惠，达成交易，并建立长期贸易关系。

强化提高二

（一）卖方：广东龙光纺织品有限公司

（二）买方：英国约克日用百货公司

（三）产品：烧烤组合玩具（KITCHEN PLAY SET）

（四）卖方产品最低目标价格：

USD 4.22/SET　FOB 广州

（五）买方目的地市场同类产品价格：USD 60.00/DOZ

（六）其他参考条件：

1. 包装：12 SETS/CTN
2. 毛重：13.2 KGS/CTN
3. 净重：8 KGS/CTN
4. 尺码：(60.5 × 33 × 49.5) CM/CTN
5. 退税率：15%
6. 信用证通知/转递费：200 元人民币
7. 议付费：0.125%
8. 托收手续费：0.1%
9. 欧洲及北美地区邮费：20 美元
10. 运费：1 × 20' FCL　3 560 美元
11. 运杂费（拖车费、报关费、码头费）：2 800 元人民币
12. 公司办公费用：按外汇净收入中每 1 美元扣 0.50 元人民币计算
13. 保险费率：平安险（0.25%），水渍险（0.30%），一切险（1.50%）
14. 国内购货价（含 17% 增值税）：烧烤组合玩具　28 元人民币/套

要求：拟订谈判计划，以价格为主要内容展开谈判并做好谈判记录，做到互利互惠，达成交易，并建立长期贸易关系。

强化提高三

（一）卖方：广东省机电产品进出口公司
（二）买方：迪拜施卡罗贸易公司
（三）产品：台灯（TABLE LAMP）
（四）卖方产品规格及最低目标价格：

FOB 广州
ART NO. 001　USD 5. 00/SET
ART NO. 002　USD 10. 00/SET
ART NO. 003　USD 12. 00/SET

（五）买方目的地市场同类产品价格：

ART NO. 001　USD 7. 00/SET
ART NO. 002　USD 13. 00/SET
ART NO. 003　USD 16. 00/SET

（六）其他参考条件：

1. 包装：6 SETS/CTN
2. 退税率：15%
3. 信用证通知/转递费：200 元人民币
4. 议付费：0. 125%
5. 托收手续费：0. 1%
6. 欧洲及北美地区邮费：20 美元
7. 运费：1 ×20’ FCL　3 560 美元
8. 运杂费（拖车费、报关费、码头费）：2 800 元人民币
9. 公司办公费用：按外汇净收入中每 1 美元扣 0. 50 元人民币计算
10. 保险费率：平安险（0. 25%），水渍险（0. 30%），一切险（1. 50%）
11. 国内购货价（含 17% 增值税）：
    ART NO. 001　32 元人民币/台
    ART NO. 002　68 元人民币/台
    ART NO. 003　96 元人民币/台
12. 货物装箱情况：

型号	净重	毛重	尺码
ART NO. 001	10 KGS/CTN	15 KGS/CTN	(35 ×45 ×30) CM/CTN
ART NO. 002	14 KGS/CTN	21 KGS/CTN	(45 ×45 ×55) CM/CTN
ART NO. 003	16 KGS/CTN	23 KGS/CTN	(55 ×45 ×60) CM/CTN

要求：拟订谈判计划，以价格为主要内容展开谈判并做好谈判记录，做到互利互惠，达成交易，并建立长期贸易关系。

第二部分　外贸英语谈判

一、实训目的

通过本模块的实训，使学生掌握外贸英语洽谈的常用句型，提高英语商务口语表达能力和熟悉外贸英语洽谈的过程和技巧。

二、实训任务

根据提供的情境，两人一组进行模拟洽谈，态度要诚恳，同时注意表情和动作。

三、实训提示

外贸英语谈判一般包括建立业务关系、询盘和报盘、价格商议、支付方式和装运等环节。

（一）建立业务关系（ESTABLISHING BUSINESS RELATIONS）

1. 洽谈要点

买方：

（1）Self-introduction.

（2）Purpose of coming.

（3）Company introduction.

卖方：

（1）Welcome and self-introduction.

（2）Company introduction.

（3）Product introduction.

2. 常用句型

句型 1　自我介绍

（1）I'm a businessman from ABC Trading Company, here is my card.

我是 ABC 贸易公司的业务员，这是我的名片。

（2）I'm a sales manager of ABC Trading Company, here is my business card.

我是 ABC 贸易公司的销售经理，这是我的名片。

(3) Hello, my name is..., I'm a trade representative of ABC Trading Company.
你好，我是××，是来自 ABC 贸易公司的业务代表。

句型 2　来访目的

(1) I'm here today is to trade with you.
我今天来这儿的目的是与你们做贸易。

(2) I'm here today is to have a business talk with you.
我今天来这是想与你们进行业务洽谈。

(3) We are desirous of entering into business relations with you.
我渴望与你们建立业务关系。

句型 3　公司介绍

(1) Our company is a state-owned enterprise, with more than 10 years experiences in this line.
我们公司是一家国有企业，在这个行业有 10 年的历史。

(2) We deal in computers and have been in this line for 10 years.
我们是经营电脑的，干这行有 10 年了。

(3) We specialize in garments and our company was founded in 1990.
我们公司成立于 1990 年，是专营服装的。

句型 4　产品介绍

(1) Our products are very popular in Canada because they are good in quality and reasonable in price.
我们的产品因为质量好、价格合理，在加拿大深受欢迎。

(2) Our products sell well in Canadian market since they are fresh in design and fine in workmanship.
我们的产品因为设计新颖、款式多样，在加拿大市场深受欢迎。

(3) Our products are of superior quality and favourable prices. This is the best seller of this year.
我们的产品质量优越，价格优惠。这是今年最畅销的产品。

(二) 询盘和报盘 (INQUIRY AND OFFER)

1. 洽谈要点

买方：

(1) Showing interest.

(2) Asking for catalogues, samples and price lists.

(3) Making specific inquiry.

卖方：

（1）Giving general information about company and products.

（2）Showing catalogues, samples and price lists.

（3）Making specific offer.

2. 常用句型

句型 1　询问对某产品感兴趣

（1）May I know what particular items you are interested in?
我想知道你们对哪个产品感兴趣？

（2）Which item are you interested in?
你们对哪个产品感兴趣？

（3）Would you tell me what articles you are keen on?
请你们告诉我们你们对哪个产品感兴趣？

句型 2　请求提供资料

（1）May I have a look at your samples?
我们可以看一看你们的样品吗？

（2）Can you show me your latest catalogues?
你可以给我看看你们最新的商品目录吗？

（3）We'd like to have your catalogues and price list for study.
我们想要一些你们的目录和价格单研究一下。

句型 3　询价

（1）Would you give me an indication of price?
你能给我一个参考价吗？

（2）May I know the prices?
我可以了解你们的价格吗？

（3）May I have an idea of your prices?
我可以了解你们的价格情况吗？

句型 4　报价

（1）We can offer you 500 tons of Soy Beans at USD 50 per ton CIFC2 New York.
我们可以向你们报 500 吨大豆，每吨 50 美元 CIFC2 纽约。

（2）Here is our offer for 1 000 pcs of Mountain Bikes.
这是我们 1 000 辆山地车的报价。

（3）We'd like to quote you our best price for 200 dozen Sport Shoes at USD 34 per pair CFR Hamburg for shipment in June.
我们给你方报 200 打运动鞋的最低价：每双 34 美元 CFR 汉堡港，6 月装运。

句型 5　无现货供应

（1）The goods you are interested in are out of stock at present.
你要的商品现在没货。

（2）We are sorry for being unable to supply Article No. 1 from stock now since they have been sold out.
很抱歉，我们现在没有一号产品，因为该产品已全部卖完。

（3）I'm afraid we can't meet your requirement for this item.
恐怕我们不能满足你们对这个产品的需求。

句型 6　推荐代用品

（1）If you are in urgent need of the goods, we'd like to recommend our new products to you.
如果你们急需这些商品，我愿意向你们推荐我们的新产品。

（2）If you are badly in need of this item, we suggest that you try our new product as a substitute for the one you required for.
如果你们急需这些商品，我建议你们试试我们的新产品来替代你们需要的产品。

（3）If you need the goods urgently, we suggest you try our new brand.
如果你们急需这些商品，我建议你们试试我们的新品牌。

句型 7　报盘有效期

（1）This offer is good for three days.
本报盘有效期三天。

（2）Our offer remains valid from this Thursday until June 3rd.
我们的报盘从本周四开始一直到 6 月 3 日有效。

（3）Our price is subject to your reply reaching here on or before June 3rd.
我们的报盘以你方的答复在 6 月 3 日或之前到达我方为准。

（三）价格商议（PRICE HAGGLING）

1. 洽谈要点

买方：

（1）Complaining about the high price with good reasons:

A. Comparing the price with the world market trend.

B. Comparing the price with other suppliers'.

C. Comparing the price with that before.

（2）Asking for a reduction in price.

卖方：

（1）Supporting the original price:

A. Good quality of the goods.

B. Cost and upward tendency in the world market.

C. Special prices for special customers.

(2) Coming to an agreement.

2. 常用句型

句型1　抱怨价格高

(1) Your price is on the high side. It's impossible for us to accept it.
你们的价格太高了，我们无法接受。

(2) Your price is out of line with the prevailing market.
你们的价格与现行市场价不符。

(3) Your price is 5% higher than the other suppliers'.
你们的价格比其他供应商的价格高出5%。

句型2　表明价格上涨的原因

(1) Price can't be taken separately from quality.
我们不能撇开质量谈价格。

(2) I'm afraid you have to take the quality into consideration when you judge a price.
当考虑价格的时候，需要对产品的质量作全面的衡量。

(3) The international market has gone up greatly in recent months.
最近几个月来，国际市场价格大幅度上涨。

句型3　价格商议

(1) May I suggest we go fifty-fifty and close the gap?
让我们各让一半来填补差价，如何？

(2) How about meeting each other half-way with the gap?
让我们各让一半来填补差价，好吗？

(3) What do you think of reducing the price by 2%?
你觉得减价2%行吗？

句型4　要求佣金或折扣

(1) Is there any commission included in your price? We are commission agent. We do business on commission.
你们的价格包含佣金吗？我们是佣金商，我们以获取佣金来做生意。

(2) We usually get 5% commission from our suppliers.
我们通常从欧洲供应商那儿得到5%的佣金。

(3) I think it is necessary to give us some rate of discount for the first order, as it's much easier to lose a customer than to get one over.
我认为第一次交易有必要给我们一定的折扣，因为失去一个客户容易而得到一个客户却很难。

句型 5　给予佣金或折扣

（1） As a rule, we don't allow any commission. But if your order is over USD5 000, we will consider giving you 2% commission.
按惯例，我们是不给佣金的。但如果你们的订单超过 5 000 美元，我们可以考虑给予 2% 的佣金。

（2） As an encouragement of business, we'll allow you 2% commission.
为了促进贸易，我们打算给予你们 2% 佣金。

（3） With an eye to our future business, we will grant you a special discount of 2%. That's the best we can do.
着眼于将来的贸易，我们将给你方 2% 的特殊折扣，这是最高点了。

（四）支付方式（PAYMENT TERMS）

1. 洽谈要点

买方：

（1） Inquiring about the terms of payment.

（2） Difficulty in accepting payment by L/C.

卖方：

（1） Introducing usual mode of payment.

（2） Reasons for payment by L/C.

2. 常用句型

句型 1　询问支付方式

（1） What mode of payment do you wish to accept?
你打算接受怎样的支付方式？

（2） Well, I'm glad to say that we've settled the price. What about the terms of payment?
很高兴我们在价格上达成协议，现在我们是否可以谈谈支付条款？

（3） This time I'd like to have your proposal about the payment terms.
这一次我们想听听你们在支付方式上的意见。

句型 2　建议某种支付方式

（1） I wonder if you would accept payment by D/P.
我想知道你们能否接受 D/P 的支付方式。

（2） It would help me greatly if you could accept payment by D/P.
如果你方能接受 D/P，这可帮了我大忙。

（3） If you agree to accept D/P, we can compromise on other terms.
如果你方能接受 D/P，我们可以在其他条件上让步。

句型 3　要求信用证支付的理由

（1） We only accept payment by irrevocable letter of credit in order to get the banker's guarantee.

为了得到银行的担保，我们只接受不可撤销信用证。

（2）As the financial market is unstable, payment by L/C will give us the bank's guarantee.

由于金融市场不稳定，信用证支付能给我们银行的担保。

（3）L/C is a reliable and safe method of payment, and it protects the seller as well as the buyer.

信用证是一种可靠、安全的支付方式，它保护了买卖双方的利益。

句型4　不愿接受信用证支付的理由

（1）Opening an L/C causes us a lot of expenses because it requires a certain sum of deposit in the bank.

开立信用证会给我们带来很多费用，因为我们得在银行存一笔押金。

（2）In opening a letter of credit, I have to pay a deposit and that will tie up my funds and add to the cost of my imports.

开立信用证我要存一笔押金，这样会占有我的资金和增加进口成本。

（3）As the world market is rather dull, it doesn't pay to adopt L/C for an order as small as ours.

因为世界市场不景气，向我们这么小的单用信用证支付很不划算。

（五）装运（SHIPMENT）

1. 洽谈要点

买方：

（1）Inquiring about the time of shipment.

（2）Asking for a timely or an early delivery.

卖方：

（1）Introducing date of shipment.

（2）Difficulty in advancing shipment.

2. 常用句型

句型1　询问装运期

（1）When at the earliest can we expect the shipment?

你们最早可以什么时间装运？

（2）When can you have the goods shipped?

你们可以什么时间装运？

（3）Shall we go on to the next item, i. e. the time of delivery?

让我们进入下一个环节——装运，好吗？

句型2　建议某时间装运

（1）I wonder if it is possible for you to effect shipment during March?

我想知道你们能否在 3 月装运？

（2） Will it be possible for you to ship the goods in March？
你们能否在 3 月装运？

（3） We'll appreciate it if you could make shipment in March.
如果你们能在 3 月装运我们将不胜感激。

句型 3　要求按时或提前装运的理由

（1） December is the selling season for this commodity in our market and we have to find someone else to do the retailing.
12 月是这个产品在我方市场的销售季节，而且我们要找人做零售。

（2） To establish a new brand in our market，early introduction is an important factor.
在我方市场建立一个新品牌，早日投放到市场是很重要的。

（3） Our customers in Europe are in urgent need of the goods.
我们在欧洲的客户急需这些商品。

句型 4　不能提前装运的原因

（1） The fact remains that our manufacturers have a heavy backlog on their hands.
事实是我们的厂家手头积压了很多订单。

（2） All the shipping space to the destination port has been fully booked up.
所有到目的港的舱位都已经订满。

（3） Since there is no direct steamer to your port from Guangzhou，we have to transship the goods in Hong Kong.
由于从广州到你方港口没有直达船，货物必须从香港转运。

（六）成交（CONCLUSION OF BUSINESS）

1. 洽谈要点

买方：

（1） Examining all the terms and conditions.

（2） Asking for amendments to the mistakes if any.

卖方：

（1） Repeating the main points.

（2） Making amendments to the mistakes if any.

2. 常用句型

句型 1　请买方检查成交条款

（1） Now we have covered all the important points，before we draft the contract，let's examine the details again.
现在我们已经谈妥了所有的要点，在我们草拟合同前，让我们把合同的细节再核对一下。

(2) The draft contract is ready, would you please check it up and see if everything is in order?

合同的草稿已经准备好，请你核对一下，看看是否一切都与我们谈的相符?

(3) Before we start to draft the contract, can we go over the terms so that no mistakes are made?

在我们草拟合同前，让我们把合同的细节再核对一下看看是否有错漏的地方?

句型 2　要求更改成交条款

(1) I'd like to amend it to read shipment in the early November.

我想你们应该将装运时间改成 11 月上旬。

(2) Please have it amended as shipment in the early November.

请你们将装运时间改成 11 月上旬。

(3) Would you please alter it reading shipment in the early November?

你们是否应该将装运时间改成 11 月上旬?

四、实训内容

MAKE A DIALOGUE BASED ON THE FOLLOWING PARTICULARS（请根据提供的情景进行模拟洽谈）:

You are ZHANG DATONG from GUANGDONG ZHONGSHAN WEIWEI LIGHTING CO., LTD. and are now having a talk with Mr. PIERRE, a customer from Le Vernet TRADE COMPANY LIMITED, PARIS FRANCE. He is quite interested in your Energy Saving Electronic Lamps. It's your first meeting, please have a face-to-face talk with Mr. PIERRE according to the following particulars and pay attention to the points marked with *.

情境：假如你是广东中山威威照明有限公司的张大同，来自法国巴黎 Le Vernet 贸易公司的 PIERRE 先生对你们的节能灯感兴趣，你正在与他进行业务洽谈。这是你们第一次见面，请根据以下提供的信息，两人为一组进行模拟商务英语洽谈，带 * 号部分是洽谈要点，请尽量展开谈。

(1) Buyer: Mr. PIERRE of Le Vernet TRADE COMPANY LIMITED, PARIS FRANCE

(2) Seller: ZHANG DATONG from GUANGDONG ZHONGSHAN WEIWEI LIGHTING CO., LTD.

(3) Commodity: Triangle Brand Energy Saving Electronic Lamps

(4) Quantities: 5 000 pieces of Art. No. TR - 3U - A 100V 5W & Art. No. TR - 3U - A 110V 7W each

(5) * prices:

Seller: To make an offer as follows:

Article Nos.	Quantities	Unit price
LY－5W－A50　110V 5W　E27/B22	20 000 pieces	USD 0. 50/piece CIF LE HAVRE
LY－5W－A60　110V 7W　E27/B22	20 000 pieces	USD 0. 60/piece CIF LE HAVRE

Buyer：To make a counter-offer（还盘）as follows：

Article Nos.	Quantities	Unit price
LY－5W－A50　110V 5W　E27/B22	29 000 pieces	USD 0. 40/piece CIF LE HAVRE
LY－5W－A60　110V 7W　E27/B22	29 000 pieces	USD 0. 50/piece CIF LE HAVRE

Agreement（协议）：To set the price at the buyer's counter-offer

（6）Payment Terms：By irrevocable sight L/C to be opened 30 days before the time of shipment

（7）Time of Shipment：In December

五、强化提高

强化提高一

MAKE DIALOGUES BASED ON THE FOLLOWING SITUATIONS（请根据提供的情境进行模拟洽谈）：

（一）ESTABLISHING BUSINESS RELATIONS（建立业务关系）

Compose a dialogue according to the given situation：

You attend the 2018 Autumn Guangzhou Fair on behalf of Guangdong Textiles Import & Export Corporation (Group). At the fair, you meet Mr. Burns, a businessman from American Overseas Trading Company. It's the first time for him to attend this fair, everything is new to him. Both of you want to have a talk on the purpose of entering into trade relations with each other.

情境：你代表广东纺织品进出口公司参加 2018 年的秋季广交会。广交会期间，你遇到了美国 ABC 海外贸易公司的业务员 Burns 先生，这是他第一次参加广交会，一切对他来说都是崭新的，你们彼此都想借此机会建立业务关系。

（二）INQUIRY AND OFFER（询盘和报盘）

Compose a dialogue according to the given situation：

Mr. Burns are interested in your carpets and he inquires for 500 pieces of Art. No. S008 for prompt shipment. Since this article is out of stock, you recommend Art. No. S009 as a substitute and assure Mr. Burns of the same quality and even better prices.

情境：Burns 先生对你们公司的地毯有兴趣，并对货号 S008 的产品进行询盘。很遗憾这个商品缺货，你向他推荐了货号 S009 的产品作为代用品。S009 号地毯价廉物美，请你说服他试订这个商品。

（三）PRICE HAGGLING（价格商议）

Compose a dialogue according to the given situation:

Your offer for 500 pieces of Art. No. S009 is USD 55/PC CIF San Francisco. Mr. Burns thinks it too high and makes a counter-offer at USD 45/PC. You stick to your original price by stressing the good quality of your carpets and the upward tendency of the market demand. Mr. Burns insists on a reduction, so you finally agree to meet each other half way.

情境：你对 500 件货号 S009 的地毯报价是每件 55 美元 CIF 旧金山，而 Burns 先生对此的还价却是每件 45 美元 CIF 旧金山。你认为你们的地毯价廉物美，而且市场正处于上涨时期。但是 Burns 先生认为你方价格偏高，最后你们各让一步，在价格上达成协议。

（四）PAYMENT TERMS（支付方式）

Compose a dialogue according to the given situation:

You have settled the quantity and price of this transaction, now you're talking about the terms of payment with Mr. Burns. Mr. Burns asks for D/P terms for his imports. You insist on L/C payment, as it is both an international practice and a customary practice of your company. Finally you persuade him to accept irrevocable L/C at sight.

情境：现在你和 Burns 先生将要进入支付方式这一环节的洽谈，Burns 先生建议以 D/P 方式支付，而你方却坚持你们公司的支付惯例信用证支付，请你说服他采用不可撤销即期信用支付。

（五）SHIPMENT（装运）

Compose a dialogue according to the given situation：

Suppose you are having a talk with Mr. Burns about the time of shipment. He asks you to make shipment in the early November. The reason is that he wants to place the goods on the market before the Christmas Day. Since the manufacturers are fully committed（任务很紧），the best you can do is in the end of November. Finally，you promise to deliver in the mid-November.

情境：现在你正在和 Burns 先生谈论装运时间，他要求你方在 11 月上旬装运，因为他要在圣诞节前将商品投放市场，而你方却由于厂家手头订单过多无法满足他的要求。最后，你方答应提前到 11 月中旬装运。

（六）CONCLUSION OF BUSINESS（成交）

Compose a dialogue according to the given situation：

You have just concluded a transaction with Mr. Burns for carpets. Before signing the contract，you are now checking up all the main points you've agreed upon. The main points are as follows：

Commodity：Carpets（Art. No. S009）

Quantity：500 pieces

Unit Price：USD 50/PC CIF San Francisco

Terms of Payment：By irrevocable L/C at sight

Time of Shipment：In mid-November

情境：经过多次协商，你公司终于与 Burns 先生谈妥了一笔地毯的生意，在草拟合同前，你们将双方谈妥的要点重新复述和核对一次。

商品：地毯（货号 S009）

数量：500 件

单价：每件 50 美元 CIF 旧金山

支付：不可撤销即期信用证

装运：11 月中旬

强化提高二

MAKE A DIALOGUE BASED ON THE FOLLOWING PARTICULARS（请根据提供的情境进行模拟洽谈）：

Mr. White from California Trading Corporation is interested in the Canned LYCHEE and Miss Zhang from Tianhong Foodstuffs Co.，Ltd. is having a business talk with him. Please have a business talk according to the given particulars and pay attention to the points marked with ＊.

情境：来自加利福尼亚贸易公司的 White 先生正在和天虹食品有限公司的张小姐进行 1 000 箱荔枝罐头的业务洽谈，请根据以下提供的信息，两人为一组进行模拟商务英语洽谈，带 * 号部分是洽谈要点，请尽量展开谈。

(1) Buyer: Mr. White form California Trading Corporation

(2) Seller: Miss Zhang from Tianhong Foodstuffs Co., Ltd.

(3) Commodity: Canned LYCHEE（荔枝罐头）

(4) Quantity: 10 000 cartons

(5) * Price: Sellers: To offer at USD 165/carton CIF San Francisco

Buyers: To counter-offer at USD 145/carton CIF San Francisco

Agreement（协议）: To set the price at USD 150/carton CIF San Francisco

(6) Payment Terms: By irrevocable L/C at sight

(7) * Time of Shipment:

Buyer: To require shipment in November

Seller: To promise delivery in December

Agreement（协议）: To ship 60% of the goods in November and the balance in December

强化提高三

MAKE A DIALOGUE BASED ON THE FOLLOWING PARTICULARS（请根据提供的情境进行模拟洽谈）:

Mr. Wang from Guangzhou Yuehua Import & Export Corporation is having a business talk about Toy Cars with Mrs. Jenkins from Australian Johnson & Son Trading Corporation. It's the first time they meet each other, please have a business talk in pairs according to the given particulars and pay attention to the points marked with *.

情境：广州粤华进出口有限公司的王先生正在和来自澳大利亚 Johnson & Son 贸易公司的 Jenkins 女士进行儿童玩具车的业务洽谈。这是他们第一次见面，请根据以下提供的信息，两人为一组进行模拟商务英语洽谈，带＊号部分是洽谈要点，请尽量展开谈。

SMF322

SMS268

（1） Buyer：Mrs. Jenkins from Australian Johnson & Son Trading Corporation

（2） Seller：Mr. Wang from Guangzhou Yuehua Import & Export Co. , Ltd.

（3） Commodity：Toy Cars

（4） ＊Art. Nos. & Quantities：

Buyer：To be interested in 3 000 pieces of Article No. SMF145 and 5 000 pieces of Article No. SMS268

Seller：To recommend Art. No. SMF322 as a substitute for Art. No. SMF145 since Art. No. SMF145 is out of stock

Agreement（协议）：To place an order for 3 000 pieces of Art. No. SMF322 and 5 000 pieces of Art. No. SMS268

（5） Prices：

Art. Nos.	Quantity	Price
SMS268	5 000 PCS	USD 2. 5/PC CIF Sydney
SMF322	3 000 PCS	USD 1. 5/PC CIF Sydney

（6） ＊Payment Terms：

Buyer：To ask for D/P at sight

Seller：To require for irrevocable L/C at sight

Agreement（协议）：To accept payment by D/P at sight as an encouragement of business.

（7） Time of Shipment：In May

实训模块三　签订合同

一、实训目的

通过本模块的实训，使学生了解国际货物买卖合同条款的主要内容，掌握拟订国际货物买卖合同条款应注意的问题，能熟练应用有关的国际贸易惯例独立拟订合同的主要条款。

二、实训任务

（1）根据提供的资料拟订国际货物买卖合同的主要条款。

（2）根据提供的资料填制销售合同（或销货确认书）。

三、实训提示

（一）商品的品名条款

1．规定品名条款的方法

（1）直接规定商品的品名，如大米、小麦等。

（2）为了明确起见，也可在商品品名前加具体的品种、等级或型号等概述性描述词。

2．规定品名条款的注意事项

（1）内容必须明确、具体，避免空泛、笼统的规定。

（2）条款中规定的品名，必须是卖方能够供应而买方所需要的商品，凡做不到或不必要的描述性的词句，都不应加入。

（3）尽可能使用国际上通用的名称，若使用地方性的名称，交易双方应事先取得共识。

（4）注意选用合适的品名，以利于降低关税、方便进出口和节省运费开支。

（二）商品的品质条款

1．表示商品品质的方法

（1）以实物表示的品质。以实物表示的品质可分为看货买卖和凭样品买卖两种。

（2）凭说明表示的品质。凭说明表示的品质又可分为凭规格买卖、凭等级买卖、凭标准买卖、凭说明书和图样买卖、凭商标或牌号买卖、凭产地名称买卖六种。

2. 条款举例

（1）“彩色灯泡，烛形，220 伏，28 瓦。”

“Colour Lamps Candle type 220V 28W.”

（2）“华凌牌空调机，型号 KFR 34GW，220 伏，50 赫兹，带遥控。”

“Hualin Brand Air Conditioner Model：KFR 34GW，220V 50Hz with remote control.”

（3）“2018 年中国产荔枝，良好平均品质。”

“Lychee of P. R. of China，2018 crop，F. A. Q.”

3. 规定品质条款应注意的问题

（1）对某些商品可规定一定的品质机动幅度，即允许卖方所交货物的质量指标在一定的幅度内有灵活性。品质公差是指国际上公认的产品品质误差。凡在品质公差范围内的货物，买方不得拒收或要求调整价格。品质公差用于工业制成品，而品质机动幅度用于农副产品。

（2）正确运用各种表示品质的方法。在实际业务中，应视商品的特性选用表示商品品质的方法。

（三）商品的数量条款

1. 商品数量条款的内容

国际货物买卖合同中商品数量条款的内容主要包括成交商品的数量和计量单位。

2. 条款举例

“500 公吨，卖方可溢装或短装 5%。”

“500m/t 5% more or less at seller's option.”

3. 拟订商品数量条款应注意的问题

（1）要注意各国使用的度量衡制度不同而导致计量单位上的差异。在国际贸易中通常采用的度量衡制度有：公制、英制、美制、国际单位制。我国现行的法定计量单位制是在国际单位制的基础上增加一些非国际单位制的单位。

（2）要注意根据货物的实际情况确定不同的计重方法。在国际贸易中，货物重量常见的计量方法有：毛重、净重、公量、法定重量和理论重量五种。

（3）规定数量条款应注意合理规定数量的机动幅度——溢短装条款，一般规定为 5%。

（4）要注意《UCP600》有关数量的规定。

根据《UCP600》第三十九条 a 款规定：凡“约”“大概”“大约”或类似词语，用于信用证、数量和单价时，应解释为有关金额、数量或单价不超过 10% 的增减幅度。若合同和信用证中未明确规定可否溢短装，则对于散装货，可根据《UCP600》第三十九条 b 款“除非信用证规定货物的数量不得有增减外，在所支付款项不超过信用证金额的条件下，货物数量准许有 5% 的增减幅度，但是，当信用证规定数量以单位或个数计数时，此项增减幅度则不适用”的规定处理。

（四）商品的包装条款

1. 商品包装条款的内容

合同中商品包装条款的内容一般包括包装材料、包装方式、包装规格、包装标志等。

运输标志（Shipping Marks）又称唛头，它是指书写、压印或刷制在外包装的图形、文字和数字。它通常由一个简单的几何图形和一些字母、数字及简单的文字组成，其主要内容包括：①收、发货人代号；②目的地；③件号、批号。

2. 条款举例

（1）“纸箱装，每箱净重约 15 千克，500 纸箱装 1 只 20 英尺集装箱运送。”

“In cartons of about 15kg net, 500 cartons transported in one 20ft container.”

（2）“布袋装，内衬聚乙烯袋，每袋净重 25 千克。”

“In cloth bags, lined with polythene bags of 25kg net each.”

3. 拟订商品包装条款应注意的问题

（1）要考虑商品的特点和不同的运输方式。

（2）对包装的规定要明确具体。

（3）包装费用一般包括在货价之内，不另行计收，若买方有特殊要求，应明确包装由谁供应和包装费用由谁负担。

（五）货物装运条款

1. 货物装运条款的内容

国际货物买卖合同中装运条款的主要内容有装运时间、装运港和目的港、分批装运和转运等。

2. 条款举例

（1）“5 月份装运，由伦敦至上海。卖方应在装运月份前 45 天将备妥货物可供装船的时间通知买方。允许分批和转船。”

“Shipment during May from London to Shanghai. The Sellers shall advise the Buyers 45 days before the month of shipment of the time the goods will be ready for Shipment. Partial shipments and transshipment allowed.”

（2）“3/4 月份分两次平均装运，允许转运。”

“During Mar. / Apr. in two equal shipments, transshipment to be permitted.”

3. 拟订货物运输条款应注意的问题

（1）装运期的规定不应使用诸如：“迅速”“立即”“尽快”之类词语，如使用此类词语，按《UCP600》第四十六条 b 款规定，银行将不予置理；《UCP600》第四十七条 b 款还规定，“以后”将理解为不包括所述日期。

（2）确定目的港和目的地时应注意：

①目的港和目的地必须明确具体。

②合同中规定以海上运输方式交运的交易，货物运往的目的港无直达班轮或航次很少的，合同中应规定允许转运的条款。

③目的港必须是船舶可以停泊的港口。对内陆国家的贸易而又采用 CIF 或 CFR 条件的，一般应选择距离该国最近的、我方能够安排船舶的港口为目的港。在采用多式联运的情况下，除非联运承运人接受全程运输，一般不可接受以内陆城市为目的港的条件。

④在规定目的港时，应注意所选择的港口是否重名问题。凡有重名的港口或城市，应加注国名，在同一个国家有同名港口或城市者，应注明所在国家的部位，以防发生因漏注而错运货物的事故。

（3）要注意《UCP600》对分批装运和转船的规定。

①第四十条 b 款的规定："运输单据表面注明货物系使用同一运输工具并经同一路线运输的，即使每套运输单据注明的装运日期不同及/或装货港、接受监管地、发运地不同，只要运输单据注明的目的地相同，也不视为分批装运。"

②除非信用证另有规定，允许分批装运和转船。

③如信用证规定在指定时期内分批装运，其中任何一批未按批装运，信用证对该批和以后各批货物均告失效。

（六）保险条款

1. 保险条款的内容

（1）按 FOB、FCA、CFR 或 CPT 条件成交的保险条款。

按 FOB、FCA、CFR 或 CPT 条件成交，合同中的保险条款只需规定："保险由买方办理。"

（2）按 CIF 或 CIP 条件成交的保险条款。

按 CIF 或 CIP 条件成交的保险条款，则需具体规定保险金额、投保险别和保险适用的条款等内容。

2. 条款举例

（1）"保险由买方办理。"

"Insurance: To be covered by the Buyer."

（2）"保险：由卖方按发票金额加乘 10% 投保一切险及战争险，以中国人民保险公司 1981 年 1 月 1 日的有关海洋运输货物保险条款为准。如果买方要求加投上述保险或保险金额超出上述金额，必须提前征得卖方的同意，超出的保险费由买方承担。"

"Insurance: To be covered by the Sellers for the full invoice value plus 10% against all risks and war risks as per and subject to the relevant ocean marine cargo clauses of the People's Insurance Company of China, dated Jan. 1, 1981. If the Buyers desire to cover for any other extra risks besides aforementioned of amount exceeding the aforementioned limited, the sellers' approval must be obtained beforehand and all the additional premiums thus incurred shall be for the Buyers' account."

3. 拟订保险条款应注意的问题

（1）必须明确保险适用的条款及生效日期。

①"中国保险条款"（China Insurance Clauses，简称 CIC）。中国人民保险公司根据我国保险业务的实际需要并参照国际保险市场的习惯做法制订。按照能否单独投保，可分为

基本险和附加险两类。基本险是可以单独投保的险别，附加险是不能单独投保的险别。

②伦敦保险协会海运货物保险条款，英文简称为ICC，该条款有六种保险险别：ICC（A）、ICC（B）、ICC（C）、战争险、罢工险和恶意损害险，其中除恶意损害险不能单独投保外，其余五种险别都可以单独投保。

ICC（A）相当于我国海运货物保险的一切险，ICC（B）相当于我国海运货物保险的水渍险，ICC（C）相当于我国海运货物保险的平安险。以上三种险别，保险公司的承保责任起讫适用于“仓至仓条款”。我保险公司可根据客户的要求，酌情按ICC条款的有关规定承保。

（2）必须明确投保险别，注意“仓至仓条款”适用的险别。

中国人民保险公司的《海洋运输货物保险条款》规定的平安险、水渍险和一切险三种险别和伦敦保险协会海运货物保险条款规定的ICC（A）、ICC（B）、ICC（C）对承保责任起讫或称保险期限，均采用国际保险业务中惯用的“仓至仓条款”（即Warehouse to Warehouse Clause，简称W/W Clause）。但战争险和罢工险不适用“仓至仓条款”。

（3）要注意被保险人必须对保险标的物具有保险利益。

保险利益又称可保权，是指投保人对保险标的物具有法律上承认的利益。就货物保险而言，反映在运输货物上的利益，主要是货物本身的价值，但也包括与此相关联的运费、保险费、关税、预期利润等。海上保险仅要求被保险人在保险标的物发生损失时必须具有保险利益。

（4）如加保战争险、罢工险，应明确“若发生有关的保险费率调整，所增加的保费由买方负担”。

（5）注意基本险与附加险的关系。

附加险只能在投保某一种基本险的基础上才可加保，但因一切险的责任范围已包括了一般附加险，故如投保人在投保时选择了一切险，则无须再加保一般附加险。

伦敦保险协会海运货物保险条款的战争险和罢工险可单独投保。

（七）价格条款

1. 价格条款的内容

进出口合同中的价格条款，一般包括商品的单价和总值两项基本内容。单价通常由计量单位、单位价格金额、计价货币和贸易术语四个部分组成。总值是单价与数量的乘积，也是一笔交易的总金额。

2. 条款举例

（1）“每件300美元CIF东京。”

“USD300 per piece CIF Tokyo.”

（2）“每公吨218英镑FOB广州。”

“GBP218 per metric ton FOB Guangzhou.”

3. 拟订价格条款应注意的问题

（1）根据国际市场行情，合理确定商品的单价，防止偏高或偏低。

（2）根据船源、货源等实际情况，选择适当的贸易术语。

（3）争取选择有利的计价货币，必要时可加订保值条款。

（4）灵活运用各种不同的作价办法。尽可能避免承担价格变动的风险。

（5）参照国际贸易的习惯做法，注意佣金和折扣的合理运用。

（6）如交货品质、交货数量有机动幅度或包装费另行计价时，应订明机动部分的作价和包装费计价的具体方法。

（八）收付条款

1. 收付条款的内容

收付条款的内容是指货款结算方式如汇付、托收、信用证或这三种的结合。

2. 条款举例

（1）“买方应通过买卖双方都接受的银行向卖方开出以卖方为受益人的不可撤销、可转让的即期付款信用证并允许分装、转船。信用证必须在装船前 30 天开到卖方，信用证有效期限延至装运日期后 21 天在中国到期。”

“The Buyers shall open with a bank to be accepted by both the Buyers and Sellers an irrevocable transferable letter of credit, allowing partial shipment, transshipment in favor of the Sellers and addressed to Sellers payable at sight against first presentation of the shipping document to Opening Bank. The covering letter of credit must reach the Sellers 30 days before shipment and remain valid in China until the 21st day (inclusive) from the date of shipment.”

（2）“买方对卖方开具的见票后 30 天付款的跟单汇票，于提示时应即予承兑，并应于汇票到期日即予付款，付款后交单。”

“The Buyers shall duly accept the documentary draft drawn by the Sellers at 30 days sight upon first presentation and make payment on its maturity. The shipping documents are to be delivered against payment only.”

（3）“买方同意在本合同签字之日起，15 天内将本合同总金额 50% 的预付款以电汇方式汇交卖方，并在收到本合同所列单据后 7 天内电汇其余货款。”

“50% of the total contract value as advance payment shall be remitted by the Buyer to the Seller through T/T within 15 days after signing this contract. Payment to be effected by the Buyer shall not be later than 7 days after receipt of the documents listed in the contract by T/T.”

3. 拟订收付条款应注意的问题

（1）要灵活运用支付方式。

①在国际贸易中使用的支付方式主要有汇付、托收和信用证，这三种支付方式虽都通过银行办理，但汇付和托收属于商业信用，而信用证属于银行信用。

②在出口贸易中，原则上采用信用证支付方式，但为了提高竞争力和降低费用，对于信誉好的客户，也可采用汇付或托收。

③一笔交易大多使用一种支付方式，但有时根据不同需要，也可把两种或两种以上的支付方式结合使用。

（2）采用信用证付款时，一般不接受可撤销信用证或以开证人为付款人的信用证。

（3）采用 T/T 付款时，必须先收取 30% 的定金，在货物装运前通知买方电汇货款，款到后方能装运出口。

(4) 采用信用证和托收付款时，全套单据必须随附托收项下的汇票，信用证项下的汇票采用光票收款。

(5) 若采用托收，拟订条款时应注意：

①事先作好客户的资信调查，掌握适当的授信额度。

②了解进口国家的贸易管制和外汇管制条例，以免货到目的地后，不准进口或收不到外汇而造成损失。

③了解进口国家的商业惯例，以免当地习惯做法影响安全迅速收汇。

④出口合同应争取 CIF 或 CIP 条件成交，由出口人办理货运保险；或可投保出口信用险，在不采取 CIF 或 CIP 条件时，应投保卖方利益险。

(九) 商品检验条款

1. 商品检验条款的内容

在国际货物买卖合同中商品检验条款的内容主要有检验时间与地点、检验机构和检验证书。

2. 条款举例

"买卖双方同意以装运港（地）中国出入境检验检疫局签发的质量和重量（数量）检验证书作为信用证项下议付所提交的单据的一部分。对货物的质量和/或重量（数量）与合同规定不符时，买方有权向卖方索赔，并提供经卖方同意的公证机构出具的检验报告。索赔期限为货物到达目的港（地）后 30 天内。"

"It is mutually agreed that the Certificate of Quality and Weight (Quantity) issued by the China Exit and Entry Inspection and Quarantine Bureau at the port/place of shipment shall be part of the documents to be presented for negotiation under the relevant L/C. The Buyers shall have the right to reinspect the quality and weight (quantity) of the cargo. The reinspection fee shall be borne by the Buyers. Should the quality and/or weight (quantity) be found not in conformity with that of the contract, the Buyers ate entitled to lodge with the Sellers a claim which should be supported by survey reports issued by a recognized surveyor approved by the Sellers. The claim, if any, shall be lodged within 30 days after arrival of the cargo at the port/place of destination."

3. 拟订商品检验条款应注意的问题

(1) 必须明确规定商品检验的时间和地点。在国际货物买卖合同中一般采用出口国检验，进口国复验，因为买方只有在复验期限内复验并取得证书，才能作为提出索赔的依据，所以要对复验的期限予以明确。

(2) 必须明确检验方法。在我国，合同无规定或规定不明确的，按国家标准检验，无国家标准的按部颁标准，无部颁标准的按企业标准。

(3) 检验条款应明确具体，并避免与信用证的规定相冲突而单证不符。

(十) 索赔条款

1. 索赔条款的内容

国际货物买卖合同中的索赔条款有两种规定方法：异议与索赔条款和罚金条款。

2. **条款举例**

"品质异议须在货到目的口岸之日起 30 天内提出，数量异议须在货到目的口岸之日起 15 天内提出，买方需同时提供双方同意的公证行的检验证明。卖方应于收到异议后 30 天内答复买方。由自然原因或船方、保险商责任造成的损失，卖方将不予考虑任何索赔。信用证未在合同指定日期内到达卖方，或在 FOB 条款下，买方未按时派船到指定港口，或信用证与合同条款不符，买方在未接到卖方通知所规定的期限内改有关条款时，卖方有权撤销合同或延迟交货，并有权提出索赔。"

"In case discrepancy on the quality of the goods is found by the Buyers after arrival of the goods at the port of destination, claim may be lodged within 30 days after arrival of the goods at the port of destination, while for quantity discrepancy, claim may be lodged within 15 days after arrival of the goods at the port of destination, being supported by Inspection Certificate issued by a reputable public surveyor agreed upon by both parties. The Sellers shall, within 30 days after receipt of the notification of the claim, send reply to the Buyers. For the losses due to natural cause or causes falling within the responsibilities of the Ship-owners or the Underwriters, the Sellers shall not consider any claim for compensation, In case the Letter of Credit does not reach the Sellers within the time stipulated in the Contract, or under FOB price terms Buyers do not send vessel to appointed ports or the Letter of Credit opened by the Buyers do not send vessel to appointed ports or the Letter of Credit opened by the Buyers does not correspond to the Contract terms and the Buyers fail to amend thereafter sits terms by shall have right to cancel the contract or to delay the delivery of the goods and shall have also the right to lodge claims for compensation of losses."

3. **拟订索赔条款应注意的问题**

（1）明确索赔的对象。根据损失的原因和责任的不同，索赔有三种不同的情况：凡属合同当事人的责任造成的损失，可向责任方提出索赔；如是承保范围内的货物损失，应向保险公司索赔；如是承运人的责任造成的货物损失，则应向承运人索赔。

（2）索赔期限的确定要适当。索赔期限是指受损害一方有权向违约方提出索赔的期限。按照法律和国际惯例，受损害一方只能在索赔的期限内提出索赔，否则即丧失索赔权。索赔的期限有约定与法定两种。一般法定期限比较长。例如《联合国国际货物销售合同公约》规定，买方向卖方提出索赔的期限是自买方实际收到货物之日起两年之内。

（十一）不可抗力条款

1. **不可抗力条款的内容**

国际货物买卖合同的不可抗力条款的内容包括不可抗力事件的范围、对不可抗力事件的处理原则和方法、不可抗力事件发生后通知对方的期限和方法，以及出具证明文件的机构等。

2. **条款举例**

"如由于战争、地震、水灾、火灾、暴风雨、雪灾或其他不可抗力的原因，致使卖方不能全部或部分装运或延迟装运合同货物，卖方对于这种不能装运或延迟装运本合同货物不负有责任。但卖方须用电报或电传通知买方，并须在 15 天以内航空挂号信件向买方提交由中国国际贸易促进委员会（中国国际商会）出具的证明此类事件的证明书。”

“If the shipment of the contracted goods is prevented or delayed in whole or in part by reason of war, earthquake, flood, fire, storm, heavy snow or other causes of Force Majeure, the Seller shall not be liable for non-shipment or late shipment of the goods of this contract. However, the Seller shall notify the Buyer by cable or telex and furnish the latter within 15 days by registered airmail with a certificate issued by the China Council for the Promotion of International Trade (China Chamber of International Commerce) attesting such event or events.”

3．拟订不可抗力条款应注意的问题

（1）在国际贸易中，对不可抗力的含义及其叫法并不统一。在英美法中，有“合同落空”原则；大陆法系中有“情势变迁”或“契约失效”原则；尽管各国对不可抗力有不同的叫法与说明，但其精神原则大体相同。

（2）不可抗力事故的范围应采用我国最常用的规定方法，即采用综合规定的办法在买卖合同中订明。

（3）明确规定不可抗力事件发生后向对方提交证明书的期限。实际业务中常规定为15天。

（4）明确规定不可抗力事件发生后出具证明文件的机构，在我国应注明由中国国际贸易促进委员会出具。

（十二）仲裁条款

1．仲裁条款的内容

国际货物买卖合同中仲裁条款的内容有提请仲裁的争议范围、仲裁地点、仲裁机构、仲裁规则、裁决的效力等。

2．条款举例

“凡因本合同引起的或与本合同有关的任何争议，均应提交中国国际经济贸易仲裁委员会按照申请仲裁时该会现行有效的仲裁规则，由申请一方选择由该会在北京或由该会深圳分会在深圳或由该会上海分会在上海进行仲裁。仲裁裁决是终局的，对双方均有约束力。”

“Any dispute arising from or in connection with this Contract shall be submitted to China International Economic and Trade Arbitration Commission for arbitration which shall be conducted by the commission in Beijing or by sits Shenzhen Sub-Commission in Shenzhen or by its Shanghai Sub-Commission in Shanghai at the Claimant's option in accordance with the Commission's arbitration rules in effect at the time of applying for arbitration. The arbitral award is final and binding upon both parties.”

3．拟订仲裁条款应注意的问题

（1）必须明确提请仲裁的争议范围。

（2）必须明确规定仲裁规则及国际公约。

（3）对仲裁地点的确定，应力争在我国仲裁。

（4）我国的常设仲裁机构是中国国际经济贸易仲裁委员会和海事仲裁委员会。

（5）在我国，凡由国际经济贸易仲裁委员会作出的裁决都是终局性的，对双方当事人都有约束力，必须依照执行，任何一方都不许向法院起诉要求变更。

（6）仲裁的费用一般规定由败诉方承担。

四、实训内容

（一）拟订售货合同

张大同于 2021 年 11 月 15 日收到接受通知并于当天拟订好合同。请你根据“实训模块一”广东中山威威照明有限公司与法国巴黎 Le Vernet 贸易有限公司“函电往来”的内容，代张大同拟订合同条款并填制合同。（合同签订日期：2021 年 11 月 15 日；合同签订地点：广州；合同号码：98SGQ468001）

售 货 合 同
SALES CONTRACT

卖方：
Sellers：________________　　Contract No：________________
Date：________________
地址：　　Signed at：________________
Address：________________　　Telex：________________
Fax：________________

Buyers：　　Telex：________________
Address：________________　　Fax：________________

This Sales Contract is made by and between the Sellers and the Buyers, whereby the Sellers agree to sell and the Buyers agree to buy the under-mentioned goods according to the terms and conditions stipulated below：

(1) 货号，品名及规格 Name of Commodity and Specifications	(2) 数量 Quantity	(3) 单位 Unit	(4) 单价 Unit Price	(5) 金额 Amount
% more or less both in amount and quantity allowed	Total Amount			

(6) Packing：________________ (7) Delivery from ________________ to ________________ (8) Shipping Marks：________________

(9) Time of Shipment：Within ________ days after receipt of L/C allowing transhipment and partial shipment.

(10) Terms of Payment：By 100% Confirmed Irrevocable Letter of Credit in favor of the Sellers to be available by sight draft to be opened and to reach China before ________________ and to remain valid for negotiation in China until the 15th days after the foresaid Time of Shipment. L/C must mention this contract number. L/C advised by BANK OF CHINA, GUANGZHOU BRANCH. TLX：444U4K GZBC CN. All banking Charges outside China (the mainland of China) are for account of the Drawee.

(11) Insurance：To be effected by Sellers for 110% of full invoice value covering ________ up to ________
To be effected by the buyers.

(12) Quality/Quantity Discrepancy and Claim：
In case the quality and / or quantity weight are found by the Buyers to be not on conformity with the Contract after arrival of the goods at the port of destination, the Buyers may lodge claim with the Sellers supported by survey report issued by an inspection organization agreed upon by both parties, with the exception, however, of those claims for which the insurance company and or the shipping company are to be held responsible, Claim for quality discrepancy should be filed by the Buyers within 30 days after arrival of the goods at the port of destination, while for quantity / weight discrepancy claim should be filed by the Buyers within 15 days after arrival of the goods at the port of destination, The Sellers shall, within 30 days after receipt of the notification of the claim, send reply to the Buyers.

(13) Force Majeure：In case of Force Majeure, the Sellers shall not be held responsible for late delivery or non-delivery of the goods but shall notify the Buyers by cable. The Sellers shall deliver to the Buyers by registered mail, if so requested by the Buyers, a certificate issued by the China Council for the Promotion of International Trade or/and competent authorities.

(14) Arbitration：All dispute arising from the execution of or in connection with this contract shall be settled amicably by negotiation. In case of settlement can be reached through negotiation the case shall then be submit China International Economic & Trade Arbitration Commission. In Shenzhen (or in Beijing) for arbitration in act with its sure of procedures. The arbitral award is final and binding upon both parties for setting the Dispute. The fee, for arbitration shall be borne by the losing party unless otherwise awarded.

The Sellers ________________　　The Buyers ________________

（二）寄合同要求会签

拟订好售货合同，张大同当天（2021 年 11 月 15 日）通过特快专递寄交法国巴黎 Le Vernet 贸易有限公司 PIERRE 先生会签，并通过电子邮件告知 PIERRE 先生，请代张大同翻译如下信函并发送邮件。

> PIERRE 先生：
>
> 事由：第 98SGQ468001 号合同
>
> 今寄上标题合同正本一式两份，请会签后寄回一份，以便存档。
>
> 张大同敬上
>
> 2021 年 11 月 15 日

____

____

____

____

（三）会签后寄回合同

PIERRE 先生于 2021 年 11 月 18 日收到合同后会签寄回一份，并通过电子邮件告知张大同。请你翻译信函，并发送邮件。

> 张大同先生：
>
> 事由：你方第 98SGQ468001 号合同
>
> 收到你方关于节能灯的上述合同，谢谢。
>
> 我们已会签，今寄回一份备存。
>
> 我们将尽快开立信用证。
>
> PIERRE 先生敬上
>
> 2021 年 11 月 18 日

____

____

____

____

五、强化提高

强化提高一

（一）请将下列合同条款翻译为英文

1. 数量及包装条款

5 000 件，卖方可溢装或短装 5%，每 10 件装 1 纸箱，500 纸箱装 1 只 20 英尺集装箱运送。

2. 装运及保险条款

11 月份装运，由广州至纽约。允许转船，不允许分批，卖方应在装运后及时通知买方。由卖方按发票金额的 110% 投保一切险及战争险。

3. 价格及支付条款

每公吨 1 500 美元 CIF 伦敦，不可撤销、可转让的信用证于 2020 年 5 月 10 日前开抵中国，以卖方为受益人，凭即期汇票在中国议付。

4. 检验及仲裁条款

由中国商检局出具的品质/重量证明书将作为装运品质数量证明。凡因执行本合同所发生的或与合同有关的一切争议，双方应友好协商解决。如果协调不能解决，应提交中国国际经济贸易仲裁委员会，根据该委员会的有关仲裁程序暂行规则在中国进行仲裁的，仲裁裁决是终局的，对双方都有约束力。仲裁费用除另有裁决外由败诉一方承担。

（二）合同审核

卖方 SINOCHEM GUANGDONG IMPORT AND EXPORT CORPORATION, 58, ZHAN QIAN ROAD, GUANGZHOU, CHINA 与买方 METCH THAI ELECTRICAL APPLANCES COMPANY, 45 -7 MAITRICHITR RD. , BANGKOK, THAILAND 经过多次洽商，于 2020 年 4 月 22 日达成一笔交易，内容主要有：威威牌电冰箱（TRIANGLE BRAND REFRIGERATOR）BCD - 184W 100 台，BCD - 184G 100 台，BCD - 184Y 100 台，每台 180.00 美元 CIF BANGKOK，即期不可撤销保兑信用证付款，允许有 5% 的溢短装，纸箱装，信用证须于 5 月 15 日开到中国，证开到后 30 天出运，不允许分批装运，投保水渍险。根据上面内容，卖方已草拟好下面的售货合同。请审核并修改合同。

售货合同
SALES CONTRACT

卖方：SINOCHEM GUANGDONG IMPORT AND EXPORT
Sellers：CORPORATION　　Contract No：98SGQ468001
Date：APR. 22, 2020
地址：　　Signed at：GUANGZHOU
Address：ZHAN QIAN ROAD, GUANGZHOU, CHINA　　Telex：0835
Fax：83556688

Buyers：METCH THAI ELECTRICAL APPLANCES COMPANY, Telex：
Address：45 - 7 MAITRICHITR RD. , BANGKOK, THAILAN　　Fax：

This Sales Contract is made by and between the Sellers and the Buyers, whereby the Sellers agree to sell and the Buyers agree to buy the under-mentioned goods according to the terms and conditions stipulated below：

（1）货号，品名及规格 Name of Commodity and Specifications	（2）数量 Quantity	（3）单位 Unit	（4）单价 Unit Price	（5）金额 Amount
TRIANGLE BRAND　REFRIGERATOR				
BCD - 184W	100	SET	USD 180. 00	USD 18 000. 00
BCD - 184G	100	SET	USD 180. 00	USD 18 000. 00
BCD - 184Y	100	SET	USD 180. 00	USD 18 000. 00
% more or less both in amount and quantity allowed	Total Amount			USD 54 000. 00

（6）Packing：CARTON（7）Delivery from GUANGZHOU to BANGKOK（8）Shipping Marks：N/M

（9）Time of Shipment：Within 30 days after receipt of L/C allowing transhipment and partial shipment.

（10）Terms of Payment：By 100% irrevocable Letter of Credit in favor of the Sellers to be available by sight draft to be opened and to reach China before MAY. 15, 2020 and to remain valid for negotiation in China until the 15th days after the foresaid Time of Shipment. L/C must mention this contract number . L/C advised by BANK OF CHINA. GUANGZHOU BRANCH. TLX：444U4K CZBC CN. All banking Charges outside China（the mainland of China）are for account of the Drawee.

（11）Insurance：To be effected by Sellers for 110% of full invoice value covering F. P. A. up to BANGKOK
To be effected by the buyers.

（12）Quality/Quantity Discrepancy and Claim：
In case the quality and / or quantity weight are found by the Buyers to be not on conformity with the Contract after arrival of the goods at the port of destination, the Buyers may lodge claim with the Sellers supported by survey report issued by an inspection organization agreed upon by both parties, with the exception, however, of those claims for which the insurance company and or the shipping company are to be held responsible, Claim for quality discrepancy should be filed by the Buyers within 30 days after arrival of the goods at the port of destination, while for quantity/weight discrepancy claim should be filed by the Buyers within 15 days after arrival of the goods at the port of destination, The Sellers shall, within 30 days after receipt of the notification of the claim, send reply to the Buyers.

（13）Force Majeure：In case of Force Majeure, the Sellers shall not be held responsible for late delivery or non-delivery of the goods but shall notify the Buyers by cable. The Sellers shall deliver to the Buyers by registered mail, if so requested by the Buyers, a certificate issued by the China Council for the Promotion of International Trade or/and competent authorities.

（14）Arbitration：All dispute arising from the execution of or in connection with this contract shall be settled amicably by negotiation. In case of settlement can be reached through negotiation the case shall then be submit China International Economic & Trade Arbitration Commission. In Shenzhen（or in Beijing）for arbitration in act with its sure of procedures. The arbitral award is final and binding upon both parties for setting the Dispute. The fee, for arbitration shall be borne by the losing party unless otherwise awarded.

The Sellers 张三　　The Buyers ________

强化提高二

根据下面信函，B 方经理刘五于 2020 年 6 月 2 日接到 A 方的接受通知，并于当天填制合同。请你代经理刘五填制如下的销货确认书（销货确认书号码为 GT03 – 25896）。

A 方：M/S. HAIDAROUS TRADING
　　　地址：P. O. BOX 2215, DUBAI, UAE
B 方：广东纺织品进出口广通贸易有限公司
　　　(GUANGDONG TEXTILES IMPORT & EXPORT GUANDTON TRADING COMPANY LIMITED)
　　　地址：广州小北路 168 号粤纺大厦 7 楼
　　　(7/F, GUANGDONG TEXTILES MANSION, 168 XIAOBEI ROAD, GUANGZHOU, CHINA)

A 方："SPORT SHOES GS12A 2 000 双，请给予我方最优惠报价。"

B 方："谢谢！SPORT SHOES GS12A 2 000 PAIRS, TEN PAIRS IN A CARTON, USD 23.00/PAIR CIFDUBAI，不可撤销跟单信用证付款，2020 年 5 月 15 日复到我方有效。"

A 方："你方报价过高，价格降为每双 21 美元可以接受。"

B 方："为使我们能建立贸易关系，我方同意降为每双 22 美元，货款的支付方式为不可撤销跟单信用证付款，在收到你方信用证后 45 天内交货。"

A 方："接受你方 2020 年 6 月 1 日的再还盘，7 月份装运，装运港为广州，目的港为迪拜，禁止分批和转运。请起草合同正本一式两份航寄我公司。"

卖　方

号　码
No. ____________________

销 货 确 认
SALES CONFIRMATION

日　期
Date: ____________________
签约地点:
Signed at: ____________________
电报挂号
Cable: ____________________
TELEX: ____________________
FAX: ____________________

买　方 ____________________
Buyers: ____________________
地　址 ____________________
Address: ____________________

电报挂号: ____________________
Cable Address: ____________________
TELEX: ____________________
FAX: ____________________

兹经买卖双方同意按下列条款成交:

The undersigned Sellers and Buyers have agreed to close the following transactions according to the terms and conditions stipulated below:

1.

货　号 Art No.	品 名 及 规 格 Description	数　量 Quantity	单　价 Unit Price	金　额 Amount

数量及总值均得有　　　　　　% 的增减，由卖方决定。

With 　　　% more or less both in amount and quantity allowed at the Sellers' option.

2. 总　值
Total Value:
3. 包　装
Packing:
4. 装运期
Time of Shipment:
5. 装运口岸和目的地
Loading Port & Destination:
6. 保　险　由卖方按发票全部金额 110% 投保至 ____________ 为止的 ____________ 险。
Insurance: To be effected by Sellers for 110% of full invoice value covering ________ up to ________ only.
7. 付款条件: 买方须于　　年　　月　　日前将不可撤销的，即期信用证开到卖方。议付有效期延至上列装运期后 15 天在中国到期，该信用证中必须注明允许分运及转运。
Terms of Payment: By Irrevocable, and Divisible Letter of Credit to be available by sight draft to reach the Sellers before ________ and to remain valid for negotiation in China until the 15th day after the aforesaid Time of Shipment. The L/C must specify that transhipment and partial shipments are allowed.
8. 装船标记
Shipping Mark:
9. 开立信用证时请注明我成交确认书号码。
When opening L/C, Please mention our S/C number.
10. 备　注
Remarks:

卖　方　　　　　　　　买　方
THE SELLERS　　　　　THE BUYERS

____________________　　　____________________

希 将 本 确 认 书 一 份 签 署 后 寄 回 本 公 司。

Please sign and one copy of this sales confirmation to us at your earliest convenience.

强化提高三

根据买方和卖方的往来信函填写“销货确认书”（销货确认书号码为 GD－2019－7885，签约日期为2019 年 8 月 15 日）。

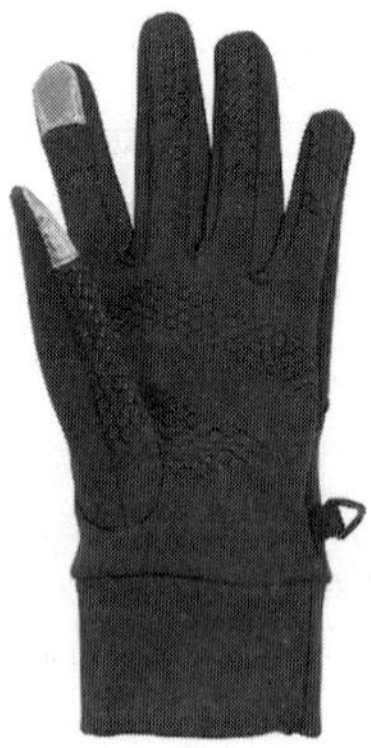

（一）询盘

July 28, 2019

Guangdong Textiles Imp. & Exp. Guandton Trading Co. , Ltd.
7/F, Guangdong Textiles Mansion,
168 Xiaobei Road, Guangzhou, China

Dear Sirs,

One of our clients in Colombo is in the market for a parcel of 3 000 pairs of Leather Dressing Gloves. We would therefore ask you to make us an offer based on CIFC 2% Colombo.

We shall appreciate it if you will arrange shipment as early as possible by direct steamer for Colombo.

As usual, our sight irrevocable L/C will be opened in your favour 30 days before the time of shipment.

Yours faithfully,
ABC TRADING CO. , LTD.

（二）发盘

August 2, 2019

ABC Trading Co. , Ltd.
No. 180 Mosque Road, Gorakana, Sir Lanka

Dear Sirs,

Thank you for your e-mail of July 28 inquiring for 3 000 pairs of Leather Dressing Gloves.

We take pleasure in making you an offer as follows, subject to your acceptance reaching here not later than August 10: 3 000 pairs of Art. No. GL9001 Leather Dressing Gloves in grey, blue and black colours, 50 pairs to a carton, at USD 26. 00 per pair CIFC2% Colombo, for shipment in Guangzhou in October.

We look forward to your early reply.

Yours faithfully,
GUANGDONG TEXTILES IMP. & EXP. GRANDTON TRADING CO. , LTD.

（三）接受

August 6, 2019

Guangdong Textiles Imp. & Exp. Guandton Trading Co. , Ltd.
7/F, Guangdong Textiles Mansion,
168 Xiaobei Road, Guangzhou, China

Dear Sirs,

Thank you for your e-mail of August 2 offering us 3 000 pairs of Leather Dressing Gloves at USD 26. 00 per pair CIFC2% Colombo.

We are glad to persuade our client to accept your price, though they found it a bit on the high side. We are now arranging with our bank for the relevant L/C.

When making shipment, kindly see to it that insurance is to be effected against All Risks and War Risk for 110% of the invoice value.

Yours faithfully,
ABC TRADING CO. , LTD.

卖 方

号 码
No. ______________
日 期
Date: ______________
签约地点:
Signed at: ______________
电报挂号
Cable: ______________
TELEX: ______________
FAX: ______________

销 货 确 认
SALES CONFIRMATION

买 方 ______________
Buyers: ______________
地 址 ______________
Address: ______________

电报挂号: ______________
Cable Address: ______________
TELEX: ______________
FAX: ______________

兹经买卖双方同意按下列条款成交:

The undersigned Sellers and Buyers have agreed to close the following transactions according to the terms and conditions stipulated below:

1.

货 号 Art No.	品 名 及 规 格 Description	数 量 Quantity	单 价 Unit Price	金 额 Amount

数量及总值均得有　　　　%的增减，由卖方决定。

With　　　% more or less both in amount and quantity allowed at the Sellers' option.

2. 总 值
Total Value:
3. 包 装
Packing:
4. 装运期
Time of Shipment:
5. 装运口岸和目的地
Loading Port & Destination:
6. 保 险　由卖方按发票全部金额110%投保至______________为止的______________险。
Insurance: To be effected by Sellers for 110% of full invoice value covering ________ up to ________ only.
7. 付款条件: 买方须于　　年　　月　　日前将不可撤销的，即期信用证开到卖方。议付有效期延至上列装运期后15天在中国到期，该信用证中必须注明允许分运及转运。
Terms of Payment: By Irrevocable, and Divisible Letter of Credit to be available by sight draft to reach the Sellers before ________ and to remain valid for negotiation in China until the 15th day after the aforesaid Time of Shipment. The L/C must specify that transhipment and partial shipments are allowed.
8. 装船标记
Shipping Mark:
9. 开立信用证时请注明我成交确认书号码。
When opening L/C, Please mention our S/C number.
10. 备 注
Remarks:

卖 方　　　　　　　　买 方
THE SELLERS　　　　　THE BUYERS

______________　　　　______________

希将本确认书一份签署后寄回本公司。

Please sign and one copy of this sales confirmation to us at your earliest convenience.

实训模块四　催证、申请开证

一、实训目的

本模块的实训，使学生了解卖方如何催开信用证和买方申请开证的具体手续以及买方申请开证时应注意的问题。

二、实训任务

（1）根据提供的资料独立草拟规范的催证英文信函。
（2）根据前期拟订的合同内容填制开证申请书。

三、实训提示

（一）催证文函

1. 写信要点

（1）有关的信用证还未收到。
（2）要求速开信用证。
（3）开证注意事项。
（4）盼早收到信用证。

2. 常用句型

句型1　有关的信用证还未收到

（1）Regarding the 500 pieces of Children' Bicycles under our Sales Contract No. 123, we would draw your attention to the fact that the date of delivering is drawing near, but we haven't received your L/C.
关于我方第123号销售合同项下的500辆童车，我们拟提请你方注意，交货期日益迫近，而有关信用证迄今仍未收到。

（2）As to our S/C No. 234, we regret to find that your L/C has failed to arrive here within the time stipulated.
关于我方第234号销售合同，我们很遗憾你方的信用证未能在规定的时间开达我方。

句型2　要求速开信用证

（1）As the goods are ready for shipment, please expedite your L/C so that we may effect shipment by S. S "Peace".

由于货已备好待装，请速开信用证，以便这批货赶上"和平"号轮。

（2）Please do your utmost to open your L/C, so that we may execute your order smoothly.

请速开信用证，以便这笔订货得以顺利执行。

句型 3　开证注意事项

（1）In order to avoid subsequent amendments, please see to it that the L/C stipulations are in exact accordance with the terms of the contract.

为了避免随后修改，务请做到信用证内规定事项与合同条款完全一致。

（2）In order to avoid subsequent L/C amendment, please pay attention to the stipulations of the S/C.

为了避免随后对信用证的修改，请留意销售合同的规定。

3. 信函范例

Dear Sirs,

In regard to our S/C No. 234, we would draw your attention to the fact that the date of shipment is approaching, but we still have not received your covering L/C. Please open the relevant L/C immediately, so that we can ship the goods in time.

In order to avoid subsequent amendments, please see to it that the L/C stipulations are in exact accordance with the terms of the contract.

We look forward to receiving your covering L/C soon.

Yours faithfully,

敬启者：

关于我方第 234 号销售合同，拟提请注意交货期日益临近，但至今我们还未收到有关的信用证。请速开信用证，以便我方及时装运。

为了避免日后的修改，请做到信用证的规定事项与合同条款完全一致。

盼早日收到你们的信用证。

敬上

（二）申请开证的具体手续

（1）递交有关合同的副本及附件。

（2）填写开证申请书。

（3）缴付保证金。

（4）支付开证手续费。

（三）申请开证应注意的问题

（1）开证申请书的填制必须以合同为依据。

（2）开证时间的掌握应以卖方在收到信用证后能在合同规定的装运期内出运为原则。

具体包括：①合同规定开证日期，就必须在规定期限内开立信用证；②合同有装运期的起止日期，则最迟必须让卖方在装运期的第一天就能收到信用证；③合同只规定最后装运期，则买方应在合理的时间内开证，一般掌握在合同规定的交货期前一个月或一个半月。

（3）证同一致。合同中规定要在信用证上明确的条款都必须列明，不能使用“参阅第×××号合同”或“第×××号合同项下货物”等条款，也不能将有关合同作为信用证附件附在信用证后。

（4）要明确规定信用证中各类单据的出单人（商业发票、保险单和运输单据除外）及各单据应表述的内容。

（5）对不准分批装运、不准转运等，要在信用证中明确规定，否则将被认为是允许分批和转运。

（6）实务中对进口业务原则上不开可转让信用证，也不开立载有电报索偿条款（T/T reimbursement clause）的信用证。

四、实训内容

（一）催开信用证

广东中山威威照明有限公司张大同为了保证在2021年12月交货，于2021年11月22日向法国巴黎Le Vernet贸易有限公司的PIERRE先生发出催证文函，请翻译下面的文函：

> PIERRE先生：
>
> 我方已收到贵方寄回的合同No. 98SGQ468001，谢谢。请你方速开信用证，以便我方顺利执行该项订单。
>
> 为了避免随后的修改，务请注意信用证的规定事项与合同条款完全一致。
>
> 此致
>
> 张大同　敬上
>
> 2021年11月22日

____

____

____

（二）填制“开证申请书”

法国巴黎Le Vernet贸易有限公司于2021年11月24日向当地的METITA BANK LTD.，FRANCE申请开证，请你代PIERRE先生，按前面双方拟订的合同，以电开证的方式，填写下面的开证申请书：

IRREVOCABLE DOCUMENTARY CREDIT APPLICATION

To:　　　　　　　　　　　　　　　　　　　　Date:

<table>
<tr><td colspan="2">Beneficiary (fullname and address)</td><td>L/C No.
Ex-Card No.
Contract No.

Date and place of expiry of the credit</td></tr>
<tr><td>Partial shipments
☐ allowed
☐ not allowed</td><td>Transhipment
☐ allowed
☐ not allowed</td><td>☐ Issue by airmail　☐ With brief advice by teletransmission
☐ Issue by express delivery
☐ Issue by teletransmission (which shall be the operative instrument)</td></tr>
<tr><td colspan="2">Loading on board/ dispatch/ taking in charge at/ from

not later than
for transportation to</td><td>Amount (both in figures and words)

Credit available with
☐ by sight payment　☐ by acceptance　☐ by negotiation
☐ by deferred payment at
against the documents detailed herein
☐and beneficiary's draft for　　% of the invoice value
at
on</td></tr>
<tr><td colspan="2">Description of goods:

Packing:</td><td>☐ FOB　☐ C&F　☐ CIF
☐ or other terms</td></tr>
</table>

Documents required: (marked with ×)
1. (　) Signed Commercial Invoice in 　　copies indicating L/C No. and Contract No.
2. (　) Full set of clean on board ocean Bills of Lading made out to order and blank endorsed, marked "freight [　] to collect/ [　] prepaid [　] showing freight amount" notifying
3. (　) Air Waybills showing "freight [　] to collect/ [　] prepaid [　] indicating freight amount" and consigned to
4. (　) Memorandum issued by 　　　consigned to
5. (　) Insurance Policy/Certificate in 　copies for 　% of the invoice value showing claims payable in China in currency of the draft, blank endorsed, covering ([　] Ocean Marine Transportation/ [　] Air Transportation/ [　] Over Land Transportation) All Risks, War Risks.
6. (　) Packing List/ Weight Memo in 　　copies issued by quantity/ gross and net weights of each package and packing conditions as called for by the L/C.
7. (　) Certificate of Quantity /Weight in 　　copies issued by an independent surveyor at the loading port, indicating the actual surveyed quantity/ weight of shipped goods as well as the packing condition.
8. (　) Certificate of Quantity in 　　copies issued by [　] manufacturer [　] public recognized surveyor [　]
9. (　) Beneficiary's certified copy of cable/ telex dispatched to the accountees within 　　hours after shipment advising [　] name of vessel/ [　] flight No. / [　] wagon No. , date, quantity, weight and value of shipment.
10. (　) Beneficiary's Certificate certifying that extra copies of the documents have been dispatched according to the contract terms.
11. (　) Shipping Co's Certificate attesting that the carrying vessel is chartered or booked by accountee or their shipping agents:
12. (　) Other documents, if any:

Additional instructions:
1. (　) All banking charges outside the opening bank are for beneficiary's account.
2. (　) Documents must be presented within 　　days after the date of issuance of the transport documents but within the validity of this credit.
3. (　) Third party as shipper is not acceptable. Short Form/ Blank Back B/L is not acceptable.
4. (　) Both quantity and amount 　　% more or less are allowed.
5. (　) Prepaid freight drawn in excess of L/C amount is acceptable against presentation of original charges voucher issued by shipping Co. / Air Line/ or it's agent.
6. (　) All documents to be forwarded in one cover, unless otherwise stated above.
7. (　) Other terms, if any:

Account No. :　　　　　　　　with ______________________ (name of bank)
Transacted by:　　　　　　　(Applicant: name, signature of authorized person)
Telephone No. :　　　　　　　(with seal)

（三）开立信用证

开证行 METITA BANK LTD.，FRANCE 根据法国巴黎 Le Vernet 贸易有限公司的申请开立如下信用证，由中国银行广州分行于 2021 年 11 月 25 日通知广东中山威威照明有限公司。

GUANGZHOU INT'L FINANCIAL BUILDING.
197 Deng Feng Xi Lu, Guangzhou, P. R. China

中国银行 广东省分行
BANK OF CHINA
GUANGDONG BRANCH
GUANGZHOU, CHINA

ORIGINAL

信 用 证 通 知 书

通知日：NOV. 25, 2021
我行号码：DN4008276T02

致：广东中山威威照明有限公司
GUANGDONG ZHONGSHAN WEIWEI LIGHTING CO., LTD.

开 证 行：
METITA BANK LTD., FRANCE

转 递 行：

信用证号：LRT9802457
开证日期：211125

金　　额：USD 29 000.00
来证方式：Full SWIFT/Telex

本证页数（不包面函）：
我行费用负担：Beneficiary Account　　我行是否加保：Unnecessary

敬启者　：
兹通知贵司，我行收自上述银行的信用证一份，现随附通知，并请注意下列打"×"条文：
(　　) 该行首次来证，请慎重处理。
(　　) 此证如需加保，请与我行联系。
(　　) 此证尚未生效，请切勿出货。
(　　) 此证印押未符，请切勿出货。

注意事项：
1. 贵司交单时，请将信用证及通知书一并提示；
2. 我行保兑信用证，限向我行交单议付，否则保兑无效；
3. 非我行保兑信用证，不构成我行任何责任；
4. 费用由受益人负担时，对我行客户，我行会主动借记其账，收取我行费用；
5. 请注意我行对信用证中有关条款的提示。

贵司负担费用：
通知费：CNY 200.00
保兑费：CNY
预先通知费：CNY
电报费：CNY

备注：

中 国 银 行 广 东 省 分 行 具
FOR BANK OF CHINA GUANGDONG BRANCH

下列项目仅供我行使用：
ADV-CHG：USD
CONFIRM：USD
PRE-ADV：USD
RLS-CHG：USD
（ $ ）

2021NOV. 25				Logical Terminal GDPF
MT S700	Issue of a Documentary Credit			Page 00001
				Func JSRVPR1
User Header	Service Code	103	:	
	Bank Priority	113	:	
	Msg User Ref.	108	:	
	Info. From CI	115	:	

Sequence of Total	*27		:	1 / 1
Form of Doc. Credit	*40	A	:	IRREVOCABLE
Doc. Credit Number	*20		:	LRT9802457
Date of Issue	31	C	:	211125
Expiry	*31	D	:	220110
Applicant	*50		:	Le Vernet TRADE COMPANY LIMITED, PARIS FRANCE 245 Avenue Foch, PARIS FRANCE
Beneficiary	*59		:	GUANGDONG ZHONGSHAN WEIWEI LIGHTING CO., LTD. 52, CUIHUA ROAD, ZHONGSHAN, CHINA
Amount	*32	B	:	Currency USD Amount 20 000. 00
Pos. / Neg. Tol. (%)	39	A	:	05 / 05
Available with/by	*41	D	:	ANY BANK BY NEGOTIATION
Draft at...	42	C	:	SIGHT
Drawee	42	D	:	METITA BANK LTD., FRANCE
Partial Shipments	43	P	:	Not Allowed
Transhipment	43	T	:	Allowed
Loading in Charge	44	A	:	GUANGZHOU
For Transport to...	44	B	:	LE HAVRE
Shipment Period	44	C	:	LATEST DEC 28, 2021
Description of Goods	45	A	:	

Weiwei Brand LED Bulb

LY-5W-A50　110V 5W　E27/B22　USD 0. 45/PC　29 000 PCS

LY-5W-A60　110V 7W　E27/B22　USD 0. 55/PC　29 000 PCS

CIF LE HAVRE　AS PER S/C 98SGQ468001 DD 15, 11, 2021

Documents required　46　A　:

+ COMMERCIAL INVOICEIN 5 COPIES
+ PACKING LIST IN 5 COPIES
+ FULL SET OF CLEAN ON BOARD MARINE BILLS OF LADING, MADE OUT TO ORDER, MARKED "FREIGHT PREPAID" AND NOTIFY APPLICANT
+ GSP CERTIFICATE OF ORIGIN FORM A, CERTIFYING GOODS OF ORIGIN IN CHINA, ISSUED BY COMPETENT AUTHORITIES
+ INSURANCE POLICY/CERTIFICATE COVERING RISKS F. P. A OF PICC. INCLUDING WAREHOUSE TO WAREHOUSE CLAUSE UP TO FINAL DESTINATION AT LE HAVRE,
  FOR AT LEAST 110 PCT OF CIF-VALUE.
+ SHIPPING ADVICES MUST BE SENT TO APPLICANT WITHIN 2 DAYS AFTER SHIPMENT ADVISING NUMBER OF PACKAGES, GROSS & NET WEIGHT, VESSEL NAME, BILL OF LADING NO. AND DATE, CONTRACT NO., VALUE.
+ BENEFICIARY'S CERTIFICATE CERTIFYING THAT ONE COPY EACH OF INVOICE, N/N B/L HAVE BEEN FAXED TO BUYER TO FAX NO. 833-675 WITHIN 3 DAYS AFTER SHIPMENT.

2021NOV25　　Logical Terminal　GDPF

MT S700　　Issue of a Documentary Credit　　Page　00002

Func　JSRVPR1

Addition Cond.　47　A　:

IF BILLS OF LADIGN ARE REQUIRED ABOVE, PLEASE FORWARD DOCUMENTS IN TWO MAILS, ORIGINALS SEND BY COURIER AND DUPLICATES BY REGISTERED AIRMAIL.

Details of Charges　71　B　:　BANK CHARGES EXCLUDING ISSUING BANKS ARE FOR ACCOUNT OF BENEFICIARY.

Presentation Period　48　:　DOCUMENTS TO BE PRESENTED WITHIN 15 DAYS FROM SHIPMENT DATE

Confirmation　*49　:　WITHOUT

Instructions　78　:

DISCREPANT DOCUMENTS, IF ACCEPTABLE, WILL BE SUBJECT TO A CISCREPANCY HANDLING FEE OF USD 50.00 OR EQUIVALENT WHICH WILL BE FOR ACCOUNT OF BENEFICIARY.

SPECIAL NOTE: ISSUING BANK WILL DISCOUNT ACCEPTANCES ON REQUEST, FOR A/C OF BENEFICIARY (UNLESS OTHERWISE STATED) AT APPROPRIATE LIBOR RATE PLUS 1.00 PERCENT MARGIN.

Send. To　Rec. Info.　72　:　THIS CREDIT IS ISSUED SUBJECT TO 1993 REVISION, I. C. C. PUBLICATIONS NO. 600

Trailer　Order is <MAC: > <PAC: > <ENC: > <CHK: > <TNG: > <PDE: >

MAC: ID20750E

CHK: 5034662F74BC

五、强化提高

强化提高一

广东纺织品进出口广通贸易有限公司（GUANGDONG TEXTILES IMP. & EXP. GRANDTON TRADING CO., LTD., 168 XIAOBEI ROAD, GUANGZHOU, CHINA）与 M/S. HAIDAROUS TRADING P. O. BOX 2215, DUBAI, UAE 签订进口合同，拟进口货物一批，根据合同要求，广东纺织品进出口广通贸易有限公司于 2018 年 12 月 26 日向中国银行申请开证，请根据销货确认书填制开证申请书：

卖　方
M/S. HAIDAROUS TRADING
P. O. BOX 2215，DUBAI，UAE

销 货 确 认 书
SALES CONFIRMATION

No. C215
日期
Date：DEC. 22，2018
签约地点：
Signed at：GUANGZHOU，CHINA
电报挂号
Cable："ARTCANTON"
TELEX：44371KTTEX CN
FAX：（020）83869360

买　方　GUANGDONG TEXTILES IMP. & EXP.
Buyers：GRANDTON TRADING CO.，LTD.
地　址　168 XIAOBEI ROAD，GUANGZHOU，CHINA
Address：

电报挂号：
Cable Address：
TELEX：
FAX：263745

兹经买卖双方同意按下列条款成交：

The undersigned Sellers and Buyers have agreed to close the following transactions according to the terms and conditions stipulated below：

1.

货　号 Art No.	品 名 及 规 格 Description	数　量 Quantity	单　价 Unit Price	金　额 Amount
	LADIES LYCRA LONG PANT		CIF GUANGZHOU	
ART NO. P97811	SIZE：M-XXL　ASSORTED	200 DOZ	@ USD 23. 00	USD 4 600. 00
ART NO. P97811(2)	SIZE：M-XXL　ASSORTED	200 DOZ	@ USD 24. 00	USD 4 800. 00
		400 DOZ		USD 9 400. 00

数量及总值均得有　5　%的增减，由卖方决定。

With　5　% more or less both in amount and quantity allowed at the Sellers' option.

2. 总　值

Total Value：USD 9 400. 00（U. S. Dollars NINE THOUSAND FOUR HUNDRED ONLY.）

3. 包　装

Packing：CARTON IN 10 DOZ

4. 装运期

Time of Shipment：NOT LATER THAN MAR. 27，2019

5. 装运口岸和目的地

Loading Port & Destination：FROM DUBAI TO GUANGZHOU

6. 保　险　由卖方按发票全部金额110%投保至＿＿＿＿为止的＿＿＿＿险。

Insurance：To be effected by Sellers for 110% of full invoice value covering F. P. A up to GUANGZHOU only.

7. 付款条件：买方须于2019年1月1日将不可撤销的，即期信用证开到卖方。议付有效期延至上列装运期后15天在中国到期，该信用证中必须注明允许分运及转运。

Terms of Payment：By Irrevocable，and Divisible Letter of Credit to be available by sight draft to reach the Sellers before JAN. 1，2019 and to remain valid for negotiation in China until the 15th day after the aforesaid Time of Shipment. The L/C must specify that transhipment and partial shipments are allowed.

8. 装船标记

Shipping Mark：MAHARAJA DEIRA/ANAND/264553/GUANGZHOU

9. 开立信用证时请注明我成交确认书号码。

When opening L/C，Please mention our S/C number.

10. 备　注

Remarks：

卖　方
THE SELLERS
MARRY

买　方
THE BUYERS
张明华

希将本确认书一份签署后寄回本公司。

Please sign and one copy of this sales confirmation to us at your earliest convenience.

IRREVOCABLE DOCUMENTARY CREDIT APPLICATION

To:　　　　　　　　　　　　　　　　　　　　　　　　Date:

<table>
<tr><td colspan="2">Beneficiary (fullname and address)</td><td>L/C No.
Ex-Card No.
Contract No.</td></tr>
<tr><td colspan="2"></td><td>Date and place of expiry of the credit</td></tr>
<tr><td>Partial shipments
□allowed□not allowed</td><td>Transhipment
□allowed □not allowed</td><td rowspan="2">□Issue by airmail　□With brief advice by teletransmission
□Issue by express delivery
□Issue by teletransmission (which shall be the operative instrument)</td></tr>
<tr><td colspan="2" rowspan="2">Loading on board/ dispatch/ taking in charge at/ from

not later than
for transportation to</td></tr>
<tr><td>Amount (both in figures and words)</td></tr>
<tr><td colspan="2" rowspan="2">Description of goods:

Packing:</td><td>Credit available with
□by sight payment □by acceptance □by negotiation
□by deferred payment at against the documents detailed herein
□and beneficiary's draft for　% of the invoice value
at
on</td></tr>
<tr><td>□FOB　□C&F　□CIF
□or other terms</td></tr>
</table>

Documents required: (marked with ×)

1. (　) Signed Commercial Invoice in　　　copies indicating L/C No. and Contract No.
2. (　) Full set of clean on board ocean Bills of Lading made out to order and blank endorsed, marked "freight [　] to collect/ [　] prepaid [　] showing freight amount" notifying
3. (　) Air Waybills showing "freight [　] to collect/ [　] prepaid [　] indicating freight amount" and consigned to
4. (　) Memorandum issued by　　　consigned to
5. (　) Insurance Policy/Certificate in　　copies for　　　% of the invoice value showing claims payable in China in currency of the draft, blank endorsed, covering ([　] Ocean Marine Transportation/ [　] Air Transportation [　] Over Land Transportation) All Risks, War Risks.
6. (　) Packing List/ Weight Memo in　　copies issued by quantity/ gross and net weights of each package and packing conditions as called for by the L/C.
7. (　) Certificate of Quantity /Weight in　copies issued by an independent surveyor at the loading port, indicating the actual surveyed quantity/ weight of shipped goods as well as the packing condition.
8. (　) Certificate of Quantity in　　copies issued by [　] manufacturer/ [　] public recognized surveyor/ [　]
9. (　) Beneficiary's certified copy of cable/ telex dispatched to the accountees within　　hours after shipment advising [　] name of vessel/ [　] flight No. / [　] wagon No. , date, quantity, weight and value of shipment.
10. (　) Beneficiary's Certificate certifying that extra copies of the documents have been dispatched according to the contract terms.
11. (　) Shipping Co's Certificate attesting that the carrying vessel is chartered or booked by accountee or their shipping agents:
12. (　) Other documents, if any:

Additional instructions:

1. (　) All banking charges outside the opening bank are for beneficiary's account.
2. (　) Documents must be presented within　　days after the date of issuance of the transport documents but within the validity of this credit.
3. (　) Third party as shipper is not acceptable. Short Form/ Blank Back B/L is not acceptable.
4. (　) Both quantity and amount　　% more or less are allowed.
5. (　) Prepaid freight drawn in excess of L/C amount is acceptable against presentation of original charges voucher issued by shipping Co. / Air Line/ or it's agent.
6. (　) All documents to be forwarded in one cover, unless otherwise stated above.
7. (　) Other terms, if any:

Account No. :　　　　　　　　with ________________________ (name of bank)

Transacted by:　　　　　　　(Applicant: name, signature of authorized person)

Telephone No. :　　　　　　　(with seal)

强化提高二

根据售货合同填制信用证申请书（申请日期为2019年3月5日）。

售 货 合 同
SALES CONTRACT

卖　方：SUNNY TRADING CO., LTD.
Sellers: ______

地　址：666 BAKE STREET, NEWYORK
Address: ______

Contract No.: CF－04－289861
Date: FEB. 25, 2019
Signed at: SHANGHAI
Telex: ______
Fax: ______

Buyers: SHANGHAI CHUNFENG IMP. & EXP. CORP.
Address: 128 NANHAI ROAD, SHANGHAI, CHINA
Telex: ______
Fax: ______

This Sales Contract is made by and between the Sellers and the Buyers, whereby the Sellers agree to sell and the Buyers agree to buy the under-mentioned goods according to the terms and conditions stipulated below:

（1）货号，品名及规格 Name of Commodity and Specifications	（2）数量 Quantity	（3）单位 Unit	（4）单价 Unit Price	（5）金额 Amount
iPhone 10	1 000	SET	CIF SHNAGHAI USD 1 100.00	USD 1 100 000.00
5% more or less both in amount and quantity allowed	Total Amount			USD 1 100 000.00

（6）Packing: CARTON （7）Delivery from NEWYORK to SHANGHAI （8）Shipping Marks: N/M

（9）Time of Shipment: Within 30 days after receipt of L/C allowing transhipment and partial shipment.

（10）Terms of Payment: By 100% Irrevocable Letter of Credit in favor of the Sellers to be available by sight draft to be opened and to reach USA before MAR. 10, 2019 and to remain valid for negotiation in USA until the 15th days after the foresaid Time of Shipment. L/C must mention this contract number. All banking Charges outside China (the mainland of China) are for account of the Beneficiary.

（11）Insurance: To be effected by Sellers for 110% of full invoice value covering ALL RISKS up to SHANGHAI
To be effected by the buyers.

（12）Quality/Quantity Discrepancy and Claim:
In case the quality and / or quantity weight are found by the Buyers to be not on conformity with the Contract after arrival of the goods at the port of destination, the Buyers may lodge claim with the Sellers supported by survey report issued by an inspection organization agreed upon by both parties, with the exception, however, of those claims for which the insurance company and or the shipping company are to be held responsible, Claim for quality discrepancy should be filed by the Buyers within 30 days after arrival of the goods at the port of destination, while for quantity / weight discrepancy claim should be filed by the Buyers within 15 days after arrival of the goods at the port of destination, The Sellers shall, within 30 days after receipt of the notification of the claim, send rely to the Buyers.

（13）Force Majeure: In case of Force Majeure, the Sellers shall not be held responsible for late delivery or non-delivery of the goods but shall notify the Buyers by cable. The Sellers shall deliver to the Buyers by registered mail, if so requested by the Buyers, a certificate issued by competent authorities.

（14）Arbitration: All dispute arising from the execution of or in connection with this contract shall be settled amicably by negotiation. In case of settlement can be reached through negotiation the case shall then be submit China International Economic & Trade Arbitration Commission. In Shenzhen (or in Beijing) for arbitration in act with its sure of procedures. The arbitral award is final and binding upon both parties for setting the Dispute. The fee, for arbitration shall be borne by the losing party unless otherwise awarded.

The Sellers BAKE　　　　The Buyers 刘五

IRREVOCABLE DOCUMENTARY CREDIT APPLICATION

To: Date:

Beneficiary (fullname and address)	L/C No. Ex-Card No. Contract No. Date and place of expiry of the credit
Partial shipments ☐allowed ☐not allowed / Transhipment ☐allowed ☐not allowed Loading on board/ dispatch/ taking in charge at/ from not later than for transportation to	☐Issue by airmail ☐With brief advice by teletransmission ☐Issue by express delivery ☐Issue by teletransmission (which shall be the operative instrument) Amount (both in figures and words) Credit available with ☐by sight payment ☐by acceptance ☐by negotiation ☐by deferred payment at against the documents detailed herein ☐and beneficiary's draft for % of the invoice value at on
Description of goods: Packing:	☐FOB ☐C&F ☐CIF ☐or other terms

Documents required: (marked with ×)
1. ( ) Signed Commercial Invoice in copies indicating L/C No. and Contract No.
2. ( ) Full set of clean on board ocean Bills of Lading made out to order and blank endorsed, marked "freight [ ] to collect/ [ ] prepaid [ ] showing freight amount" notifying
3. ( ) Air Waybills showing "freight [ ] to collect [ ] prepaid [ ] indicating freight amount" and consigned to
4. ( ) Memorandum issued by consigned to
5. ( ) Insurance Policy/Certificate in copies for % of the invoice value showing claims payable in China in currency of the draft, blank endorsed, covering ([ ] Ocean Marine Transportation/ [ ] Air Transportation/ [ ] Over Land Transportation) All Risks, War Risks.
6. ( ) Packing List/ Weight Memo in copies issued by quantity/ gross and net weights of each package and packing conditions as called for by the L/C.
7. ( ) Certificate of Quantity /Weight in copies issued by an independent surveyor at the loading port, indicating the actual surveyed quantity/ weight of shipped goods as well as the packing condition.
8. ( ) Certificate of Quantity in copies issued by [ ] manufacturer / [ ] public recognized surveyor / [ ]
9. ( ) Beneficiary's certified copy of cable/ telex dispatched to the accountees within hours after shipment advising [ ] name of vessel/ [ ] flight No. / [ ] wagon No., date, quantity, weight and value of shipment.
10. ( ) Beneficiary's Certificate certifying that extra copies of the documents have been dispatched according to the contract terms.
11. ( ) Shipping Co's Certificate attesting that the carrying vessel is chartered or booked by accountee or their shipping agents:
12. ( ) Other documents, if any:

Additional instructions:
1. ( ) All banking charges outside the opening bank are for beneficiary's account.
2. ( ) Documents must be presented within days after the date of issuance of the transport documents but within the validity of this credit.
3. ( ) Third party as shipper is not acceptable. Short Form/ Blank Back B/L is not acceptable.
4. ( ) Both quantity and amount % more or less are allowed.
5. ( ) Prepaid freight drawn in excess of L/C amount is acceptable against presentation of original charges voucher issued by shipping Co. / Air Line/ or it's agent.
6. ( ) All documents to be forwarded in one cover, unless otherwise stated above.
7. ( ) Other terms, if any:

Account No.: with ____________________ (name of bank)
Transacted by: (Applicant: name, signature of authorized person)
Telephone No.: (with seal)

强化提高三

根据下面提供的合同审核信用证申请书，把与合同规定不符的地方指出来并修改。

SALES CONTRACT

Sellers: HONGDA MOTOR CO. LTD.
Address: NO. 1 – 1, 2 – CHOME, MINAMI – AOYAMA, MINATO-KU, TOKYO, JAPAN

Contract No: 001 – 32A – 5202 – 12
Date: FEB. 2, 2001
Signed at: GUANGZHOU
Telex:
Fax:

Buyers: GUANGZHOU HONDA AUTOMOBILE CO. LTD.
Address: HENGSHA, HUANGPU, GUANGZHOU P. R. CHINA

Telex:
Fax:

This Sales Contract is made by and between the Sellers and the Buyers, whereby the Sellers agree to sell and the Buyers agree to buy the under-mentioned goods according to the terms and conditions stipulated below:

(1) Name of Commodity and Specifications	(2) Quantity	(3) Unit	(4) Unit Price	(5) Amount
HONDA AUTOMOBILE ENGINE				
MODLE GL – 3.0	100	SET	USD 13 000.00	USD 1 300 000.00
MODLE GX – 2.4	130		USD 10 000.00	USD 1 300 000.00
MODLE GT – 1.3	100		USD 7 000.00	USD 700 000.00
5% more or less both in amount and quantity allowed	Total Amount			USD 3 300 000.00

(6) Packing: IN CONTAINERS　(7) Shipping Marks: N/M

(8) Delivery from ANY JAPANESE SEA PORT to XINGANG HUANGPU, GUANGZHOU, CHINA

(9) Time of Shipment: Not later than 2001/03/10, allowing transhipment and partial shipment.

(10) Terms of Payment: By 100% Irrevocable Letter of Credit in favor of the Sellers to be available by sight draft to be opened and to reach Japan before FEB. 15, 2001 and to remain valid for negotiation in Japan until the 15th days after the foresaid Time of Shipment. L/C must mention this contract number. L/C advised by INDDUSTRIAL AND COMMERCIAL BANK OF CHINA TOKYO BRANCH.

(11) Insurance: To be effected by Sellers for 110% of full invoice value covering INSTITUTE CARGO CLAUSE (A), INSTITUTE STRIKE CLAUSES, INSTITUTE WAR CLAUSE up to XINGANG, HUANGPU, GUANGZHOU, CHINA including warehouse to warehouse.

(12) Quality/Quantity Discrepancy and Claim:
In case the quality and / or quantity weight are found by the Buyers to be not on conformity with the Contract after arrival of the goods at the port of destination, the Buyers may lodge claim with the Sellers supported by survey report issued by an inspection organization agreed upon by both parties, with the exception, however, of those claims for which the insurance company and or the shipping company are to be held responsible, Claim for quality discrepancy should be filed by the Buyers within 30 days after arrival of the goods at the port of destination, while for quantity / weight discrepancy claim should be filed by the Buyers within 15 days after arrival of the goods at the port of destination, The Sellers shall, within 30 days after receipt of the notification of the claim, send rely to the Buyers.

(13) Force Majeure: In case of Force Majeure, the Sellers shall not be held responsible for late delivery or non-delivery of the goods but shall notify the Buyers by cable. The Sellers shall deliver to the Buyers by registered mail, if so requested by the Buyers, a certificate issued by competent authorities.

(14) Arbitration: All dispute arising from the execution of or in connection with this contract shall be settled amicably by negotiation. In case of settlement can be reached through negotiation the case shall then be submit China International Economic & Trade Arbitration Commission. In Shenzhen (or in Beijing) for arbitration in act with its sure of procedures. The arbitral award is final and binding upon both parties for setting the Dispute. The fee, for arbitration shall be borne by the losing party unless otherwise awarded.

The Sellers ________　　　　The Buyers ________

不可撤销跟单信用证申请书

APPLICATION FOR IRREVOCABLE DOCUMENTARY CREDIT

ATTENTION: NO NET WEIGHT

To: THE INDUSTRIAL AND COMMERCIAL BANK OF CHINA, GUANGZHOU BRANCH Dated: FEB.12, 2001

Please establish [X] By SWIFT/Telex [ ] By airmail an Irrevocable Credit as per followings

Advising Bank INDUSTRIAL AND COMMERCIAL BANK OF CHINA, TOKYO BRANCH	(20) IRREVOCABLE DOCUMENTARY CREDIT No. (31D) Expiry Date 2001/04/10 Expiry Place TOKYO, JAPAN
(50) Applicant GUANGZHOU HONDA AUTOMOBILE CO., LTD. HENGSHA, HUANGPU, GUANGZHOU P.R. CHINA	(59) Beneficiary HONDA MOTOR CO., LTD. NO.1-1, 2-CHOME, MINAMI-AOYAMA, MINATO-KU, TOKYO, JAPAN

(32B) Currency code, Amount (in figures): USD3,258,393.60

(In words): SAY IN U.S.DOLLARS THREE MILLION TWO HUNDRED FIFTY-EIGHT THOUSAND THREE HUNDRED AND NINETY-THREE AND CENTS SIXTY ONLY

Quantity and Credit amount tolerance____%

(41a) Credit available with [X] ANY BANK [ ] Issuing Bank

By [X] Negotiation [ ] Acceptance [X] Sight Payment [ ] Deferred Payment at

(42C) Draft at sight For 100 % of Invoice Value.

(43P) Partial Shipment [ ] allowed [X] not allowed (43T) Transhipment [X] allowed [ ] not allowed

(44A) Loading on board From Any Japanese sea port (44B) For Transportation to XINGANG, HUANGPU, GUANGZHOU, CHINA

(44C) Latest Date of Shipment: 2001/03/20

(45A) Description of Goods: Automobile Parts as per proforma invoice/contract No.001-32A-5202-12.

Price term: CIF XINGANG, HUANGPU, GUANGZHOU, CHINA

Packing: IN CONTAINERS

(46A) Documents required: (marked with x)

(X) Signed Commercial invoice in 3 originals ~~copies~~ indicating L/C No.and Contract No. as mentioned above.

(X) 2/3 set of clean on board ocean Bills of Lading made out to order and blank endorsed marked "freight prepaid .

[ ] showing freight amount" notifying [X] Applicant [ ]

( ) Air Waybills showing "freight [ ] to collect [ ] prepaid [ ] indicating freight amount" and consigned to [ ] Applicant [ ]

Issuing Bank [ ]

(X) Insurance Policy/Certificate in 2 originals for 110 % of the invoice value showing claims payable in Guangzhou China in currency of the draft blank endorsed, covering([X] Ocean Maring Transportation [ ] Air Transportation [ ] Over Land Transportation) All Risks,War Risks,Strike Risks, including warehouse to warehouse as per Institute Cargo Clauses (A), Institute Strike Clauses, Institute War Clauses

(X) Packing List/Weight Memo in 2 originals ~~Copies~~ indicating quantity/gross ~~and net~~ weights of each package and packing conditions as called for by the L/C.

( ) Certificate of Quantity/Weight in Copies.

(X) Certificate of Quality in 2 Copies issued by [X] Beneficiary [ ] public recognized surveyor [ ] manufacturer

( ) Beneficiary's certified copy of cable/telex dispatched to the accountees within hours after shipment advising [ ] name of vessel [ ] B/L No. [ ] flight No. [ ] wagon No. [ ] Shipping date [ ] contract No. [ ] L/C No.,commodity, quantity ,weight and value of shipment.

( ) ~~Certificate of origin in copies~~. Beneficiary's certificate certifying that they have sent documents to the applicant by courier service including 1/3 set of original B/L,commercial invoice in one original and one copy, packing list in one original and one copy indicating cases'No., containers'No.,parts'No./description/quantity of each case and gross weights of each case,certificate of Origin in one original,insurance policy/certificate in one copy and the courier receipt should be attached for negotiation.

(X) Plant Inspection Certificate issued by Inspection and Quarantine Department of Official Authority in the country of the shipper if the goods are packed into coniferous wood package; Statement of non- coniferous wood packing material issued by the shipper in the use of non-coniferous wood packing material; Statement of no wood packing material issued by the shipper in the use of non-wood packing material.

All documents must be issued in English.

(47A) Additional conditions

( ) Documents issued earlier than L/C issuing date are not acceptable.

(X) All banking charges and interest if any outside opening bank are for account of beneficiary

(X) All documents to be forwarded in one cover, unless otherwise stated.

( ) The remaining ________________ % of invoice value________________

( ) Third party as shipper is not acceptable.

(48) Period for presentation: Documents to be presented within 21 days after the date of issuance of the transport document(s) but within the validity of the credit

(71B) Charges [X] Beneficiary [ ] Applicant

实训模块五　审核信用证及改证

一、实训目的

本模块的实训，使学生了解审证的主要内容，能依据合同和《UCP600》审核信用证，并进行修改。掌握改证信函的写信要点和常用句型。

二、实训任务

（1）根据前期拟订的合同和《UCP600》审核信用证。

（2）根据提供的资料草拟改证英文信函。

三、实训提示

（一）信用证审核的主要内容

1．开证银行

开证行的政治背景、资信状况、印鉴、密押是否相符，索汇路线是否正确，是否符合支付协定，是否要加具保兑或由偿付银行确认偿付。

2．信用证的类型

来证不论是即期的、远期的、保兑的、可转让的、循环的或备用的信用证，都应该有“IRREVOCABLE”字样。根据《UCP600》规定，若信用证没有明示是否可撤销，应理解为不可撤销。

当合同规定开出的是保兑信用证时，应检查证内是否有注明“CONFIRMED”字样。

3．开证人

开证人一般情况下是订立货物买卖合同的买方，也可能是买方的客户或买方委托的开证人。

4．受益人

受益人应是订立货物买卖合同的卖方。审证时应以合同为依据，逐字查核受益人的名称和地址是否写错。

5．币制和金额

原则上来证的币别和币值应与合同的币别和币值相符。如用其他货币开证，应按汇率折算是否与合同金额相符，否则要改证。如来证金额因含折扣或佣金与合同不一致，应核算来证的净值是否与合同的净值相一致。若来证规定数量增减，应注意来证金额也应该有相同比例的增减。

6. **有效期、地点**

来证应规定一个有效期，到期地点应在我国国内。根据《UCP600》规定，若信用证没有规定有效期，视为无效信用证。如来证规定的有效期的最后 1 天适逢法定假日或银行例假日，该期限可顺延至下一个营业日。

7. **汇票条款**

若信用证为即期付款，其汇票条款一般为“CREDIT AVAILABLE BY YOUR DRAFT（S）AT SIGHT FOR 100 PERCENT OF INVOICE VALUE DRAWN ON ...”。若信用证为远期付款，要分清是真远期还是假远期，真远期的汇票条款一般为“AVAILABLE BY YOUR DRAFT（S）AT 30 DAYS SIGHT DRAWN ON THE ISSUING BANK FOR 100% OF INVOICE VALUE”，假远期的汇票条款一般为“THE NEGOTIATON BANK IN AUTHARISED TO NEGOTIATE THE USANCE DRAFTS ON SIGHT BASIS; DISCOUNT CHARGES, ACCEPTANCE COMMISSION ARE FOR BUYER'S ACCOUNT”。

8. **分批装运及转运**

根据《UCP600》规定，运输单据表面注明货物系使用同一运输工具并经同一路线运输的，即使每套运输单据注明的装运日期不同及/或装货港、接受监管地、发运地不同，只要运输单据注明的目的地相同，也不视为分批装运。

根据《UCP600》规定，除非信用证另有规定，允许分批装运和转船。

根据《UCP600》规定，除非信用证特别授权，如信用证规定在指定时期内分批装运，其中任何一期未按期装运，则信用证对该期和以后各期均告失效。

来证不准分批，又没有数量增减条款，则实际装运数量不得少装。但对于散装货而言，根据《UCP600》规定，即使信用证不准分批，数量也可有 5% 的增减幅度。

来证不准转运的，要确定能否取得直达提单，否则必须改证。

来证规定在某个港口转船，有的指定由某个船公司接转或在某港转装集装箱等，收证后都要核实能否按来证要求办理，是否使得额外的费用（如 ORC、THC）大量增加。

9. **装运港和目的港**

来证规定海运的起运港为中国港口（CHINESE PORTS）或当地港口，甚至规定亚洲口岸（ASIAN PORTS）都可以，但不能是一个内陆城市如乌鲁木齐、拉萨或北京等。

来证的目的港应与合同一致，除非是分运几个港口，否则目的港只能列一个。

来证笼统规定目的港为欧洲主要口岸（EUROPEAN MAIN PORT），只需按合同或买方通知的港口发货即可，不必改证。

10. **装运期**

信用证的装运期一般应规定为最迟（LATEST）某月某日。

来证没有规定装运期，根据《UCP600》的规定，可理解为双到期，即装运期与信用证的有效期相同。

来证规定尽快装运（ASAP），根据《UCP600》的规定银行将不予置理。

来证如在规定装运日期时使用“于”或“约于”之类词，按惯例银行将理解为在所述日期前后各5天内装运，起讫日包括在内。

11．货物描述

来证的品名、货号、规格、包装和合同号码等必须与合同一致。

来证所列单价和数量应与合同一致。

12．单据要求

（1）商业发票（COMMERCIAL INVOICE）。

来证要求出具两份不同买主名称的商业发票时，应要求改证。

（2）装箱单（PACKING LIST）。

来证要求提供中性包装单（NEUTRAL PACKING LIST），装箱单上不显示受益人名称和地址即可，不必改证。

（3）提单（BILL OF LADING，简称B/L）。

以FOB交易，提单应注明FREIGHT COLLECT，如来证误开为FREIGHT PREPAID，应要求改证。

来证要求提单上列出集装箱号和/或铅封号，则需以集装箱船装运并在提单上列出集装箱号和/或铅封号。

来证要求提供直达提单或某船公司提单时，应考虑实际和可能，无法提供时应要求改证。

（4）保险单（INSURANCE POLICY）。

来证要求保险单中的保险条款、险别、保险加成、保险人和理赔人等方面内容应与合同一致。

来证规定由于任何原因引起的灭失或残损（LOSS OR DAMAGE FROM ANY CAUSE HOWSOEVER ARISING）都赔偿的，应要求改证，改为任何外部原因（ANY EXTERNAL CAUSE），方能被保险公司承保。

除非信用证另有规定，保险单据必须使用与信用证相同的货币开立。

保险加成，保险公司一般可承保加成到30%，如来证规定加成高于30%又不是投保关税险，要取得保险公司同意，否则应该改证。

（5）产地证（CERTIFICATE OF ORIGIN）。

来证指定由出入境检验检疫局或贸促会出具产地证的可以接受，但要求上述两家机构互相加具证明的不能接受。

（6）普惠制产地证格式A（GENERALISED SYSTEM OF PREFERENCES CERTIFICATE OF ORIGIN FORM A，简称G. S. P.）。

出入境检验检疫局是我国签发普惠制产地证的唯一机构，来证指定其他机构如贸促会签发普惠制产地证的，应要求改证。

（7）品质证（CERTIFICATE OF QUALITY）和检验证（INSPECTION CERTIFICATE）。

品质证和检验证是检验货物的证明文件，其检验项目有品质、数量和重量等，来证未指定出证机构的，可由出口公司或生产厂出证，也可由出入境检验检疫局出证。

来证要求由贸促会出证的，应要求改证。

（8）受益人证明书（BENEFICIARY'S CERTIFICATE）。

受益人证明书主要有寄单证明、电抄本和履约证明等。来证要求出具的受益人证明书应是受益人实际已完成或受益人力所能及的任务的证明。

（9）装船通知。

来证规定在装运前若干天发装船通知并且要列明装运日期的，应要求改证，改为装运后发电（IMMEDIATELY AFTER SHIPMENT）。

（10）海关发票（CUSTOMS INVOICE）。

如来证指定某种格式或编号的海关发票，应核查能否提供，否则应改证。

（11）领事发票（CONSULAR INVOICE）。

来证规定要求提供领事发票的，应要求改证删除。

13. 交单期限

来证一般规定一个装运后的交单期限，如来证没有要求，根据《UCP600》的规定，最长的交单期限为装船后21天，但不能超过信用证的有效期。

14. 跟单信用证统一惯例文句

来证一般规定有依照惯例声明，如“除非另有规定外，本证根据国际商会1993年修订本第600号小册‘跟单信用证统一惯例’办理”。但对于SWIFT开证，可以省略该声明。

（二）修改信用证应注意的问题

信用证经过全面的审核后，如发现有问题，应及时通知国外客户通过开证行进行修改。改证时一般应掌握以下几点：

（1）一份信用证如有几处需要修改，应集中一次通知开证人办理修改，避免一改再改，既增加双方的费用又浪费时间，而且还会引起不良影响。

（2）修改信用证的要求一般应用电讯通知开证人，同时应规定一个修改书的到达时限。

（3）对收到的信用证修改通知书应认真进行审核，如发现修改内容有误或我方不能同意的，出口企业有权拒绝接受，但应及时作出拒绝修改的通知送交通知行，以免影响合同的顺利履行。

（4）根据《UCP600》规定，一份信用证的修改通知书的内容要么全部接受，要么全部拒绝，不能接受其中一部分拒绝另一部分。

（5）信用证修改通知书必须由原通知行转递或通知，由开证人或开证行直接寄给出口企业的应提请原证通知行证实。

（三）改证信函

1. 写信要点

（1）确认收到信用证，指出不符点。

（2）不符点内容的修改。

（3）要求尽快修改。

2. 常用句型

句型1 确认收到信用证，指出不符点

（1）We have received your L/C No. 123, but find it contains the following discrepancies and would request you to make the following amendments:
我们已收到你方第 123 号信用证，但发现其中有下列不符点，请对信用证作如下修改：
（2）Thank you for your L/C No. 123, but we regret to say that we have found a number of discrepancies. Please amend the L/C as follows:
收到你方第 123 号信用证，谢谢，但我们遗憾地发现其中有一些不符点，请对信用证作如下修改：
（3）Referring to L/C No. 123, we must point out that the unit of quantity does not conform to the contract.
关于第 123 号信用证，我们必须指出数量的单位与合同不符。

句型 2　不符点内容的修改

（1）To add the clause "..."
增加"……条款"
（2）To insert the word (s) "..." before/after/between "..."
在"……"之前/之后/中间加上"……"
（3）To increase the amount of...from...to...
把金额由……增加到……
（4）To delete the clause/the words "..."
删除"……"条款/词
（5）"..." should read "..."
"……"应改为"……"
（6）Please amend "..." instead of "..."
请将"……"修改为"……"

句型 3　要求尽快修改

（1）Please amend the L/C as soon as possible so as to enable us to effect shipment in time.
请尽快修改信用证以便我方按时装运。
（2）Please adjust the credit immediately so that we can make arrangements to ship the goods in time.
请马上修改信用证，以便我们按时装运。
（3）Your early amendment to the L/C will be highly appreciated.
请尽快修改信用证为谢。

3. 信函范例

Dear Sirs,

Thank you for your L/C No. 123, but we regret to say that there are some discrepancies in it. Please amend the L/C as follows:

（1）The amount both in figures and in words should respectively be USD 55 000 and "Say US Dollars Fifty-five Thousand Only".

(2) Insert "Children" before "Bicycles".

(3) Delete the clause of insurance.

We look forward to your early amendments to the L/C.

Yours faithfully,

敬启者：

感谢你方第123号信用证，但是我们感到很遗憾，该证有一些与合同不符之处。请将该证作如下修改：

(1) 金额的数字和文字表示都应该是"55 000美元"。

(2) 在"自行车"前加上"Children"一词。

(3) 删除保险条款。

盼望早日收到你们的信用证修改书。

敬上

四、实训内容

(一) 审证

请你根据合同98SGQ468001审核LRT9802457号信用证，指出信用证与合同不符之处，并进行修改。

不符点	改正

(二) 申请改证

广东中山威威照明有限公司张大同经审证，发现信用证有错，于2021年11月27日发函要求法国巴黎Le Vernet贸易有限公司的PIERRE先生通过开证行METITA BANK LTD., FRANCE修改信用证。请将下面的信函翻译成英文。

PIERRE 先生：

关于你方 11 月 25 日开出的 LRT9802457 号信用证，我们必须指出，该信用证有两点与合同不符，请你方作出以下修改：①信用证的金额应为 USD 67 500.00；②信用证应允许分批装运。由于装运期临近，希望你方立即修改信用证以便我们能按时安排发运。

此致

张大同　敬上

2021 年 11 月 27 日

（三）开证行改证

开证行 METITA BANK LTD.，FRANCE 根据法国巴黎 Le Vernet 贸易有限公司的改证申请，开来如下修改好的信用证。请你替张大同核对是否与改证要求一致。

2021NOV29			Logical Terminal　GDPF
MT S700	Issue of a Documentary Credit		Page　00001
			Func　JSRVPR1

User Header	Service Code	103	:
	Bank Priority	113	:
	Msg User Ref.	108	:
	Info. From CI	115	:

Sender's Ref.	*20		: 1 / 1
Receiver's Ref.	*21		: LRT9802457
Date of Issue	31	C	: 211125
Date of Amendment	30		: 211129
Number of Amendment	26	E	01
Beneficiary	*59		: GUANGDONG ZHONGSHAN WEIWEI LIGHTING CO., LTD. 152, CUIHUA ROAD, ZHONGSHAN, CHINA
Increase Doc. Credit	32	B	: Currency USD Amount 9 000.00
New Amount	34	B	: Currency USD Amount 29 000.00
Pos. / Neg. Tol.（%）	39	A	: 05 / 05
Narrative	79		: * PARTIAL SHIPMENTS ARE ALLOWED * ALL OTHER TERMS AND CONDITIONS OF THIS CREDIT REMAIN UNCHANGED
Trailer			Order is <MAC: > <PAC: > <ENC: > <CHK: > <TNG: > <PDE: > MAC: ID20750E CHK: 5034662F74BC

五、强化提高

强化提高一

根据售货合同审核并修改信用证。

售 货 合 同
SALES CONTRACT

卖方： GUANGDONG LIGHT ELECTRICAL.
Sellers: APPLANCES CO. ,LTD.

地址：
Address: 52,DEZHENG ROAD SOUTH,GUANGZHOU,CHINA

Contract No. : 98SGQ468001
Date: APR. 22,2019
Signed at: GUANGZHOU
Telex: 0835
Fax: 83556688

Buyers: A. B. C. CORP.
Address: AKEDSANTERINK AUTO P. O. BOX. 9,FINLAND

Telex: ____
Fax: ____

This Sales Contract is made by and between the Sellers and the Buyers, whereby the Sellers agree to sell and the Buyers agree to buy the under-mentioned goods according to the terms and conditions stipulated below:

(1)货号, 品名及规格 Name of Commodity and Specifications	(2)数量 Quantity	(3)单位 Unit	(4)单价 Unit Price	(5)金额 Amount
HALOGEN FITTING W500 10% more or less both in amount and quantity allowed	9 600	PC	CIF HELSINKI USD 3. 80/PC	USD 36 480. 00
	Total Amount			USD 36 480. 00

(6) Packing: CARTON (7) Delivery from GUANGZHOU to HELSINKI (8) Shipping Marks:

(9) Time of Shipment: Within 30 days after receipt of L/C allowing transshipment and partial shipment.

(10) Terms of Payment: By 100% Confirmed irrevocable Letter of Credit in favor of the Sellers to be available by sight draft to be opened and to reach China before MAY 1,2019 and to remain valid for negotiation in China until the 15th days after the foresaid Time of Shipment. L/C must mention this contract number. L/C advised by BANK OF CHINA. GUANGZHOU BRANCH. TLX:444U4K GZBC CN. ALL banking Charges outside China(the mainland of China) are for account of the Drawee.

(11) Insurance: To be effected by Sellers for 110% of full invoice value coveringF. P. A. up toHELSINKI

(12) Arbitration: All dispute arising from the execution of or in connection with this contract shall be settled amizedly the friendly negotiation. In case of settlement can be reached through negotiation the case shall then be submit China International Economic & Trade Arbitration Commision. In Shenzhen (or in Beijing) for arbitration in act with its sure of procedures. The arbitral award is final and binding upon both parties for setting the disputes. The fee, for arbitration shall be borne by the losing party unless Otherwise awarded.

The Sellers 张三　　　　The Buyers PAUL

Issue of Documentary Credit

Issuing Bank	:	STANDARD BANK LTD. , FINLAND
Doc. Credit No.	:	REVOCABLE
Credit Number	:	9802457. 42
Date of Issue	:	190428
Expiry	:	Date 190416 Place FINLAND
Applicant	:	A. B. C. CO. AKEKSANTERINK AUTO P. O. BOX 9, FINLAND
Beneficiary	:	GUANGDONG LIGHT ELECTRICAL CO. LTD. 52, DEZHENG ROAD SOUTH, GUANGZHOU, CHINA
Amount	:	USD 3 648. 00 (SAY U. S. DOLLARS THIRTY SIX THOUSAND FOUR HUNDRED AND EIGHT ONLY)
Pos. / Neg. Tol. (%)	:	5/5
Available with/by	:	ANY BANK IN ADVISING COUNTRY BY NEGOTIATION
Draft at...	:	DRAFTS AT 20 DAYS' SIGHT FOR FULL INVOICE VALUE
Partial Shipments	:	Not Allowed
Transhipment	:	Allowed
Loading in Charge	:	GUANGZHOU
For Transport to	:	HELSINKI
Shipment Period	:	AT THE LATEST MAY 30, 2019
Descrip. of Goods	:	960 PCS OF HALOGEN FITTING W500, USD 6. 80 PER PC AS PER SALES CONTRACT 98SG468001 DD 22, 4, 2019 CIF HESINKI
Documents Required	:	* COMMERCIAL INVOICE 1 SIGNED ORIGINAL AND 5 COPIES * PACKING LIST IN 2 COPIES * FULL SET OF CLEAN ON BOARD MARINE BILLS OF LADING, MADE OUT TO ORDER, MARKED "FREIGHT PREPAID" AND NOTIFY APPLICANT (AS INDICATE ABOVE) * GSP CERTIFICATE OF ORIGIN FORM A, CERTIFYING GOODS OF ORIGIN IN CHINA, ISSUED BY COMPETENT AUTHORITIES * INSURANCE POLICY/CERTIFICATE COVERING ALL RISKS AND WAR RISKS OF PICC. INCLUDING WAREHOUSE TO WAREHOUSE CLAUSE UP TO FINAL DESTINATION AT HELSINKI, FOR AT LEAST 120 PCT OF CIF-VALUE * SHIPPING ADVICES MUST BE SENT TO APPLICANT WITH 2 DAYS AFTER SHIPMENT ADVISING NUMBER OF PACKAGES, GROSS & NET WEIGHT, VESSEL NAME, BILL OF LADING NO. AND DATE, CONTRACT NO. , VALUE.
Presentation Period	:	6 DAYS AFTER ISSUANCE DATE OF SHIPPING DOCUMENT
Confirmation	:	WITHOUT

强化提高二

根据下面提供的合同审核并修改信用证。

卖方
GUANGDONG FOREIGN TRADE IMP.
AND EXP. CORPORATION.
267 TIANHE ROAD GUANGZHOU,
CHINA

销 货 确 认 书
SALES CONFIRMATION

No. AB44001
日期
Date: FEB. 12, 2020
签约地点:
Signed at: GUANGZHOU, CHINA
电报挂号
Cable: "ARTCANTON"
TELEX: 44371 KTTEX CN
FAX:

买方
Buyers: A. B. C. TRADING CO., LTD., HONGKONG
地址
Address: 312 SOUTH BRIDGE STREET, HONGKONG

电报挂号:
Cable Address:
TELEX:
FAX:

兹经买卖双方同意按下列条款成交:
The undersigned Sellers and Buyers have agreed to close the following transactions according to the terms and conditions stipulated below:

1.

货　号 Art No.	品 名 及 规 格 Description	数　量 Quantity	单　价 Unit Price	金　额 Amount
	AIR CONDITIONER (HUALING BRAND)		FOB C2% GUANGZHOU	
ART NO. P97811	KF-23GW	500 PCS	@HKD 1 000.00	HKD 500 000.00
ART NO. P97801	KF-25GW	500 PCS	@HKD 1 000.00	HKD 500 000.00
		1 000 PCS		HKD 1 000 000.00

数量及总值均得有　　%的增减，由卖方决定。
With　5　% more or less both in amount and quantity allowed at the Sellers' option.

2. 总值
Total Value: HKD 1 000 000.00 (H. K. Dollars ONE MILLION ONLY)

3. 包装
Packing: CARTON IN 1 PC

4. 装运期
Time of Shipment: APR. 30, 2020

5. 装运口岸和目的地
Loading Port & Destination: FROM GUANGZHOU TO DUBAI

6. 保险　　由卖方按发票全部金额110%投保至　　　　为止的　　　　险。
Insurance: To be effected by Sellers for 110% of full invoice value covering　　　　up to　　　　only.

7. 付款条件：买方须于　2020　年3　月　10　日将不可撤销的，即期信用证开到卖方，信用证，议付有效期延至上列装运期后15天在中国到期，该信用证中必须注明允许分运及转运。
Terms of Payment:
By Irrevocable, and Confirmed Letter of Credit to be available by sight draft to reach the Sellers before MAR. 10, 2020 and to remain valid for negotiation in China until the 15th day after the aforesaid Time of Shipment. The L/C must specify that transhipment and partial shipments are allowed.

8. 装船标记
Shipping Mark: A. B. C. /DUBAI/NOS1-1000/MADE IN CHINA

9. 开立信用证时请注明我成交确认书号码。
When opening L/C, Please mention our S/C number.

10. 备注
Remarks: THE CREDIT IS SUBJECT TO UCP600 (2007 REVISION)

卖　方
THE SELLERS
苏华

买　方
THE BUYERS
BACK

希 将 本 确 认 书 一 份 签 署 后 寄 回 本 公 司
please sign and send one copy of this sales confirmation to us at your earliest convenience.

香港南洋商业银行

NANYANG COMMERCIAL BANK LTD. , HONGKONG

HONGKONG 1ST MARCH, 2020

TO: BANK OF CHINA, GUANGZHOU. CHINA

REVOCABLE DOCUMENTARY CREDIT NO. 97 – 34985

FOR THE ACCOUNT OF A. B. C. TRADING CO. LTD. , HONGKONG. 312 SOUTH BRIDGE STREET, HONGKONG.

DEAR SIRS,

WE OPEN AN REVOCABLE DOCUMENTARY CREDIT IN FAVOUR OF GUANGDONG FOREIGN TRADE IMP. AND EXP. CO. 267 TIANGHE ROAD GUANGZHOU, CHINA. FOR A SUM NOT EXCEEDING USD 980 000. 00 (SAY HONGKONG DOLLARS NINE HUNDRED AND EIGHTY THOUSAND ONLY.) AVAILABLE BY THE BENEFICIARY'S DRAFT (S) AT 30 DAYS SIGHT DRAWN ON APPLICAN BEARING THE CLAUSE: "DRAWN UNDER NANYANG COMMERCIAL BANK LTD. , HONGKONG. DOCUMENTARY CREDIT NO. 34985 DATED 1ST MAY, 2020. " ACCOMPANIED BY THE FOLLOWING DOCUMENTS:

(1) MANUAL SIGNED COMMERCIAL INVOICE IN TRIPLICATE. ALL INVOICES MUST SHOW FOB, FREIGHT AND INSURANCE COSTS SEPARATELY.

(2) 3/3 ORIGINAL + 3 NN COPIES CLEAN ON BOARD BILL OF LADING MADE OUT TO ORDER OF NANYANG COMMERCIAL BANK LTD. , HONGKONG, MARKED "FREIGHT PREPAID", INDICATING L/C NO. , S/C NO. AND NOTIFY ACCOUNTEE.

(3) INSURANCE POLICY / CERTIFICATE IN DULICATE IN FAVOUR OF NANYANG COMMERCIAL BANK LTD. , HONGKONG FOR 110% OF THE INVOICE VALUE BLANK ENDORSED. COVERING P. I. C. C. OCEAN MARINE CARGO CLAUSES (W. A.) AND WAR RISKS DATED 1ST JANUARY, 1981. INCLUDING WAREHOUSE TO WAREHOUSE CLAUSE UP TO FINAL DESTINATION AT DUBAI.

(4) CERTIFICATE OF ORIGIN ISSUED BY GUANGZHOU IMPORT AND EXPORT COMMODITY INSPECTION BUREAU OF THE PEOPLES REPUBLIC OF CHINA IN TRIPLICATE. EVIDENCING SHIPMENT OF THE FOLLOWING MERCHANDISE:

AIR CONDITIONER (HUALING BRAND), 500 PCS KR – 23GW AND 500 PCS KF – 25GW, PACKING: IN CARTON BOX, 50 KILOS NET EACH CARTON, 1PC/CARTON, @ HKD1, 000. 00, FOBC2% DUBEI, OTHER TERMS AND CONDITIONS AS S/C NO. AB97/44001, FROM GUANGZHOU TO DUBAI VIA HONGKONG. PARTIAL SHIPMENT PROHIBITED. TRANSHIPMENT PERMITIED. LATEST DATE FOR SHIPMENT: 30TH APPIL, 2020. EXPIRY DATE: 15TH APRIL, 2020. IN PLACE OF OPENER FOR NEGOTIATION.

OTHER TERMS AND CONDITIONS:

BENEFICIARY'S DECLARATION ON THE INVOICE THAT THE PRODUCTION COMPANY IS A STATE-OWNED ENTERPRISE AND AS NO RELATION WITH ISRAEL WHATSOEVER.

SHIPPER MUST SEND ONE COPIES OF SHIPPING DOCUMENTS DIRECT TO BUYER AND CERTIFICATE TO THIS EFFECT IS REQUIRED.

DOCUMENTS MUST BE PRESENTED WITHIN 5 DAYS AFTER SHIPPING DATE SHOWN ON B/L, BUT WITHIN THE VALIDITY OF THE L/C.

DISCREPANCY FEE OF USD 50. 00 WILL BE DEDUCTED FROM THE PROCEEDS OF ANY DRAWING IF DISCREPANT DOCUMENTS ARE PRESENTED.

SHIPPING MARKS: A. B. C. / DUBAI/ NOS1 – 100/ MADE IN CHINA

WE HEREBY ENGAGE WITH THE DRAWERS, ESDORSERS AND BONARIDE HOLDERS OF DRAFT (S) DRAWN UNDER AND COMPLIANCE WITH THE TERMS OF THIS CREDIT THAT SUCH DRAFT (S) SHALL BE DULLY HONOURED ON DUE PRESENTATION.

YOURS FAITHFULLY,

NANYANG COMMERCIAL BANK LTD. , HONGKONG

强化提高三

根据下面提供的合同审核并修改信用证。

售 货 合 同
SALES CONTRACT

卖方：GUANGDONG TEXTILES IMPORT AND
Sellers：EXPORT CO.

地址：14/F GUANGDONG TEXTILES MANSIONS
Address：168 XIAOBEI ROAD. GUANGZHOU，CHINA.

Contract No.：98SGQ468001
Date：APR. 22，2012
Signed at：GUANGZHOU
Telex：0835
Fax：

Buyers：A. B. C. CANTWELL，CC FITTINGS
Address：MEADOWLANDS GRANTSTOWN CO. WATERFORD

Telex：
Fax：

This Sales Contract is made by and between the Sellers and the Buyers，whereby the Sellers agree to sell and the Buyers agree to buy the under-mentioned goods according to the terms and conditions stipulated below：

（1）货号，品名及规格 Name of Commodity and Specifications	（2）数量 Quantity	（3）单位 Unit	（4）单价 Unit Price	（5）金额 Amount
DRAWER SLIDES AND HANDLES	1 000	SET	CIF DUBLIN USD 25. 00	USD 25 000. 00
5 % more or less both in amount and quantity allowed	Total Amount			USD 25 000. 00

（6）Packing：CARTON （7）Delivery from GUANGZHOU to DUBLIN （8）Shipping Marks：N/M

（9）Time of Shipment：Within 30 days after receipt of L/C allowing transhipment and partial shipment.

（10）Terms of Payment：By 100% irrevocable Letter of Credit in favor of the Sellers to be available by sight draft to be opened and to reach China before MAY 15，2012 and to remaind valid for negotiation in China until the 15th days after the foresaid Time of Shipment. L/C must mention this contract number. L/C advised by BANK OF CHINA. GUANGZHOU BRANCH. TLX：444U4K GZBC CN. ALL banking Charges outside China（the mainland of China）are for account of the Drawee.

（11）Insurance：To be effected by Sellers for 110% of full invoice value covering F. P. A. up to DUBLIN . To be effected by the buyers.

（12）Arbitration：All dispute arising from the execution of or in connection with this contract shall be settled amizedly the friendly negotiation. In case of settlement can be reached through negotiation the case shall then be submit China International Economic & Trade Arbitration Commision. In Shenzhen（or in Beijing）for arbitration in act with its sure of procedures. The arbitral award is final and binding upon both parties for setting the. Disputes. The fee，for arbitration shall be borne by the losing party unless otherwise awarded.

The Sellers 张三　　　　The Buyers Salong

```
2012APR25 07:55:54                                      Logical Terminal GDPF
MT S700                  Issue of a Documentary Credit             Page 00001
                                                                   Func JSRVPRI
MSGACK  DWS765I Auth OK, key B0020421064AF648, BKCHCNBJ AIBK**** record797208
Basic Header         F  01 BKCHCNBJA400 0649 494074
Application Header   0 700 1715 120424 AIBKIE2DAXXX 3189 448014 020425 0015 N
                                          *AIB BANK
                                          *DUBLIN
User Header          Service Code     103:
                     Bank. Priority   113:
                     Msg User Ref.    108:
                     Info. from CI    115:                 ORIGINAL
Sequence of Total    *27    : 1 / 1
Form of Doc. Credit  *40 A  : IRREVOCABLE
Doc. Credit Number   *20    : AIB.IM02023502
Date of Issue         31 C  : 120424
Expiry               *31 D  : Date 120619 Place CHINA
Applicant Bank        51 A  : AIBKIE2DXXX
                             *AIB BANK
                             *DUBLIN
Applicant            *50    : C AND D CANTWELL, CC FITTINGS,
                              MEADOWLANDS
                              GRANTSTOWN
                              CO WATERFORD
Beneficiary          *59    : GUANGDONG TEXTILES IMPORT AND
                              EXPORT.COTTON MANUFACTURED GOODS CO
                              14/F GUANGDONG TEXTILES MANSIONS
                              168 XIAO BEI RD GUANGZHOU CHINA
Amount               *32 B  :            Currency USD Amount 20000.00
Available with/by    *41 A  : AIBKIE2DXXX
                             *AIB BANK
                             *DUBLIN
                              BY ACCEPTANCE
Drafts at ...         42 C  : 30 DAYS SIGHT
Drawee                42 A  : AIBKIE2DXXX
                             *AIB BANK
                             *DUBLIN
Partial Shipments     43 P  : PROHIBITED
Transshipment         43 T  : PERMITTED
Loading in Charge     44 A  :
             GUANGZHOU CHINA
For Transport to ...  44 B  :
             DUBLIN,IRELAND.
Descript. of Goods    45 A  :
             +DRAWER SLIDES AND HANDLES
             CIF DUBLIN,IRELAND.
Documents required    46 A  :
             +SIGNED INVOICES IN TRIPLICATE
             +FULL SET OF CLEAN ON BOARD MARINE BILLS OF LADING CONSIGNED TO
             ORDER, BLANK ENDORSED, MARKED FREIGHT PREPAID AND CLAUSED NOTIFY
             APPLICANT.
             +INSURANCE POLICY/CERTIFICATE BLANK ENDORSED COVERING ALL RISKS
             FOR 10 PER CENT ABOVE THE CIF VALUE.
             +CERTIFICATE OF CHINA ORIGIN ISSUED BY A RELEVANT AUTHORITY.
             +PACKING LIST
Additional Cond.      47 A  :
             +PLEASE FORWARD ALL DOCUMENTS TO ALLIED IRISH BANKS, TRADE
             FINANCE SERVICES, CARRISBROOK HOUSE, BALLSBRIDGE, DUBLIN 4.
             +IF BILLS OF LADING ARE REQUIRED ABOVE, PLEASE FORWARD
             DOCUMENTS IN TWO MAILS, ORIGINALS SEND BY COURIER AND
             DUPLICATES BY REGISTERED AIRMAIL.
```

2012APR25 07:55:56 Logical Terminal GDPF
MT S700 Issue of a Documentary Credit Page 00002
Func JSRVPR1

Details of Charges	71 B	: BANK CHARGES EXCLUDING ISSUING BANKS ARE FOR ACCOUNT OF BENEFICIARY.
Presentation Period	48	: DOCUMENTS TO BE PRESENTED WITHIN 21 DAYS FROM SHIPMENT DATE
Confirmation	*49	: WITHOUT
Instructions	78	:

DISCREPANT DOCUMENTS, IF ACCEPTABLE, WILL BE SUBJECT TO A DISCREPANCY HANDLING FEE OF EUR100.00 OR EQUIVALENT WHICH WILL BE FOR ACCOUNT OF BENEFICIARY.
SPECIAL NOTE: ISSUING BANK WILL DISCOUNT ACCEPTANCES ON REQUEST, FOR A/C OF BENEFICIARY (UNLESS OTHERWISE STATED) AT APPROPRIATE LIBOR RATE PLUS 1.00 PER CENT MARGIN.

Send. to Rec. Info.	72	: THIS CREDIT IS ISSUED SUBJECT TO THE U.C.P. FOR DOCUMENTARY CREDITS, 1993 REVISION, I.C.C. PUBLICATIONS NO.500
Trailer		Order is <MAC:> <PAC:> <ENC:> <CHK:> <TNG:> <PDE:> MAC:1D20750E CHK:5034662F748C

实训模块六　租船订舱

一、实训目的

本模块的训练，要求学生能正确理解信用证或合同以及各国际贸易惯例对运输的有关规定，掌握杂货班轮和集装箱运输出口托运的有关做法。

二、实训任务

（1）根据合同、信用证和提供的资料填写出口货物联合单证（或称出口货物明细单或九联单）。

（2）根据合同、信用证和提供的资料填写出口托运单。

三、实训提示

（一）集装箱装货数量估算

1. 20 英尺集装箱装货数量估算

20 英尺集装箱长为 6.058 米，宽和高各为 2.438 米，集装箱和货物的最大总重量为 24 公吨。实际业务中，20 英尺集装箱的有效载重量为 17.5 公吨，有效容积为 28 立方米。当已知包装箱的毛重和尺码后，即可分别按重量和体积计算出 20 英尺集装箱对该批货物可装的最大数量。例如，本实训案例中，张大同与外商成交的商品，纸箱规格为 63 厘米 × 32 厘米 × 24 厘米，纸箱毛重为 4.5 千克，按重量 17.5/0.004 5 = 3 888（箱）；按体积 28/（0.63 × 0.32 × 0.24） = 583（箱）。取较少的整数数量 583 箱，即为估算数量，考虑到货物装柜的实际情况，本实训案例的实际装箱数为 580 箱。

2. 40 英尺集装箱装货数量估算

40 英尺集装箱长为 12.192 米，宽和高各为 2.438 米，集装箱和货物的最大总重量为 30.48 公吨。实际业务中，40 英尺集装箱的有效载重量为 24.5 公吨，有效容积为 55 立方米。当已知包装箱的毛重和尺码后，即可分别按重量和体积估算出 40 英尺集装箱对该批货物大约可装的最大数量。

（二）中远集装箱运输有限公司集装箱货物托运单

中远集装箱运输有限公司集装箱货物托运单共有六联。

第一联：装货单。

第二联：货主留底。

第三联：船代留底。

第四联：场站收据。

第五联：运费计算。

第六联：海关副本。

（三）集装箱货物整箱货出口托运程序

（1）托运人填写托运单证，及时订舱。

（2）船公司将有关订舱信息通知托运人。

（3）托运人申请用箱，取得设备交接单（equipment interchange receipt，EIR）后就可以凭以到空箱堆场提取所需的集装箱。

（4）托运人提空箱，装箱后制作集装箱装箱单（container load plan，CLP），并按要求及时将重箱送码头堆场，即集中到港区等待装船。

（5）托运人报检、报关，办妥有关手续后将单证交码头堆场配载。

（6）配载部门制订装船计划，经船公司确认后实施装船作业。

（7）货物装船后取得场站收据（dock receipt，D/R）正本。

（8）托运人凭 D/R 正本到船方签单部门换取 B/L 或其他单据。

（9）托运人凭 B/L 及有关单证到议付银行议付。

（四）杂货班轮出口托运程序

（1）托运人向船公司提出货物装运申请，递交托运单（booking note），填写装货联单（主要由装货单、收货单和留底组成）。

（2）船公司同意承运后，指定船名，核对装货单（shipping order，S/O）与托运单（B/N）上的内容无误后，签发 S/O，将留底（counterfoil）联留下后退还给托运人，要求托运人将货物及时送至指定的码头仓库。

（3）托运人向检验检疫机构报检，经检验检疫后出具商检证书或“通关单”。

（4）托运人持 S/O 及有关单证向海关办理货物出口报关、验货放行手续，海关在 S/O 上加盖放行图章后，货物准予装船出口。

（5）托运人按要求将货物送至指定的码头仓库准备装船。

（6）货物装船后，现场理货员核对，在 S/O 上签注实装数量、装船位置、装船日期并签名，再由理货长审查并签名后，将 S/O 交大副，大副核实无误后留下 S/O 并签发收货单（mate’s receipt，M/R）。

（7）理货长将大副签发的 M/R 转交给托运人。

（8）托运人持 M/R 到船公司付清运费（预付运费情况下），船公司审核无误后，留下 M/R 签发正本已装船提单（B/L）给托运人。

（9）托运人持 B/L 及有关单证到议付银行结汇（在信用证支付方式下），取得货款，议付银行将 B/L 及有关单证邮寄开证银行。

（五）跟单信用证统一惯例对运输的有关规定

（1）除非信用证另有规定，允许分批支款及/或分批装运。

（2）运输单据上表面注明货物系使用同一运输工具并经同一路线运输的，即使每套运输单据注明的装运日期不同及/或装货港、接受监管地、发运地不同，只要运输单据注明的目的地相同，也不视为分批装运。

（3）如信用证规定在指定时期内分期支款及/或分期装运，其中任何一期未按信用证所规定的期限支款及/或装运，则信用证对该期及以后各期货物均告失效，信用证另有规定者除外。

（4）如运输单据未注明出具单据份数，银行将接受所提交的运输单据，并视为全套正本，不论运输单据是否注明为正本，银行将作为正本予以接受。

（5）运输单据上出现“运费可预付”或“运费应预付”或类似意义的词语，不能视为运费付讫的证明，将不予接受。

（6）海运或包括海运在内的一种以上运输方式，未注明货物已装或将装于舱面，然而，运输单据内有货物可能装于舱面的规定，但未特别注明货物已装舱面或将装舱面的，银行对该运输单据予以接受。

（7）对装运期不应使用诸如“迅速”“立即”“尽快”之类词语，如使用此类词语，银行将不予置理。

（8）如使用“于或约于”之类词语限定装运日期，银行将视为在所述日期前后各5天内装运，起讫日包括在内。

四、实训内容

（一）填制出口货物联合单证（九联单）

根据前面广东中山威威照明有限公司签订的合同和信用证，张大同设计唛头“Le Vernet/LE HAVRE/NO. 1 –580”。请你代张大同填写公司的九联单。

广东中山威威照明有限公司
出 口 货 物 联 合 单 证

出 口 口 岸：________	运输工具名称：________	核 销 单 号：________
起 运 地 点：________	目 的 港：________	收 汇 方 式：________
贸易国别或地区：________	对外合同号码：________	收 货 人：________
消费国别或地区：________	装 运 日 期：________	地址及电挂：________

商品货号	品名及规格	包装			数量		重量（公斤）		价格		箱件尺寸（cm）	备注
		唛头	种类	件数	数量	单位	单位毛重	单位净重	单价	外币总值		
合计						重合计			总额			
险别	保费		总尺码		外币运费			人民币杂费		F. O. B. 总值	托运日期	
注意事项										要求出货日期：		
										出货仓库：		

填报单位：　　　　年　月　日　　　仓库：　　　　出运：　　　　复核：　　　　业务：

（二）填制托运单

根据前面的九联单，张大同于 2021 年 12 月 1 日填写托运单，请你代张大同填写托运单（装货单、收货单）。

Shipper（发货人）	B/L No.
Consignee（收货人）	中远集装箱运输有限公司 COSCO CONTAINER LINES
Notify Party（通知人）	集装箱货物托运单

Pre-carriage by（前程承运人）	Place of Receipt（收货地点）	
Ocean vessel（船名）Voy. No.（航次）	Port of Loading（装运港）	装货单 SHIPPING ORDER
Port of Discharge（卸货港）	Place of Delivery（交货地点）	Final Destination for the Merchant's Reference（目的地）

Container No.（集装箱号）	Seal No.（铅封号）Marks & Nos.（标记与号码）	No. of containers or p'kgs（箱数或件数）	Kind of Package; Description of Goods（包装种类与货名）	Gross Weight 毛重（公斤）	Measurement 尺码（立方米）
TOTAL NUMBER OF CONTAINERS OR PACKAGES (JIN WORDS) 集装箱数或件数合计（大写）					

FREIGHT & CHARGES（运费与附加费）	Revenue Tons（运费吨）	Rate（运费率）	Per（每）	Prepaid（运费预付）	Collect（运费到付）

Service Type on Receiving	Service Type on Delivery	Reeger Temperature Required（冷藏温度）	℉	℃

TYPE OF GOODS（货类）	□Ordinary（普通）　□ Reeger（冷藏）　□ Dangerous（危险品）　□ Auto（裸装车辆） □Liquid（液体）　□ Live Animal（活动物）　□ Bulk（散货）	危险品	IMCO Class. UN No.: IMDG Code Page: Property:

可否转船:	可否分批:	装期:	Received by the Carrier the total number of containers or other packages or units stated above to be transported subject to the terms and conditions of the Carrier's regular form of Bill of Lading (for combined Transport to Port shipment) which shall be deemed to be incorporated herein Date:　　as Agent only
货价:	信用证号码:	No. of original B(S)/L	
特约事项:	合同号码:	托运人盖章:	

（三）船公司签发装货单

张大同于 2021 年 12 月 3 日从船公司取回已签发的装货单，提取空集装箱，获知如下资料，请你将这些资料填写在前面的托运单（装货单）上并缮制商业发票和装箱单。

船名	SUISUN V. 103	托运日期	2021 年 12 月 1 日
装运日期	2021 年 12 月 13 日	集装箱号	MAEU6150875

（四）填制商业发票

发票号码为 LH03 – 29038，发票日期为 2021 年 12 月 3 日。

广东中山威威照明有限公司

GUANGDONG ZHONGSHAN WEIWEI LIGHTING CO. , LTD.

52，CUIHUA ROAD，ZHONGSHAN，CHINA

商业发票

COMMERCIAL INVOICE

ORIGINAL

Messrs：

Invoice No. ：

Invoice Date：

S/C NO. ：

Transport details：

标记 Marks & Numbers	货名 Description of Goods	数量 Quantity	单价 Unit Price	总值 Amount

（五）填制装箱单

广东中山威威照明有限公司

GUANGDONG ZHONGSHAN WEIWEI LIGHTING CO. , LTD.

52，CUIHUA ROAD，ZHONGSHAN，CHINA

装箱单

PACKING LIST

ORIGINAL

Exporter：

Date :

Invoice No. :

S/C No. :

Transport details：

标记 Shipping Marks	件数 Quantity	货名 Description	净重 N. W.	毛重 G. W.	尺码 Measurement

五、强化提高

强化提高一

根据下列信用证和有关资料，填制出口托运单。

Form of Doc. Credit	* 40	A	:	IRREVOCABLE
Doc. Credit Number	* 20		:	BT298346
Date of Issue	31	C	:	180301
Expiry	* 31	D	:	180625 PLACE CHINA
Applicant	* 50		:	HOPE BRIDGE CO. , LTD. 152 NORTH BRIDGE STREET, SINGAPORE
Beneficiary	* 59		:	RED TREE IMP. & EXP. CO. , LTD. 25, ZHONGSHAN ROAD, SHENZHEN, CHINA
Amount	* 32	B	:	Currency USD Amount 68 000. 00
Available with/by	* 41	D	:	ANY BANK BY NEGOTIATION
Draft at …	42	C	:	SIGHT
Partial Shipments	43	P	:	Not Allowed
Transhipment	43	T	:	Allowed
Loading in Charge	44	A	:	YANTIAN, SHENZHEN
For Transport to…	44	B	:	SINGAPORE
Shipment Period	44	C	:	NOT LATER THAN MAY. 20, 2018
Description of Goods	45	A	:	

800 DOZ CHILDREN'S CAPS KH5607

PACKING: 2DOZ/CTN. OTHER DETAILS AS PER S/C NO. : RT－04－891

USD 85. 00 / DOZCIF SINGAPORE

Documents Required　　46　　A　　:

+ FULL SET OF CLEAN ON BOARD MARINE BILLS OF LADING, MADE OUT TO ORDER OF SHIPPER, MARKED "FREIGHT PREPAID", NOTIFY APPLICANT

Special Cond. ALL DOCUMENTS MUST BE SHOWN THE NUMBER AND THE DATE OF THIS L/C.

毛重	5 KGS/CTN	尺码	(40 × 25 × 30) CM/CTN
净重	3. 5 KGS/CTN	唛头	HB/SINGAPORE/NO. 1－400

Shipper（发货人）	B/L No.
Consignee（收货人）	中远集装箱运输有限公司 COSCO CONTAINER LINES 集装箱货物托运单
Notify Party（通知人）	装货单 SHIPPING ORDER

Pre-carriage by（前程承运人）	Place of Receipt（收货地点）	
Ocean vessel（船名）Voy. No.（航次）	Port of Loading（装运港）	
Port of Discharge（卸货港）	Place of Delivery（交货地点）	Final Destination for the Merchant's Reference（目的地）

Container No.（集装箱号）	Seal No.（铅封号）Marks & Nos.（标记与号码）	No. of containers or p'kgs（箱数或件数）	Kind of Package; Description of Goods（包装种类与货名）	Gross Weight 毛重（公斤）	Measurement 尺码（立方米）
TOTAL NUMBER OF CONTAINERS OR PACKAGES (JIN WORDS) 集装箱数或件数合计（大写）					

FREIGHT & CHARGES（运费与附加费）	Revenue Tons（运费吨）	Rate（运费率）	Per（每）	Prepaid（运费预付）	Collect（运费到付）

Service Type on Receiving	Service Type on Delivery	Reeger Temperature Required（冷藏温度）	℉	℃

TYPE OF GOODS（货类）	□Ordinary（普通）　□ Reeger（冷藏）　□ Dangerous（危险品）　□ Auto（裸装车辆） □Liquid（液体）　□ Live Animal（活动物）　□ Bulk（散货）	危险品：IMCO Class. UN No.: IMDG Code Page: Property:

可否转船：	可否分批：	装期：	Received by the Carrier the total number of containers or other packages or units stated above to be transported subject to the terms and conditions of the Carrier's regular form of Bill of Lading (for combined Transport to Port shipment) which shall be deemed to be incorporated herein Date:　　　as Agent only
货价：	信用证号码：	No. of Original B(S)/L	
特约事项：	合同号码：	托运人盖章：	

强化提高二

根据出口货物联合单证提供的内容，填制出口托运单（托运日期为2019年1月24日）。

广东省纺织品进出口广通贸易有限公司联合单证______出口货物明细单

合约号：C215　核销单号：18/4782591　发票号：TW17505　流水编号：________

订货人所在
国家或地区：DUBAI，UAE　装运日期：2019. 1. 28　装货地点：广州

收货人名称：M/S. HAIDAR OUS TRADING.　船名：JI CHANG/AL IHSA'A　贸易性质：一般贸易

海关编号	货号品名及规格	数量及单位	件数及包装	毛重KG	净重KG	尺码吨	单价	外币金额	离岸价格	折美元
6204. 6300	LADIES LYCRA LONG PANT ART NO. P 97811 ART NO. P 97811（2）	600 DOZ 600 DOZ	60 CTNS 60 CTNS	@60. 00 @60. 00	@30. 00 @30. 00		USD 23. 00 USD 23. 00			
合计		1 200 DOZ	120 CTNS	7 200	3 600	14. 40 M3		USD 27 600	USD 25 305	

①业务员存

唛头：
MAHARAJA　DEIRA
ANAND
DUBAI
NO. 1－120

收汇方式：L/CNO：SK/25067/97　本票号码：　D/PD/A ____天
价格条款：CIF DUBAI　财会编号：

托收银行：保险：　1. 投保险别：F. P. A.　2. 投保金额 USD 215

L/C 装运期：MAR. 7，2019　有效结汇期：MAR. 27，2019

能否分批：ALLOWED 能否转运：ALLOWED

付款人名称、地址：HABIB BANK AG ZURICH，SIKKAT AL KHALL ROAD BRANCH，DUBAI，UAE

其他事项要求：
①提单做成"TO ORDER"
②货物装于20'集装箱整柜
③提单显示信用证号码

提单：
可提货日期：
发货仓库：罗涌仓库

按　退佣金　计佣金　给
客户名称：M/S HAIDAR OUS TRADI ING
地址：P. O. BOX 2215，DUBAI，UAE
付佣方式：

业务经办人：

中国外运广东公司
出口货物托运单

提单编号＿＿＿＿＿＿＿＿　托运日期＿＿＿＿＿＿＿＿　托运单位编号＿＿＿＿＿＿＿＿

合约编号＿＿＿＿＿＿＿＿

船　　名＿＿＿＿＿＿＿＿　船期＿＿＿＿＿＿＿＿　运往地点＿＿＿＿＿＿＿＿

托 运 人＿＿＿＿＿＿＿＿＿＿＿＿＿＿＿＿＿＿＿＿＿＿＿＿

收 货 人＿＿＿＿＿＿＿＿＿＿＿＿＿＿＿＿＿＿＿＿＿＿＿＿

通　　知＿＿＿＿＿＿＿＿＿＿＿＿＿＿＿＿＿＿＿＿＿＿＿＿

标记及号码	件　数	货　　名	重量（公斤）		容积吨
			净	毛	
合计		共重			

特约事项		

可否转船				（托运人盖章）	
可否分批		需要提单正本　　份副本　　份			
货物堆存地点		装船期限		结汇期限	
运费缴付方式		运费账单开送			
信用证号码		货价	F. O. B.	C. I. F.	
运往香港船名		实际装船日期			

运费吨：　　运费率：　　运费金额：

强化提高三

广东省机械进出口（集团）公司利用电脑填制好如下托运单，请根据提供的信用证和有关资料，审核托运单的内容是否有错漏，如有错漏请指出并进行修改。

Form of Doc. Credit	*40	A	:	IRREVOCABLE
Doc. Credit Number	*20		:	TT4658. 25
Date of Issue	31	C	:	19. 09. 25
Expiry	*31	D	:	19. 11. 25 PLACE CHINA
Applicant	*50		:	K-MART AUSTRALIA LIMITED 800 TOORONGA VIC3416 AUSTRALIA
Beneficiary	*59		:	GUANGDONG MACHINERY IMP. & EXP. CORP. (GROUP) 726 DONGFENG ROAD EAST, GUANGZHOU, CHINA
Amount	*32	B	:	Currency USD Amount 60 000. 00
Available with/by	*41	D	:	ANY BANK BY NEGOTIATION
Draft at …	42	C	:	SIGHT
Partial Shipments	43	P	:	Not Allowed
Transhipment	43	T	:	Allowed
Loading in Charge	44	A	:	GUANGZHOU
For Transport to…	44	B	:	MELBOURNE
Shipment Period	44	C	:	NOT LATER THAN NOV. 15, 2019
Descript. of Goods	45	A	:	

1 200 DOZ EDGING KNIFE WITH METAL HANDLE
PACKING: 10DOZ /BAG. OTHER DETAILS AS PER S/C NO. : A97AU22300287
USD 50. 00 / DOZCIF MELBOURNE

Documents Required 46 A :

+ FULL SET OF CLEAN ON BOARD MARINE BILLS OF LADING, MADE OUT TO ORDER OF SHIPPER, MARKED "FREIGHT PREPAID", SHOWED THE CONTAINER NO. AND NOTIFY APPLICANT

Special Cond.

ALL DOCUMENTS MUST BE SHOWN THE NUMBER AND THE DATE OF THIS L/C.

毛重	100 KGS/BAG	总尺码	3. 672 CBM
净重	90 KGS/BAG	唛头	K-MATR/CTN NO. 1 – 120/ MELBOURNE
发票号码	YSM199901	托运日期	NOV. 1, 2019
货存地点	大松岗		

广东省机械进出口（集团）公司

GUANGDONG MACHINERY IMPORT AND EXPORT CORP. （GROUP）

726 **DONGFENG ROAD EAST，GUANGZHOU，CHINA**

托　运　单

SHIPPING NOTE

托运单：GUANG DONG MACHINERY
IMPORT AND
Exporter：EXPORT CORP. （GROUP）

托运单号 No.　：YSM199901
日期 Date　：NOV. 11，2019
装运港 Loading Port：GUANGZHOU
目的港 Destination　：MELBOURNE W/T HONGKONG
提单号 B/L No.　：MANE97/2435

收货人：TO ORDER OF K-MART AUSTRALIA
Consignee：LIMITED 800 TOORONGA VIC 3416
AUSTRALIA

通知人：K-MART AUSTRALIA LIMITED 800 TOORAK
Notify：ROAD，TOORONGA VIC 3416 AUSTRALIA。

标记 Shipping Marks	件数 Quantity	货名 Description of Goods	净重 Net Weight	毛重 Gross Weight	尺码 Measurement
KMART NO. 1 – 120 MELBOURNE	120 BAGS	EDGING KNIFE WITH METAL HANDLE	10 800. 00KGS	12 000. 00KGS	3. 672CBMS
TOTAL:	120 BAGS		10 800. 00KGS	12 000. 00KGS	3. 672CBMS

可否分批 Partial Shipment　：不允许
可否转船 Transhipment　：不允许
装船期限 Latest Shipment Date：2019. 11. 15
结汇期限 Expiry Date　：NOV. 25，2019
运费缴付方式　：FREIGHT CLLECT
发票号 Invoice NO.　：YSM199901
货证情况　：
运输方式　：江．海运

正本 Original B/L：3
副本 Copy of B/L：3
货存地点 Goods in：大松岗
发票金额 Amount：USD 6 000. 00
L/C 号　：TT4658. 25
合同号 S/C No.　：A97AU22300287

运费吨：　运费率：　运费金额：

特殊条款：

GUANGDONG MACHINERY IMPORT
AND EXPORT CORP. （GROUP）

实训模块七 出口报检

一、实训目的

本模块的实训，使学生熟悉出口商品报检的一般程序，能根据合同和信用证填制出境货物检验检疫申请单。

二、实训任务

（1）根据提供的资料填制出境货物检验检疫申请单。

（2）根据提供的资料填制一般原产地证明书和普惠制原产地证明书格式 A。

三、实训提示

（一）申请出口报检的一般程序

1. 出口报检申请

属于法定检验的出口商品，报检员应填写出境货物报检单，随附合同、信用证、发票和装箱单等文件提交海关出入境检验检疫部门。报检时间一般在装运前 10 天。

2. 抽样、制样

除委托检验外，抽样的样品不得由报检员送样。而应由抽样员按规定的标准和方法随机抽样。

3. 检验

4. 签证

出口商品的签证一般在 10 个工作日内完成。用于结汇的商检证书一般使用英文签发一份正本，其签证日期不得迟于提单日期。

（二）填制出境货物检验检疫申请单应注意的问题

（1）“出境货物检验检疫申请”所列各栏必须填写完整、准确、清晰，没有内容填写的栏目应以斜杠“/”表示，不得留空。

（2）“发货人”栏是指本批货物贸易合同中卖方名称或信用证中受益人名称。如需要出具英文证书的，填写中英文。

（3）“收货人”栏是指本批出境货物贸易合同中或信用证中买方名称。如需要出具英文证书的，填写中英文。

（4）货物名称不得填写笼统的商品类，如“陶瓷”“玩具”等，必须填写具体的类别名称，“日用陶瓷”“塑料玩具”。不够位置填写的，可用附页的形式填报。

（5）“数/重量”栏填写报检货物的数/重量，重量一般填写净重。如填写毛重，或以毛重作净重则需注明。

（6）同一报检单报检多批货物，需列明每批货物的总值。（如申报货物总值与国内、国际市场价格有较大差异，检验检疫机构保留核价权力）

（7）贸易合同或信用证中贸易双方对本批货物特别约定而订立的质量、卫生等条款和报检单位对本批货物检验检疫的特别要求，须在“合同、信用证订立的检验检疫条款或特殊要求”中标出。

（8）对检验检疫申请单上未标出的，如“通关单”等，须自行填写所需证单的名称和数量。

（9）检验检疫申请单必须有申请人的亲笔签名。

（三）填制原产地证应注意的问题

（1）必须按信用证或合同的要求出证，不要把一般原产地证明书或普惠制原产地证明书 FORM A 混为一谈。

（2）签证机构必须符合信用证或合同的要求。

（3）注意一般原产地证明书或普惠制原产地证明书 FORM A 的第 1 项和第 2 项不能漏填出口国和进口国的名称。

（4）注意一般原产地证明书第 7 项的包装数量和第 9 项的计价数量不能混淆。

（5）普惠制原产地证明书 FORM A 第 12 项的出口国和进口国不能错填为装运港和目的港。

（6）一般原产地证明书或普惠制原产地证明书 FORM A 的签发日期不得早于申请日期。

四、实训内容

（一）填制出境货物检验检疫申请

张大同于 2021 年 12 月 3 日根据合同和信用证填制出境货物检验检疫申请，并于当天向海关出入境检验检疫部门报送。请你替张大同填写出境货物检验检疫申请（报验单位登记号：4401091349）。

中华人民共和国海关
出境货物检验检疫申请

电子底账数据号：

申请单位（加盖公章）：　　　　＊编号：________

申请单位登记号：　　联系人：　　电话：　　申请日期：　　年　　月　　日

发货人	（中文）					
	（外文）					
收货人	（中文）					
	（外文）					
货物名称（中/外文）	H. S. 编码	产地	数/重量	货物总值	包装种类及数量	
运输工具名称号码		贸易方式		货物存放地点		
合同号		信用证号		用途		
发货日期		输往国家（地区）		许可证/审批号		
启运地		到达口岸		生产单位注册号		
集装箱规格、数量及号码						
合同、信用证订立的检验检疫条款或特殊要求	标记及号码	随附单据（画"√"或补填）				
		□合同 □信用证 □发票 □换证凭单 □装箱单 □厂检单	□包装性能结果单 □许可/审批文件 □ □ □ □			

需要证单名称（画"√"或补填）		＊检验检疫费	
□品质证书　__正__副 □重量证书　__正__副 □数量证书　__正__副 □兽医卫生证书　__正__副 □健康证书　__正__副 □卫生证书　__正__副 □动物卫生证书　__正__副	□植物检疫证书　__正__副 □熏蒸/消毒证书　__正__副 □出境货物换证凭单　__正__副 □ □ □ □	总金额（元人民币）	
		计费人	
		收费人	

申请人郑重声明： 1. 本人被授权申请检验检疫。 2. 上列填写内容正确属实、货物无伪造或冒用他人的厂名、标志、认证标志，承担货物质量责任。 签名：________	领取证单	
	日期	
	签名	

注：有"＊"号栏由海关填写。

（二）填制普惠制原产地证明书格式 A

FORM A 编号为 GZ8/80266/0113。

Original

<table>
<tr><td colspan="3">1. Goods consigned from (Exporter's business name, address, county)</td><td colspan="3" rowspan="2">Reference No.

GENERALIZED SYSTEM OF PREFERENCES
CERTIFICATE OF ORIGIN
(Combined declaration and certificate)
FORM A
issued in THE PEOPLE'S REPUBLIC OF CHINA
(COUNTRY)
See Notes overleaf</td></tr>
<tr><td colspan="3">2. Goods consigned to (Consignee's name, address, country)</td></tr>
<tr><td colspan="3">3. Means of transport and route (as far as known)</td><td colspan="3">4. For official use</td></tr>
<tr><td>5. Item number</td><td>6. Marks and numbers of packages</td><td>7. Number and kind of packages; description of goods</td><td>8. Origin criterion (see Notes overleaf)</td><td>9. Gross weight or other quantity</td><td>10. Number and date of invoices</td></tr>
<tr><td colspan="3">11. Certification
It is hereby certified, on the basis of control carried out, that the declaration by the exporter is correct.

Place and date, signature and stamp of certifying authority</td><td colspan="3">12. Declaration by the exporter
The undersigned hereby declares that the above details and statements are correct; that all the goods were produced in
----
(country)
and that they comply with the origin requirements specified for those goods in the Generalized System of Preferences for goods exported to
----
(importing country)

Place and date, signature of authorized signatory</td></tr>
</table>

五、强化提高

强化提高一

根据给定的资料填写出境货物检验检疫申请和一般原产地证明书。

Credit Number：	SK/25067/97
Date of Issue：	DEC. 27，2018
Applicant：	ABC TRADING CO.，LTD. DUBAI（UAE）. P. O. BOX No. 6093，DUBAI（UAE），FAX NO. 263745
Beneficiary：	GUANGDONG TEXTILES IMP AND EXP GRANDTON TRADING CO. LTD，. 7/F GUANGDONG TEXTILES MANSION， NO. 168 XIAOBEI ROAD，GUANGZHOU，CHINA
Amount：	USD 99 960.00（US DOLLARS NINETY-NINE THOUSAND NINE HUNDRED AND SIXTY ONLY）
Covering：	4 000 DOZEN EMBROIDERED TABLE CLOTH NO. B4010 – A502 CIFC2 DUBAI USD 25.5 PER DOZEN PACKING：10DOZ/CTN ALL OTHER DETAILS ARE AS PER S/C No. 97/2495
Shipping Marks：	MAHARAJA / 264553/ DUBAI/NO. 1 – 400

发票号码	GD – TX – 9057	发票日期	JAN. 2，2019	产地证号码	GZC1/12002/5649
许可证号码	25 KD257	装运港	广州港	货物存放地点	大朗仓库
船名	MAEK335 V. 002	商品编码	6204.1300	集装箱号码	MALU2004023/20’
报检日期	JAN. 15，2019	提单日期	JAN. 22，2019	报检单位登记号	4401W13490

生产厂家：广东中山服装厂，2019 年 1 月 15 日由检验检疫申请员向海关出入境检验检疫部门报检，1 月 21 日海关出入境检验检疫部门审核放行。

中华人民共和国海关
出境货物检验检疫申请

电子底账数据号：

申请单位（加盖公章）：　　　　＊编号：__________

申请单位登记号：　　　联系人：　　　电话：　　　申请日期：　　年　　月　　日

发货人	（中文）	
	（外文）	
收货人	（中文）	
	（外文）	

货物名称（中/外文）	H. S. 编码	产地	数/重量	货物总值	包装种类及数量

运输工具名称号码		贸易方式		货物存放地点	
合同号		信用证号		用途	
发货日期		输往国家（地区）		许可证/审批号	
启运地		到达口岸		生产单位注册号	
集装箱规格、数量及号码					

合同、信用证订立的检验检疫条款或特殊要求	标记及号码	随附单据（画“√”或补填）	
		□合同	□包装性能结果单
		□信用证	□许可/审批文件
		□发票	□
		□换证凭单	□
		□装箱单	□
		□厂检单	□

需要证单名称（画“√”或补填）				＊检验检疫费	
□品质证书	__正__副	□植物检疫证书	__正__副	总金额（元人民币）	
□重量证书	__正__副	□熏蒸/消毒证书	__正__副		
□数量证书	__正__副	□出境货物换证凭单	__正__副		
□兽医卫生证书	__正__副	□		计费人	
□健康证书	__正__副	□			
□卫生证书	__正__副	□		收费人	
□动物卫生证书	__正__副	□			

申请人郑重声明：	领取证单	
1. 本人被授权申请检验检疫。	日期	
2. 上列填写内容正确属实、货物无伪造或冒用他人的厂名、标志、认证标志，承担货物质量责任。		
签名：________	签名	

注：有“＊”号栏由海关填写。

Original

<table>
<tr><td colspan="2">1. Exporter</td><td colspan="3" rowspan="2">Certificate No.

CERTIFICATE OF ORIGIN
OF
THE PEOPLE'S REPUBLIC OF CHINA</td></tr>
<tr><td colspan="2">2. Consignee</td></tr>
<tr><td colspan="2">3. Means of transport and route</td><td colspan="3" rowspan="2">5. For certifying authority use only</td></tr>
<tr><td colspan="2">4. Country/region of destination</td></tr>
<tr><td>6. Marks and numbers</td><td>7. Number and kind of packages; description of goods</td><td>8. H. S. Code</td><td>9. Quantity</td><td>10. Number and date of invoices</td></tr>
<tr><td colspan="2">11. Declaration by the exporter
The undersigned hereby declares that the above details and statements are correct, that all the goods were produced in China and that they comply with the Rules of Origin of the People's Republic of China.

Place and date, signature and stamp of authorized signatory</td><td colspan="3">12. Certification
It is hereby certified that the declaration by the export is correct.

Place and date, signature of authorized signatory</td></tr>
</table>

强化提高二

根据给定的资料填写出境货物检验检疫申请和 FORM A。

L/C No. : TB25078
Applicant : HALSSEN & LYON GMBH
PICKHUBEN 9
20457 HAMBURG
Beneficiary : CHINA TUHSU GUANGDONG TEA IMPORT & EXPORT CORP.
26 - 30FLOOR, GUANGDONG FOREIGN ECONOMICS & TRADE BUILDING
351 TIANHE ROAD, GUANGZHOU
Amount : EUR 130 000. 00 (EUROS ONE HUNDRED AND THIRTY THOUSAND ONLY.)
Loading in Charge : GUANGZHOU, CHINA
For Transport to : HAMBURG
Descript. of Goods : 2 000 PCS OF GUITAR, ART NO. A EUR 65. 00/PC CIFC 3% HAMBURG
PACKED IN CARTONS AND CONTAINERIZED
AS PER THE SALES CONFIRHATION NO. BT7095
THE PRICE IS TO BE UNDERSTOOD PER KILO NET SHIPPED WEIGHT CIF HAMBURG
LESS 3 PERCENT COMMISSION, INCLUDING PACKING.

发票号码：TA7149
发票日期：11th August, 2019
商品编码：9202. 9000
FORM A 号码：GZ05/3223/22223
集装箱号码：EASU9608490
船名：SUKE V. 001
货物存放地点：大朗仓库
报检单位登记号：4401YP3490
生产厂家：广州华辉乐器厂
唛头：HAMBURG/65805/NO. 1 - 1000

商品型号	数量	包装	毛重	净重	尺码
A	2 000 PCS	2 PC/CTN	4. 5 KGS/CTN	2. 5 KGS/CTN	(102 × 50 × 55) CM/CTN

2019 年 8 月 21 日由报验员张大同向海关出入境检验检疫部门申请检验，8 月 29 日海关出入境检验检疫部门审核放行，8 月 30 日在广州港装运出口。

中华人民共和国海关
出境货物检验检疫申请

电子底账数据号：

申请单位（加盖公章）： ＊编号：__________

申请单位登记号： 联系人： 电话： 申请日期： 年 月 日

发货人	（中文）				
	（外文）				
收货人	（中文）				
	（外文）				
货物名称（中/外文）	H. S. 编码	产地	数/重量	货物总值	包装种类及数量
运输工具名称号码		贸易方式		货物存放地点	
合同号		信用证号		用途	
发货日期		输往国家（地区）		许可证/审批号	
启运地		到达口岸		生产单位注册号	
集装箱规格、数量及号码					

合同、信用证订立的检验检疫条款或特殊要求	标记及号码	随附单据（画“√”或补填）	
		□合同	□包装性能结果单
		□信用证	□许可/审批文件
		□发票	□
		□换证凭单	□
		□装箱单	□
		□厂检单	□

需要证单名称（画“√”或补填）				＊检验检疫费	
□品质证书	_正_副	□植物检疫证书	_正_副	总金额（元人民币）	
□重量证书	_正_副	□熏蒸/消毒证书	_正_副		
□数量证书	_正_副	□出境货物换证凭单	_正_副		
□兽医卫生证书	_正_副	□		计费人	
□健康证书	_正_副	□			
□卫生证书	_正_副	□		收费人	
□动物卫生证书	_正_副	□			

申请人郑重声明：	领取证单	
1. 本人被授权申请检验检疫。	日期	
2. 上列填写内容正确属实、货物无伪造或冒用他人的厂名、标志、认证标志，承担货物质量责任。		
签名：________	签名	

注：有“＊”号栏由海关填写。

Original

<table>
<tr>
<td>1. Goods consigned from (Exporter's business name, address, county)</td>
<td rowspan="2">Reference No.

GENERALIZED SYSTEM OF PREFERENCES
CERTIFICATE OF ORIGIN
(Combined declaration and certificate)
FORM A
issued in THE PEOPLE'S REPUBLIC OF CHINA
(COUNTRY)
See Notes overleaf</td>
</tr>
<tr>
<td>2. Goods consigned to (Consignee's name, address, country)</td>
</tr>
<tr>
<td>3. Means of transport and route (as far as known)</td>
<td>4. For official use</td>
</tr>
</table>

<table>
<tr>
<td>5. Item number</td>
<td>6. Marks and numbers of packages</td>
<td>7. Number and kind of packages; description of goods</td>
<td>8. Origin criterion (see Notes overleaf)</td>
<td>9. Gross weight or other quantity</td>
<td>10. Number and date of invoices</td>
</tr>
<tr><td></td><td></td><td></td><td></td><td></td><td></td></tr>
</table>

<table>
<tr>
<td>11. Certification
It is hereby certified, on the basis of control carried out, that the declaration by the exporter is correct.

____
Place and date, signature and stamp of certifying authority</td>
<td>12. Declaration by the exporter
The undersigned hereby declares that the above details and statements are correct; that all the goods were produced in

____
(country)
and that they comply with the origin requirements specified for those goods in the Generalized System of Preferences for goods exported to

____
(importing country)
____
Place and date, signature of authorized signatory</td>
</tr>
</table>

强化提高三

根据给定的资料填写出境货物检验检疫申请和 FORM A。

ISSUING BANK: DONTUSU COMMERCIAL BANK TOKYO, JAPAN

L/C NO.: KKT5846172

ISSUING DATE: 05/11/2018

BENEFICIARY: GUANGDONG MACHINERY IMPORT AND EXPORT CORP. (GROUP) 726 DONGFENG ROAD EAST, GUANGZHOU, CHINA

APPLICANT: SHITAYA KINZOKU CO., LTD. 6 - 11 7 - CHOME UENO TAITO - KU TOKYO, JAPAN

AMOUNT: USD 15 880.00

SHIPMENT FROM GUANGZHOU PORT FOR TRANSPORTATION TO YOKOHAMA. COVERING SHIPMENT OF 'RABBIT' BRAND SHOVEL WITH METAL HANDLE, S501MH 210 DOZ AND S503MH 200DOZ FOR 20FT CONTAINER. AS PER S/C NO. A97JP19900247. TRADE TERM: CIF YOKOHAMA

SHIPPING MARKS: A9700247/YOKOHAMA/NO. 1 - 410

发票号码：GD920029　　发票日期：NOV. 2, 2018

生产厂家：广东中山威星农具厂　　包　装：1DOZ/CTN

船　　名：HANGTU V. 0134　　集装箱号码：1×20' FCL　SCZU7854343

商品编码：7216. 6100　　FORM A 号码：GZ07/2345/12345

商品型号	单价	净重	毛重	尺码
S501MH	USD 40. 00/DOZ	24. 00 KGS/CTN	25. 00 KGS/CTN	(97×36×23)CM/CTN
S503MH	USD 37. 40/DOZ	22. 00 KGS/CTN	23. 00 KGS/CTN	(97×36×25)CM/CTN

该批货物存于罗涌仓库，拟于 2018 年 11 月 21 日装运，2018 年 11 月 14 日由报验员向海关出入境检验检疫部门申请检验。出口公司的报检单位登记号为 4401AA490。

中华人民共和国海关
出境货物检验检疫申请

电子底账数据号：

申请单位（加盖公章）： ＊编号：__________

申请单位登记号： 联系人： 电话： 申请日期： 年 月 日

发货人	（中文）	
	（外文）	
收货人	（中文）	
	（外文）	

货物名称（中/外文）	H. S. 编码	产地	数/重量	货物总值	包装种类及数量

运输工具名称号码		贸易方式		货物存放地点	
合同号		信用证号		用途	
发货日期		输往国家（地区）		许可证/审批号	
启运地		到达口岸		生产单位注册号	
集装箱规格、数量及号码					

合同、信用证订立的检验检疫条款或特殊要求	标记及号码	随附单据（画“√”或补填）	
		□合同	□包装性能结果单
		□信用证	□许可/审批文件
		□发票	□
		□换证凭单	□
		□装箱单	□
		□厂检单	□

需要证单名称（画“√”或补填）		＊检验检疫费	
□品质证书 __正__副	□植物检疫证书 __正__副	总金额（元人民币）	
□重量证书 __正__副	□熏蒸/消毒证书 __正__副		
□数量证书 __正__副	□出境货物换证凭单 __正__副		
□兽医卫生证书 __正__副	□	计费人	
□健康证书 __正__副	□		
□卫生证书 __正__副	□	收费人	
□动物卫生证书 __正__副	□		

申请人郑重声明：	领取证单	
1. 本人被授权申请检验检疫。	日期	
2. 上列填写内容正确属实、货物无伪造或冒用他人的厂名、标志、认证标志，承担货物质量责任。		
签名：________	签名	

注：有“＊”号栏由海关填写。

Original

<table>
<tr><td colspan="3">1. Goods consigned from (Exporter's business name, address, county)</td><td colspan="3" rowspan="2">Reference No.

GENERALIZED SYSTEM OF PREFERENCES
CERTIFICATE OF ORIGIN
(Combined declaration and certificate)
FORM A
issued in THE PEOPLE'S REPUBLIC OF CHINA
(COUNTRY)
See Notes overleaf</td></tr>
<tr><td colspan="3">2. Goods consigned to (Consignee's name, address, country)</td></tr>
<tr><td colspan="3">3. Means of transport and route (as far as known)</td><td colspan="3">4. For official use</td></tr>
<tr><td>5. Item number</td><td>6. Marks and numbers of packages</td><td>7. Number and kind of packages; description of goods</td><td>8. Origin criterion (see Notes overleaf)</td><td>9. Gross weight or other quantity</td><td>10. Number and date of invoices</td></tr>
<tr><td colspan="3">11. Certification
It is hereby certified, on the basis of control carried out, that the declaration by the exporter is correct.

Place and date, signature and stamp of certifying authority</td><td colspan="3">12. Declaration by the exporter
The undersigned hereby declares that the above details and statements are correct; that all the goods were produced in

----
(country)
and that they comply with the origin requirements specified for those goods in the Generalized System of Preferences for goods exported to

----
(importing country)

Place and date, signature of authorized signatory</td></tr>
</table>

实训模块八　出口报关

一、实训目的

本模块的实训，使学生了解出口通关的业务程序，学生能根据合同、发票、装箱单和装货单填制装货单和出口货物报关单。

二、实训任务

（1）根据提供的资料填制装货单。

（2）根据提供的资料填制出口货物报关单。

三、实训提示

（一）一般出口货物通关的业务程序

1. 申报前备齐出口货物

2. 如实申报，交验单证

3. 查验货物

查验的方法：①彻底查验；②抽查；③外形查验。

海关查验进出口货物时，报关员必须在场，并按照海关的要求负责搬移货物、开拆和重封货物的包装，并应随时答复海关查验人员提出的问题或提供海关需要的相关单证，积极配合海关的查验监管活动。

对海关在查验进出口货物造成损坏的，报关员应向负责查验的海关提出赔偿要求，并办理有关手续。

4. 计征税费

（1）出口货物以海关审定的货物售予境外的离岸价格（FOB 价格）扣除出口关税作为完税价格。其公式为：

$$出口关税税额 = 完税价格 \times 出口税税率$$

$$完税价格 = \frac{FOB}{1 + 出口税率}$$

（2）消费税、增值税。

$$从价消费税额 = \frac{关税完税价格 + 关税额}{1 - 消费税税率} \times 消费税税率$$

$$从量消费税额 = 应税消费品数量 \times 消费税单位税额$$

$$滞纳金金额 = （关税额 + 增值税 + 消费税） \times 滞纳天数 \times 1\%$$

纳税义务人应自海关开出税单的次日起 15 日内向指定银行缴纳税款。逾期缴纳的应按税额的 0.1%，按日征收，星期日、节假日亦不能除外，均应按日计数。

5. 签印放行

出口货物经过申报、查验和缴纳税费后，海关便在装货单或运单上签印放行。

6. 提保放行

海关在发货人缴纳相当于税款的保证金或相应的担保后可对规定情况的货物予以放行。

（二）填制出口货物报关单应注意的问题

（1）“境内发货人”栏目应填报发货单位名称及海关注册登记编码。

（2）“出口日期”和“申报日期”栏目填写 8 位数，顺序为年、月、日各 2 位。如 2018 年 9 月 15 日填为 20180915。

（3）一份报关单只允许填报一个备案号。无登记手册或无备案审批文件的报关单，本栏目免于填报。

（4）“运输工具名称”栏目填制载运货物出境的运输工具的名称或运输工具编号。对于需要中转的运输，只填制第一程运输工具的名称。江海运输填报船舶呼号（来往港澳小型船舶为监管簿编号）+“/”+航次号；一份报关单只允许填报一个运输工具名称。

（5）一份报关单只允许填报一个提运单号，一票货物对应多个提运单时，应分单填报。

（6）一份报关单只允许填报一个许可证号。

（7）“离境口岸”栏目应填报口岸海关名称及代码。不能只填口岸海关名称或代码，且口岸海关名称必须按《关区代码表》统一规定的称谓填写。

（8）“件数”栏目应填报有外包装的出口货物的实际件数。舱单件数为集装箱（TEU）的，填报集装箱个数；舱单件数为托盘的，填报托盘数；裸装货物填报为 1。

（9）“毛重”和“净重”栏目填报出口货物实际毛重和净重，计量单位为公斤，不足一公斤的填报为 1。

（10）运费可按运费单价、总价或运费率三种方式之一填报，同时注明运费标记，并按海关规定的“货币代码表”选择填报相应的币种代码。运保费率合并计算的，运保费填报在本栏目中。

（11）保费可按保险费总价或保险费率两种方式之一填报，同时注明保险费标记，并按海关规定的“货币代码表”选择填报相应的币种代码。运保费合并计算的，运保费填报在运费栏目中。

（12）应计入完税价格的杂费填报为正值或正率，应从完税价格中扣除的杂费填报为负值或负率。杂费标记“1”表示杂费率，“3”表示杂费总价。

（13）合同、发票、装箱单、许可证等必备的随附单证不在“随附单据及编号”栏目填报。

（14）“商品名称及规格型号”栏目分两行填报。第一行填报出口货物规范的中文商品名称，第二行填报规格型号，必要时可加注原文。

（15）申报单位指对申报内容的真实性直接向海关负责的企业或单位。自理报关的，应填报出口货物的境内发货人名称及代码；委托代理报关的，应填报经海关批准的专业或代理报关企业名称及代码。

四、实训内容

张大同报检，取得出境货物通关单后，于 2021 年 12 月 10 日通过新凤罗冲口岸向海关申报。请你替张大同填制如下的单据。（出口核销单位代码：251128998－0，报关单预录入编号：002102133，广东中山威威照明有限公司海关注册登记编码：4401A13217）

（一）填制装货单

Shipper（发货人）		B/L No.
Consignee（收货人）		中远集装箱运输有限公司 COSCO CONTAINER LINES 集装箱货物托运单 装货单 SHIPPING ORDER
Notify Party（通知人）		
Pre-carriage by（前程承运人）	Place of Receipt（收货地点）	
Ocean vessel（船名）Voy. No.（航次）	Port of Loading（装运港）	
Port of Discharge（卸货港）	Place of Delivery（交货地点）	Final Destination for the Merchant's Reference（目的地）

Container No.（集装箱号）	Seal No.（铅封号）Marks & Nos.（标记与号码）	No. of containers or p'kgs（箱数或件数）	Kind of Package; Description of Goods（包装种类与货名）	Gross Weight 毛重（公斤）	Measurement 尺码（立方米）
TOTAL NUMBER OF CONTAINERS OR PACKAGES（JIN WORDS）集装箱数或件数合计（大写）					

FREIGHT & CHARGES（运费与附加费）	Revenue Tons（运费吨）	Rate（运费率）	Per（每）	Prepaid（运费预付）	Collect（运费到付）

Service Type on Receiving	Service Type on Delivery	Reeger Temperature Required（冷藏温度）	℉	℃

TYPE OF GOODS（货类）	□Ordinary（普通）　□ Reeger（冷藏）　□ Dangerous（危险品）　□ Auto（裸装车辆） □Liquid（液体）　□ Live Animal（活动物）　□ Bulk（散货）	危险品	IMCO Class. UN No.: IMDG Code Page: Property:

可否转船：	可否分批：	装期：	Received by the Carrier the total number of containers or other packages or units stated above to be transported subject to the terms and conditions of the Carrier's regular form of Bill of Lading (for combined Transport to Port shipment) which shall be deemed to be incorporated herein Date:　　　　as Agent only
货价：	信用证号码：	No. of Original B(S)/L	
特约事项：	合同号码：	托运人盖章：	

（二）填制出口货物报关单

中华人民共和国海关出口货物报关单

预录入编号：　　　　　　　　海关编号：

<table>
<tr><td>境内发货人</td><td colspan="2">出境关别</td><td colspan="2">出口日期</td><td colspan="2">申报日期</td><td>备案号</td></tr>
<tr><td>境外收货人</td><td colspan="2">运输方式</td><td colspan="2">运输工具名称及航次号</td><td colspan="3">提运单号</td></tr>
<tr><td>生产销售单位</td><td colspan="2">监管方式</td><td colspan="2">征免性质</td><td colspan="3">许可证号</td></tr>
<tr><td>合同协议号</td><td colspan="2">贸易国（地区）</td><td colspan="2">运抵国（地区）</td><td>指运港</td><td colspan="2">离境口岸</td></tr>
<tr><td>包装种类</td><td>件数</td><td>毛重（千克）</td><td>净重（千克）</td><td>成交方式</td><td>运费</td><td>保费</td><td>杂费</td></tr>
<tr><td colspan="8">随附单证及编号</td></tr>
<tr><td colspan="8">标记唛码及备注</td></tr>
<tr><td colspan="8">项号　商品编号　商品名称及规格型号　数量及单位　单价/总价/币制　原产国（地区）　最终目的国（地区）　境内货源地　征免</td></tr>
<tr><td colspan="8"></td></tr>
<tr><td colspan="8"></td></tr>
<tr><td colspan="8"></td></tr>
<tr><td colspan="8"></td></tr>
<tr><td colspan="8"></td></tr>
<tr><td colspan="8"></td></tr>
<tr><td colspan="8">特殊关系确认：　　价格影响确认：　　支付特许权使用费确认：　　自报自缴：</td></tr>
<tr><td colspan="7">报关人员　报关人员证号　电话　　兹申明对以上内容承担如实申报、依法纳税之法律责任
申报单位　　　　　　　　　　　　　　　　　申报单位（签章）</td><td>海关批注及签章</td></tr>
</table>

五、强化提高

强化提高一

根据所给的商业发票和海运提单，就下面出口货物报关单的各项内容，选择最佳答案。

1. 离境口岸（　　）

A. 上海海关　　B. 广州黄埔

C. 上海宝山　　D. 新凤罗冲

2. 出口日期（　　）

A. 98.06.20　　B. 98/6/18

C. 98.06.18　　D. 98/6/20

3. 申报日期（　　）

A. 1998年6月18日　　B. 6/18/1998

C. 98.06.20　　D. 98.06.18

4. 生产销售单位（　　）

A. 东方贸易发展公司　　B. 广东东方贸易发展公司

C. 上海东方贸易发展公司　　D. 上海荣华食品加工厂

5. 运输方式（　　）

A. 船运　　B. 海运

C. 汽车　　D. 其他

6. 运输工具名称及航次（　　）

A. JOHN　　B. JOHN V.9805

C. JOHN/9805　　D. S.S.JOHN

7. 提运单号（　　）

A. GPR05346　　B. 98/2500367

C. SC98B0125　　D. 05346

8. 申报单位（　　）

A. 东方贸易发展公司　　B. 上海荣华食品加工厂

C. 上海东方贸易发展公司　　D. 上海浦发报关行

9. 贸易方式（　　）

A. 补偿贸易　　B. 来料加工

C. 进料加工　　D. 一般贸易

10. 征免性质（　　）

A. 一般征税　　B. 全免

C. 减免 D. 许可证

11. 运抵国（ ）
A. 日本 B. 横滨
C. 东京 D. 中国

12. 指运港（ ）
A. 东京 B. 横滨
C. 门司 D. 大板

13. 境内货源地（ ）
A. 上海 B. 广州
C. 厦门 D. 中国广东

14. 成交方式（ ）
A. CFR B. FOB
C. CIF D. FCA

15. 运费（ ）
A. 502/1800/3 B. 502/1800/2
C. 110/1800/3 D. 110/1800/2

16. 合同协议号（ ）
A. 98/250036 B. SC98B0125
C. GPR05346 D. RH98B1205

17. 监管方式（ ）
A. 一般贸易 B. 易货贸易
C. 补偿贸易 D. 寄售代销

18. 毛重（ ）
A. 84 000 B. 98 000
C. 7 000 D. 147 000

19. 成交方式（ ）
A. CFR B. CIF
C. FOB C. CIP

20. 征免（ ）
A. 照章征税 B. 全免
C. 许可证 D. 减免

上海东方贸易发展公司

DONGFANG TRADE DEVELOPMENT CO. , LTD.

商业发票

COMMERCIAL INVOICE

Messrs:

S. O. CONSULTANT CO. , LTD.
12 OTEMON-KU FUKUOKA
JAPAN

INVOICE NO. : RH98B1205

INVOICE DATE : JUNE 15TH, 2018

L/C NO. : 515668

L/C DATE: MAY 12TH, 2018
S/C NO : SC98B0125

Exporter:

DONGFANG TRADE DEVELOPMENT
CO. , LTD.

Transport details:
FROM SHANGHAI TO MOJI
BY VESSEL

Terms of payment:
BY L/C

MARKS & NUMBERS	DESCRIPTION OF GOODS	GUANTITY	UNIT PRICE	AMOUNT
S. O. SC98B0125 MOJI MADE IN CHINA	HALF DRIED PRUNE 2018CROP	7 000 CASE	USD 21. 00	USD 147 000. 00
		7 000 CASE	CFR MOJI	USD 147 000. 00

TOTAL QUANTITY: 7 000 CASE PACKING: 7 000 CASE
TOTAL WEIGHT: NET WT. : 84 000 KGS GROSS WT. : 98 000 KGS
TOTAL: U. S. DOLLARS ONE HUNDRED AND FORTY-SEVEN THOUSAND ONLY.
WE CERTIFY THAT ALL THE SHIPPED GOODS ARE OF CHINESE ORIGIN.

上海东方贸易发展公司
DONGFANG TRADE DEVELOPMENT CO. , LTD.

外汇核销单编号：98/2500367
经营单位海关注册编号：3502110278　发货单位与经营单位相同
预录入编号：58711223
生产厂家：上海荣光食品加工厂
运费：USD 1 800. 00
2018 年 6 月 18 日由上海浦发报关行向上海宝山海关申报，2018 年 6 月 20 日出口。

BILL OF LADING

Shipper DONGFANG TRADE DEVELOPMENT CO. LTD.	B/L No. GPR05346
Consignee TO ORDER OF ABC BANK LTD. JAPAN	Combined Transport BILL OF LADING RECEIVED in apparent good order and condition except as otherwise noted the total number of containers or other packages or units enumerated below for transportation from the place of receipt to the place of delivery subject to the terms and conditions hereof. One of the Bills of Lading must be surrendered duly endorsed to the Carrier by or on behalf of the Holder of the Bill of Lading, the rights and liabilities arising in accordance with the terms and conditions hereof shall, without prejudice to any rule of common law or statute rendering them binding on the Merchant, become binding in all respects between the Carrier and the Holder of the Bill of Lading as though the contract evidenced hereby had been made between them. IN WITNESS whereof the number of original Bills of Lading stated under have been signed. All of this tenor and date, one of which being accomplished, the other (s) to be void.
Notify Address S. O. CONSULTANT CO., LTD. 12 OTEMON-KU FUKUOKA JAPAN	For delivery of goods please apply to:

Pre-carriage by	Place of Receipt		
Ocean Vessel Voy. No. JOHN V9805	Port of Loading SHANGHAI		
Port of Discharge MOJI, JAPAN	Place of Delivery		Final Destination for the Merchant's Reference only

Particulars Furnished by Merchants

Container, Seal No. & Marks & Nos.	No. of Package & Description of Goods	Gross Weight Kgs	Measurement m^3
S. O. SC98B0125 MOJI MADE IN CHINA CONTAINER NO.: MARES850015(40')	7 000 CASE HALF DRIED PRUNE 2018 CROP TOTAL: SEVEN THOUSAND CASE ONLY. CY/CY --------	29 656 KGS FREIGHT PREPAID	14 M^3

Freight & Charges	Revenue Tons.	Rate	Per	Prepaid	Collect

Ex. Rate:	Prepaid at	Payable at	Place and date of issue SHANGHAI JUNE 20, 2018
	Total Prepaid	No. of Original B (s) /L 3 (THREE)	Stamp & Signature

LADEN ON BOARD THE VESSEL
Date

By································

(TERMS CONTINUED ON BACK HEREOF)　　(KENWA STANDARD FORM 01)

强化提高二

根据所给的商业发票和海运提单，就下面出口货物报关单的各项内容，选择最佳答案。

1. 离境口岸（　　）
   A. 广州海关　　B. 广州黄埔
   C. 广州新风　　D. 新风罗冲
2. 出口日期（　　）
   A. 00.12.1　　B. 00－12－1
   C. 00.12.01　　D. 1－12－00
3. 运输方式（　　）
   A. 船运　　B. 海运
   C. 邮运　　D. 其他
4. 运输工具名称（　　）
   A. MELBOURNE　　B. MARN V001
   C. JANSONG VO23　　D. MARN V001/JANSONG V023
5. 提运单号（　　）
   A. A97AU22300287　　B. MANE97/2435
   C. YSM199901　　D. MANE97
6. 生产销售单位（　　）
   A. 天津东方红农具厂　　B. 广东省机械进出口（集团）公司
   C. SANYEI HONG KONG
7. 贸易方式（　　）
   A. 补偿贸易　　B. 来料加工
   C. 进料加工　　D. 一般贸易
8. 征免性质（　　）
   A. 一般征税　　B. 全免
   C. 减免　　D. 许可证
9. 运抵国（　　）
   A. 澳大利亚　　B. 奥地利
   C. 墨尔本　　D. 中国
10. 指运港（　　）
    A. 香港　　B. 澳大利亚
    C. 广州　　D. 墨尔本
11. 境内货源地（　　）
    A. 广东　　B. 天津

C. 中国　　D. 上海

12. 成交方式（　　）

A. CFR　　B. FOB

C. CIF　　D. FCA

13. 运费（　　）

A. 502/535/3　　B. 502/535/2

C. 110/535/3　　D. 110/535/2

14. 境内发货人（　　）

A. 天津东方红农具厂　　B. 广东省机械进出口（集团）公司

C. SANYEI HONG KONG

15. 毛重（　　）

A. 10 800　　B. 12 000

C. 1 200　　D. 120

16. 总价（　）

A. 502/6 000/3　　B. 6 000. 00

C. USD 6 000. 00　　D. 6 000. 00 USD

广 东 省 机 械 进 出 口（集团）公 司

GUANGDONG MACHINERY IMPORT AND EXPORT CORP. （GROUP）

726 DONGFENG ROAD EAST，GUANGZHOU，CHINA.

商业发票

COMMERCIAL　INVOICE

Messrs　:　SANYEI HONG KONG
14/F.，KAISER　ESTATE 1，　MAN　YUE
STREET，　HUNG　HOM，　KOWLOON
AUSTRALIA

INVOICE NO.　：YSM199901

INVOICE DATE　：NOV. 11，2000

L/C　NO.　：T/T

L/C　DATE　：

Exporter　GUANGDONG MACHINERY IMPORT AND
EXPORT CORP. （GROUP）
726 DONGFENG ROAD
EAST，GUANGZHOU，　CHINA.

S/C　NO.　：　A97AU22300287

Transport details：
FROM GUANGZHOU TO MELBOURNE
W/T HONG KONG BY VESSEL

Terms of payment：
T/T

MARKS AND NUMBERS	DESCRIPTION OF GOODS	QUANTITY	UNIT PRICE	AMOUNT
KMART CTN NO. 1 – 120 AUSTRIALIA	EDGING KNIFE WITH METAL HANDLE C810	1 200 PCS	USD 5. 00/PC	USD 6 000. 00

FOB GUANGZHOU.... USD 6 000. 00

TOTAL QUANTITY：　1 200 PCS　　PACKING：　120 BAGS

TOTAL WEIGHT：NET WT.：10 800 KGS　　GROSS WT.：1 200 KGS

TOTAL：U. S. DOLLARS　SIX THOUSAND ONLY.

GUANGDONG MACHINERY IMPORT AND
EXPORT CORP. （GROUP）

预录入编号：20007803

外汇核销单号码：45/7890172

由广东省机械进出口（集团）公司自行报关，在新风罗冲办理出口报关。

生产厂家：天津东方红农具厂

经营单位：广东省机械进出口（集团）公司

BILL OF LADING

<table>
<tr><td colspan="3">Shipper

GUANGDONG MACHINERY IMPORT AND
EXPORT CORP. （GROUP）
726 DONGFENG ROAD
EAST, GUANGZHOU, CHINA</td><td colspan="3">B/L No. MANE97/2435</td></tr>
<tr><td colspan="3">Consignee

TO ORDER OF K-MART AUSTRALIA
LIMITED 800 TOORONGA VIC 3416
AUSTRALIA</td><td colspan="3">Combined Transport BILL OF LADING
RECEIVED in apparent good order and condition except as otherwise noted the total number of containers or other packages or units enumerated below for transportation from the place of receipt to the place of delivery subject to the terms and conditions hereof. One of the Bills of Lading must be surrendered duly endorsed to the Carrier by or on behalf of the Holder of the Bill of Lading, the rights and liabilities arising in accordance with the terms and conditions hereof shall, without prejudice to any rule of common law or statute rendering them binding on the Merchant, become binding in all respects between the Carrier and the Holder of the Bill of Lading as though the contract evidenced hereby had been made between them. IN WITNESS whereof the number of original Bills of Lading stated under have been signed. All of this tenor and date, one of which being accomplished, the other （s） to be void.</td></tr>
<tr><td colspan="3">Notify Address

K-MART AUSTRALIA LIMITED 800 TOORAK
ROAD, TOORONGA VIA 3416 AUSTRALIA</td><td colspan="3" rowspan="3">For delivery of goods please apply to :</td></tr>
<tr><td colspan="2">Pre-carriage by
MARN V001</td><td>Place of Receipt</td></tr>
<tr><td colspan="2">Ocean Vessel　Voy. No.
JANSONG V023</td><td>Port of Loading
GUANGZHOU</td></tr>
<tr><td colspan="2">Port of Discharge
MELBOURNE W/T HONG KONG</td><td>Place of Delivery</td><td></td><td colspan="2">Final Destination for the Merchant's Reference only</td></tr>
<tr><td>Container, Seal No. & Marks & Nos.
KMART
CTN NO. 1 – 120
AUSTRALIA

CONTAINER NO.
TGHU2115234 （20'）</td><td colspan="3">No. of Package & Description of Goods

120 BAGS　EDGING KNIFE WITH METAL HANDLE

TOTAL: ONE HUNDRED AND TWENTY BAGS ONLY

FREIGHT COLLECT</td><td>Gross Weight Kgs

1 200.00 KGS</td><td>Measurement m^3

3.672 M^3
AMOUNT:
USD 535.00</td></tr>
<tr><td>Freight & Charges</td><td>Revenue Tons.</td><td>Rate　Per</td><td colspan="2">Prepaid</td><td>Collect</td></tr>
<tr><td></td><td>Prepaid at</td><td colspan="2">Payable at</td><td colspan="2">Place and date of issue
GUANGZHOU DEC. 01, 2019</td></tr>
<tr><td></td><td>Total Prepaid</td><td colspan="2">No. of Original B （s） /L
3 （THREE）</td><td colspan="2">Stamp & Signature</td></tr>
</table>

LADEN ON BOARD THE VESSEL

Date

By................................

（TERMS CONTINUED ON BACK HEREOF）　　（KENWA STANDARD FORM 01）

强化提高三

请仔细阅读以下资料，然后根据《中华人民共和国海关报关单填制规范》的要求，填制报关单。

广东省纺织品针织品有限公司

GUANGDONG TEXTILES IMP. AND EXP. KNITWEARS COMPANY LIMITED.

168 XIAOBEI ROAD, GUANGZHOU 510045, CHINA

商业发票

COMMERCIAL INVOICE

MESSRS: M/S ALAMOUDI SPORT CENTER P. O. BOX 40616 JEDDAH K. S. A.	INVOICE NO. : KTT978643 INVOICE DATE : OCT. 28, 2019 L/C NO. :
EXPORTER: GUANGDONG TEXTILES IMP. AND EXP. KNITWEARS COMPANY LIMITED. 168 XIAOBEI ROAD, GUANGZHOU 510045, CHINA	S/C NO. : KT9727985
TRANSPORT DETAILS: FROM GUANGZHOU TO JEDDAH BY VESSEL	TERMS OF PAYMENT: T/T

MARKS& NUMBERS	DESCRIPTION OF GOODS	QUANTITY	UNIT PRICE	AMOUNT
ALAMOUDI JEDDAH	男童运动衣 BOY'S PORT SUIT	6 000 DOZ	USD 63. 00	USD 378 000. 00
			CIF…JEDDAH….	USD 378 000. 00

TOTAL QUANTITY: 6 000 DOZ PACKING: 1 500 CTNS

TOTAL WEIGHT: N. WT: 45 000 KGS G. WT: 54 000 KGS

TOTAL : U. S. Dollars THREE HUNDRED SEVENTY - EIGHT THOUSAND ONLY.

GUANGDONG TEXTILES IMP. AND EXP.
KNITWEARS COMPANY LIMITED.
168 XIAOBEI ROAD, GUANGZHOU 510045, CHINA

商品编码：6112. 1100
核销单号：2999546
预录入号：2250866
总运费：5 120 美元
总保费：334 美元
生产单位：广东新会东华服装厂
境内发货单位为广东省纺织品有限公司，单位海关注册编号：4401AB1234
2019 年 11 月 1 日出口，2019 年 10 月 29 日由发货单位向广州海关申报。

BILL OF LADING

Shipper

GUANGDONG TEXTILES IMP. AND EXP.
KNITWEARS COMPANY LIMITED.
168 XIAOBEI ROAD, GUANGZHOU 510045,
CHINA

B/L No. GT2579

Combined Transport BILL OF LADING

RECEIVED in apparent good order and condition except as otherwise noted the total number of containers or other packages or units enumerated below for transportation from the place of receipt to the place of delivery subject to the terms and conditions hereof. One of the Bills of Lading must be surrendered duly endorsed to the Carrier by or on behalf of the Holder of the Bill of Lading, the rights and liabilities arising in accordance with the terms and conditions hereof shall, without prejudice to any rule of common law or statute rendering them binding on the Merchant, become binding in all respects between the Carrier and the Holder of the Bill of Lading as though the contract evidenced hereby had been made between them. IN WITNESS whereof the number of original Bills of Lading stated under have been signed. All of this tenor and date, one of which being accomplished, the other (s) to be void.

Consignee

TO ORDER OF SHIPPER

Notify Address

M/S ALAMOUDI SPORT CENTER
P. O. BOX 40616 JEDDAH K. S. A.

For delivery of goods please apply to:

Pre-carriage by

Place of Receipt

Ocean Vessel Voy. No
CHANG HER　V. 001

Port of Loading
GUANGZHOU

Port of Discharge
JEDDAH

Place of Delivery

Final Destination for the Merchant's Reference only

Container, Seal No. & Marks &Nos.	No. of Package & Description of Goods	Gross Weight Kgs	Measurement m^3
ALAMOUDI JEDDAH 2×20' FCL GATU8034814 HJCU8747654	1 500 CTNS　BOY'SPORT SUIT TOTAL: ONETHOUSAND FIVE HUNDRED CARTONS ONLY FREIGHT PREPAID	54 000	55 M^3

Freight & Charges	Revenue Tons.	Rate	Per	Prepaid	Collect

Prepaid at	Payable at	Place and date of issue GUANGZHOU NOV. 01, 2019
Total Prepaid	No. of Original B (s) /L 3 (THREE)	Stamp & Signature

LADEN ON BOARD THE VESSEL
Date
By................................

(TERMS CONTINUED ON BACK HEREOF)　　(KENWA STANDARD FORM 01)

中华人民共和国海关出口货物报关单

预录人编号：　　　　　　　　海关编号：

境内发货人	出境关别	出口日期	申报日期	备案号	
境外收货人	运输方式	运输工具名称及航次号	提运单号		
生产销售单位	监管方式	征免性质	许可证号		
合同协议号	贸易国（地区）	运抵国（地区）	指运港	离境口岸	
包装种类	件数	毛重（千克）	净重（千克）	成交方式	运费	保费	杂费
随附单证及编号					
标记唛码及备注					

项号	商品编号	商品名称及规格型号	数量及单位	单价/总价/币制	原产国（地区）	最终目的国（地区）	境内货源地	征免

特殊关系确认：　　价格影响确认：　　支付特许权使用费确认：　　自报自缴：

报关人员　报关人员证号　电话　　兹申明对以上内容承担如实申报、依法纳税之法律责任 申报单位 申报单位（签章）	海关批注及签章

实训模块九　投　保

一、实训目的

本模块的实训，使学生了解出口货物投保的一般程序，熟悉中国保险条款和伦敦协会条款的各种保险险别，能根据合同、发票和装货单等单据的资料填制保险单。

二、实训任务

（1）根据提供的资料规范填制出口货物投保单。
（2）根据提供的资料规范填制出口货物保险单。

三、实训提示

（一）出口货物投保的一般程序

（1）出口公司办理完托运手续，取得装货单，在货物装船前，填制投保单，向保险公司投保。
（2）保险公司依投保单出具保险单。
（3）出口公司按规定缴纳保险费。
（4）出口公司缮制保险单交保险公司签署，确认保单生效。

（二）险别

海洋运输货物保险，主要有中国人民保险公司条款和伦敦学会条款（ICC），根据2009年中国人民保险公司修改的条款，计有基本险别、一般附加险和特别附加险。

1. 基本险别

（1）平安险（Free From Particular Average，简称 F. P. A.）。
（2）水责险（With Particular Average or with Average，简称 W. A. 或 W. P. A.）。
（3）一切险（ALL RISKS，简称 A. R.）。

2. 一般附加险

（1）偷窃提货不着险（Theft Pilferage & Non-Delivery Risk，简称 T. P. N. D.）。
（2）淡水雨淋险（Fresh &/or Rain Water Damage，简称 F. R. W. D.）。

（3）碰损破碎险（Clash and Breakage Risk）。

（4）渗漏险（Leakage Risk）。

（5）钩损险（Hook Damage）。

（6）混杂沾污险（Inter-Mixture and Contamination Risk）。

（7）生锈险（Rust Risk）。

（8）短量险（Shortage Risk）。

（9）串味险（Taint of Odour Risk）。

（10）包装破裂险（Breakage of Packing Risk）。

（11）受潮受热险（Sweating and Heating Damage）。

3. 特别附加险

（1）战争险（War Risks）。

（2）罢工险（Strikes Risk）。

（3）舱面险（On Deck Risk）。

（4）进口关税险（Import Duty Risk）。

（5）拒收险（Rejection Risk）。

（6）海关检验险（Survey in Customs Risk）。

（7）码头检验险（Survey at Jetty Risk）。

（8）交货不到险（Failure to Delivery Risk）。

4. 伦敦协会条款（ICC）

伦敦协会条款得到了世界保险界和贸易界的广泛接受，西方国家保险业务大都采用伦敦协会条款。该条款共有6种险别，具体为：

（1）Institute Cargo Clause（A），协会货物条款（A），大致相当于ALL RISKS。

（2）Institute Cargo Clause（B），协会货物条款（B），大致相当于W. A.。

（3）Institute Cargo Clause（C），协会货物条款（C），大致相当于F. P. A.。

（4）Institute War Clause-Cargo，协会战争险条款（货物）。

（5）Institute Strikes Clause-Cargo，协会罢工险条款（货物）。

（6）Malicious Damage Clauses，恶意损害险条款。

除恶意损害险外，其余5种险别都可单独投保。

（三）填制保险单应注意的问题

（1）除非合同或信用证特别规定，被保险人一般填出口公司名称。

（2）保险金额货币单位应与信用证（托收时为合同）一致，且保险金额的大小要一致。

（3）保险金额应包含要求的保险加成率。除非信用证或合同特别规定，一般为10%。

（4）承保险别应按信用证的描述填写，以保证单证相符。

（5）保险单中的船名、航次、装运港、目的港应与提单严格一致。

（6）赔款偿付地点一般为目的港（地），投保地点一般为装运港（地），应避免混淆。

（7）一般情况下，保险单应空白背书。信用证或合同另有规定的除外。

四、实训内容

张大同2021年12月10向海关申报，海关查验后放行。张大同于2021年12月12日向保险公司投保。请你根据合同和信用证的要求替张大同填制保险单（保险单号次为PICC－98－225）。

（一）填制货物运输保险投保单

PICC 中国人民财产保险股份有限公司
PICC PROPERTY AND CASUALTY COMPANY LIMITED

货物运输保险投保单
PROPOSAL FOR CARGO TRANSPORTATION INSURANCE

投保人（APPLICANT）：________________

被保险人（INSURED）：________________

地址（ADD）：________________

邮政编码（POSTCODE）：________________

电话（TEL）：________________ 联系人（Contact person）：________________

发票号（INVOICENO.）：________________合同号（CONTRACT NO.）：________________信用证号（L/CNO.）：________________

发票金额（INVOICEAMOUNT）：________________投保加成（PLUS）：________________

兹有下列物品向中国人民财产保险股份有限公司广东省分公司国际部投保：

标记 MARKS & NOS.	包装及数量 QUANTITY	保险货物项目 DESCRIPTION OF GOODS	保险金额 AMOUNT INSURED

启运日期：
DATE OF COMMENCEMENT：________________ 装载运输工具：
PER CONVEYANCE：________________

自
FROM ________________ 经
VIA ________________ 至
TO ________________

提单号：
B/L NO.：________________ 赔款偿付地点：
CLAIM PAYABLE AT：________________

投保险别：（PLEASE INDICATE THE CONDITIONS &/ OR SPECIAL COVERAGES：）

____

请如实告知下列情况：

1. 货物种类：袋装【　】散装【　】冷藏【　】机器/汽车【　】液体【　】活动物【　】危险品等级【　】
BULKREEFERGOODS：BAG/JUMBOLIQUID LIVE ANIMAL MACHINE/AUTODANGEROUS CLASS
2. 集装箱种类：普通【✓】开顶【　】框架【　】平板【　】冷藏【　】
FLATFRAMEOPENCONTAINER：ORDINARYREFRIGERATOR
3. 转运工具：海轮【✓】飞机【　】驳船【　】火车【　】汽车【　】
BY TRANSIT：SHIPPLANE BARGETRAINTRUCK
4. 船舶资料：船籍【　】船龄【　】
REGISTRYPARTICULAR OF SHIP：AGE
5. 货物是否装载于甲板上（ONDECK）【　】
6. 其他要说明的情况：

中国广州广州大道中303号　　303 Guangzhou Road Central, Guangzhou, China
TEL：86 20 83969518－030101；Email：linxinbiao@ guangd. picc. com. cn

PICC 中国人民财产保险股份有限公司
PICC PROPERTY AND CASUALTY COMPANY LIMITED

货物运输保险投保单
PROPOSAL FOR CARGO TRANSPORTATION INSURANCE

投保人声明	保险人已向本人提供并详细介绍了条款内容，并对其中免除保险人责任的条款（包括但不限于责任免除、投保人被保险人义务、赔偿处理、其他事项等），以及本保险合同中付费约定和特别约定的内容向本人做了明确说明，本人已充分理解并接受上述内容，同意以此作为订立保险合同的依据，自愿投保本保险。
保费支付	保险合同自被保险人缴清保费之日起生效。被保险人未按合同约定缴付保费的，在此期间发生保险事故，保险人不承担保险责任。
保险销售事项确认书	本人就本货物运输保险，向中国人民此财产保险股份有限公司广东省分公司，投保货物运输保险，确认以下事项：产险销售人员姓名：＿＿＿＿＿＿＿＿，职业证号：＿＿＿＿＿＿＿＿＿＿＿＿。 已向本人详细解释有关保险条款内容，并清楚说明免除保险人责任的条款。 产险销售人员签字： 保险中介机构销售人员： 保险中介机构盖章： 投保人签章： 年　月　日

中国广州广州大道中 303 号　　303 Guangzhou Road Central，Guangzhou，China
TEL：86 20 83969518－030101；　　Email：1inxinbiao@ guangd. picc. com. cn

（二）填制货物运输保险单

中国人民财产保险股份有限公司
PICC Property and Casualty Company Limited

ORIGINAL

总公司设于北京 Head Office Beijing　　一九四九年创立 Established in 1949　　保险单号(Policy No.)

货物运输保险 保险单 CARGO TRANSPORTATION INSURANCE POLICY

发票号(Invoice No.)　　提单号(B/L NO.)
合同号(Contract No.)　　信用证号(L/C No.)
被保险人(Insured):

中国人民财产保险股份有限公司(以下简称本公司)根据被保险人要求，以 被保险人向本公司缴付约定的保险费为对价，按照本保险单列明条款承保下述货物运输 保险，特订立本保险单。

THIS POLICY OF INSURANCE WITNESSES THAT PICC PROPERTY AND CASUALTY COMPANY LIMITED (HEREINAFTER CALLED "THE COMPANY") AT THE REQUEST OF THE INSURED AND IN CONSIDERATION OF THE AGREED PREMIUM PAID TO THE COMPANY BY THE INSURED, UNDERTAKES TO INSURE THE UNDERMENTIONED GOODS IN TRANSPORTATION SUBJECT TO THE CONDITIONS OF THIS POLICY AS PER THE CLAUSES PRINTED BELOW.

标 记(MARKS & NOS)	包装及数量(PACKAGE &QUANTITY)	保险货物项目(GOODS)	保险金额(AMOUNT INSURED)

总保险金额(TOTALAMOUNT INSURED):

保费(PREMIUM): AS ARRANGED　　启运日期(DATE OF COMMENCEMENT):

装载运输工具(PER CONVEYANCE):

自(FROM): ______ 经(VIA): ______ 至(TO): ______

所保货物如发生保险单项下可能引起索赔的 损失,应立即通知本公司或下述代理人查勘。如有索赔，应向本公司提交正本保险单(本保险单共有__份正本)及有关文件。如一份 正本已用于索赔，其余正本自动失效。

IN THE EVENT OF LOSS OR DAMAGE WHICH MAY RESULT IN A CLAIM UNDER THIS POLICY, IMMEDIATE NOTICE MUST BE GIVEN TO THE COMPANY OR AGENT AS MENTIONED. CLAIMS, IF ANY, ONE OF THE ORIGINAL POLICY WHICH HAS BEEN ISSUED IN______ORIGINAL(S) TOGETHER WITH THE RELEVANT DOCUMENTS SHALL BE SURRENDERED TO THE COMPANY. IF ONE OF THE ORIGINAL POLICY HAS BEEN ACCOMPLISHED, THE OTHERS TO BE VOID.

保险服务请联系:
CONTACT INFORMATION OF INSURANCE SERVICE:
中国人民财产保险股份有限公司广东省分公司
PICC Property and Casualty Company
Limited, GUANGDONG Branch
电话(TEL):020-95518
传真(FAX):
EMAIL:
地址(ADD):广东省广州市广州大道中303号3楼

赔款偿付地点(CLAIM PAYABLE AT) ______

签单日期(Issuing DATE) ______

保险人:
UNDERWRITER:

五、强化提高

强化提高一

我国广东省机械进出口公司（集团）向荷兰罗娜茵贸易公司出口不锈钢铲头 12 000 件，每件 9.60 美元 CIF 鹿特丹，纸箱包装，每箱 12 件。合同规定投保一切险和战争险，运输标志（唛头）为：

F. V. /ART NO29099/ROTTERDAM/NOS1 - 1000

该货物于 2019 年 3 月 20 日在广州装“东方”号轮运往鹿特丹。请根据上列条件填制一份保险单。

强化提高二

GUANGDONG FOREIGN TRADE IMP. AND EXP. CORP. 向英国 ABC 贸易公司出口 LADIES LYCRA LONG PANT 共 2 400 件，每件 20 美元 CIF 伦敦，纸箱包装，每箱 12 件。合同规定投保英国伦敦保险协会 ICC（A）和战争险，运输标志（唛头）为：

ABC/LONDON/NOS1 - 200

该货物于 2019 年 5 月 20 日在广州装“东方红”号轮运往伦敦。请根据上列条件用英文填制一份保险单。

强化提高三

广东省机械进出口公司（集团）向日本东森贸易有限公司出口一批“白兔”牌铁铲（RABBIT BRAND SHOVEL WITH METAL HANDLE），数量为 4 000 件，每件 4.5 美元，CIF YOKOHAMA，投保一切险，每 10 件为 1 捆，共 400 捆，2019 年 1 月 25 日出运，该公司已填制好保险单，请审核并修改。

中保财产保险有限公司

The people insurance (Property) Company of China, Ltd.

PICC PROPERTY

发票号码　　　　　　　　　　保险单号次
Invoice No.　YSM1999C　　　　Policy No. 0071925

海洋货物运输保险单
MARINE CARGO TRANSPORTATION INSURANCE POLICY

被保险人：　GUANGDONG MACHINERY IMPORT AND EXPORT CORP. (GROUP)
Insured:

中保财产保险有限公司（以下简称本公司）根据被保险人的要求，及其所缴付约定的保险费，按照本保险单承担险别和背面所载条款与下列特别条款承保下列货物运输保险，特签发本保险单。

This policy of Insurance witnesses that The People Insurance (Property) Company of China, Ltd. (hereinafter called the Company), at the request of the Insured and in consideration of the agreed premium paid by the Insured, undertakes to insure the undermentioned goods in transportation subject to the conditions of this Policy as per the Clauses printed overleaf and other special clauses attached hereon.

保险货物项目 Descriptions of Goods	包装 单位 数量 Packing Unit Quantity	保险金额 Amount Insured
RABBIT BRAND SHOVEL WITH METAL HANDLE TOTAL: 400 BUNDLES	4 000 PCS	USD 18 000. 00

承 保 险 别
Conditions

COVERING ALL RISKS　AS PER OCEAN MARINE CARGO CLAUSES (WAREHOUSE TO WAREHOUSE CLAUSE IS INCLUDED) AND OCEAN MARINE CARGO WAR RISK CLAUSES OF THE PEOPLES INSURANCE COMPANY OF CHINA (1/1/1981).

ORIGINAL

货　物　标　记
Marks of Goods
A98JP1990006
YOKOHAMA

总　保　险　金　额：　U. S. DOLLARS EIGHTEEN THOUSAND　ONLY
Total Amount Insured:

保费　　　　　　　载运输工具　　　　　　　　　　　开航日期
Premium As arranged Per conveyance S. S　JING AN CHENG V. 0224E　Slg. on or abt　JAN. 25, 2019

起运港　　　　　　目的港
From　GUANGZHOU　To　YOKOHAMA

所保货物，如发生本保险单项下可能引起索赔的损失或损坏，应立即通知本公司下述代理人查勘。如有索赔，应向本公司提交保险单正本（本保险单共有　　份正本）及有关文件。如一份正本已用于索赔，其余正本则自动失效。

In the event of loss or damage which may result in a claim under this Policy, immediate notice must be given to the Company Agent as mentioned hereunder. Claims, if any, one of the Original Policy which has been issued in　TWO　Original (s) together with the relevant documents shall be surrendered to the Company. If one of the Original Policy has been accomplished, the others to be void.

中保财产保险有限公司
THE PEOPLE INSURANCE (PROPERTY) COMPANY OF CHINA, LTD.

赔款偿付地点
Claim payable at　GUANGZHOU

日期　　　　　　　　　　在
Date　JAN. 25, 2019　at　YOKOHAMA

地址：
Address:

保险单空白背书：　GUANGDONG MACHINERY IMPORT AND EXPORT CORP. (GROUP)
（签名）

实训模块十　装运及制单

一、实训目的

本模块的实训，使学生了解出口货物装运的程序，能根据收货单（或场站收据）填制海运提单，制作装船通知；并在此基础上，缮制全套结汇单据。

二、实训任务

（1）根据收货单填制海运提单。
（2）根据信用证、合同和海运提单填制装船通知。
（3）根据信用证和合同填制汇票、受益人证明书和客户交单联系单。

三、实训提示

（一）填制海运提单应注意的问题

（1）提单的收货人应按信用证的要求填制。一般作成空白抬头或记名指示抬头较多，合同或信用证没有特别要求，不能把发票的抬头人当成提单的抬头人。

（2）被通知人应按信用证的要求填制。一般为开证人，信用证没说明时可不填或填写开证人名称。

（3）FOB 出口成交时，提单运费缴付方式填为"运费待付"（FREIGHT COLLECT）；CFR 或 CIF 出口成交时，提单运费缴付方式填为"运费预付"（FREIGHT PREPAID）。

（4）当实际运输的船只不但有船名，而且还有航次时，必须在提单中列明。防止投保时单与单之间不符。

（5）提单日期不得早于投保日期；提单日期不得迟于信用证规定的最迟装运日期。

（6）信用证或合同对提单内容有特殊要求时（如注明信用证号码、合同号码、集装箱号码或承运人代理的名称及电话），应一一列明。

（二）装船通知

装船通知有多种形式，当以电报或电传形式传送时称为电报抄本（CABLE COPY）和电传抄本（TELEX COPY）两种形式。电报抄本根据内容又可分为两种：一种是通知买方购买保险，其内容主要包括：货名、数量、唛头、装运港名称、目的港名称、买方名称或买方指定的保险公司、预约保单号码、装船的具体时间、装载船名、航次和转船及开航时间等。另一种是通知装船，以利买方报关接货或筹措资金，必须把装船详情电告买方，如合同号、信用证号、船名、装船日期、装运港、目的港、品名、规格、件数、重量、金额、唛头等，更改船名或开船日期也应通知买方。

信用证内有时规定卖方应于装船后“立即”或“马上”将装船情况电告买方，中国银行规定“立即”“马上”为三天时间内，所以电报抄本的日期只能迟于提单日期三天之内。

（三）填制汇票应注意的问题

（1）除非合同或信用证特别规定，汇票的金额应与商业发票的金额一致。

（2）汇票的付款人不能是开证人，而应该是开证行或信用证指定的付款行。

（3）付款人的名称、地址应填写齐备。

（4）出票人的名称、地址、签章应填写齐备。

（5）当汇票须背书时，应严格按合同或信用证的要求处理。

（6）汇票的出票日期应在信用证规定的有效期内。

（四）受益人证明书

受益人证明书的特点是自己证明自己履行某项义务。一份受益人证明书一般有几个栏目：

（1）受益人中文、英文名称。

（2）单据名称。一般标明“BENEFICIARY'S CERTIFICATE”（受益人证明）或“BENEFICIARY'S STATEMENT”（受益人声明）。

（3）发票号码。

（4）信用证号码。

（5）出证日期。

（6）证明内容。

（7）受益人名称及签字。

（五）制单

1. 手工制单

手工制单是指利用英文打字机，制作各种商务单据。

2. WORD 制单

WORD 制单是指利用 WORD 在电脑上制作单据，一般一套单据设置一个文件名，为便于查询，通常以商业发票的号码作为文件名。

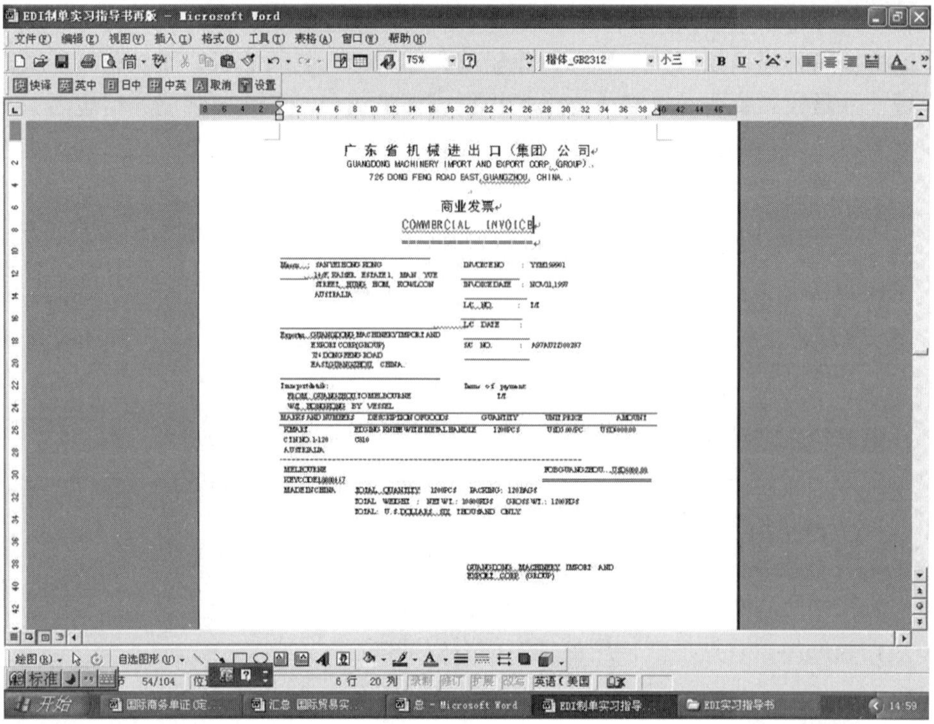
EDI制单实习指导书再版 - Microsoft Word
广 东 省 机 械 进 出 口（集团）公 司
GUANGDONG MACHINERY IMPORT AND EXPORT CORP. (GROUP).
726 DONG FENG ROAD EAST,GUANGZHOU, CHINA.
商业发票
COMMERCIAL INVOICE

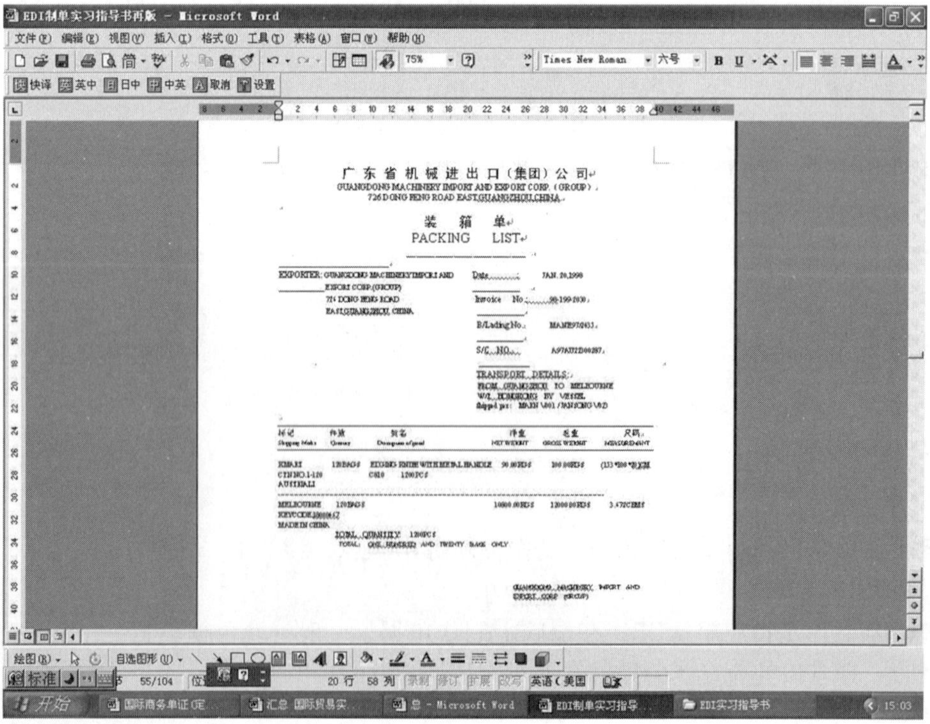
EDI制单实习指导书再版 - Microsoft Word
广 东 省 机 械 进 出 口（集团）公 司
装 箱 单
PACKING LIST

3. EXCEL **制单**

EXCEL 制单是指利用 EXCEL 在电脑上制作单据，一般一套单据设置一个文件名，为便于查询，通常以商业发票的号码作为文件名。

由于 EXCEL 可预先设置好表格，并有统计功能，每一个 shift 可直接命名为汇票、商业发票、装箱单、受益人证明书、装船通知、提单、原产地证等，直观且方便操作，每一个出口公司可根据自己的实际情况设置表格，并在一台普通电脑上即可完成，故在实际业务中运用最广。

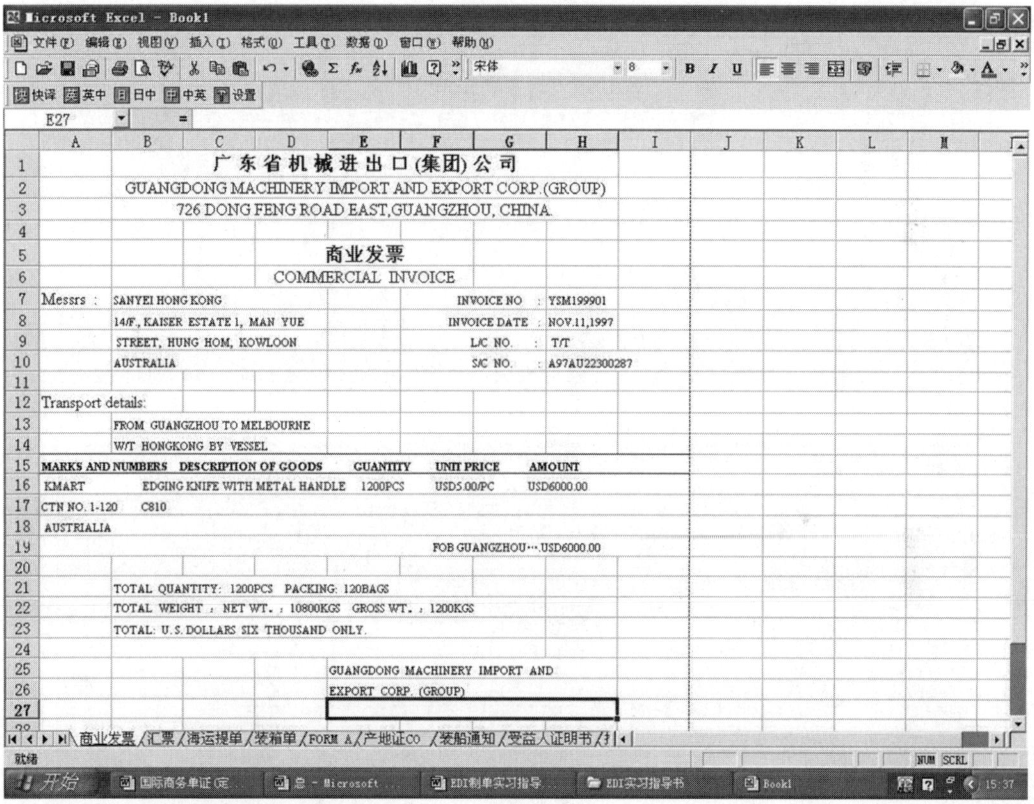

4. **外贸制单管理系统制单**

外贸制单管理系统制单是指选用已开发的制单软件，只要输入有关数据，系统即可根据用户的指令组合成相应的符合国家有关出口单证标准的单据。

外贸制单系统的特点之一是同一套单证的资料只需一次输入，就可以按用户要求制作各种单证。可以避免数据的重复输入，保证单证之间数据的一致性，减少出错，避免单与单之间不符。

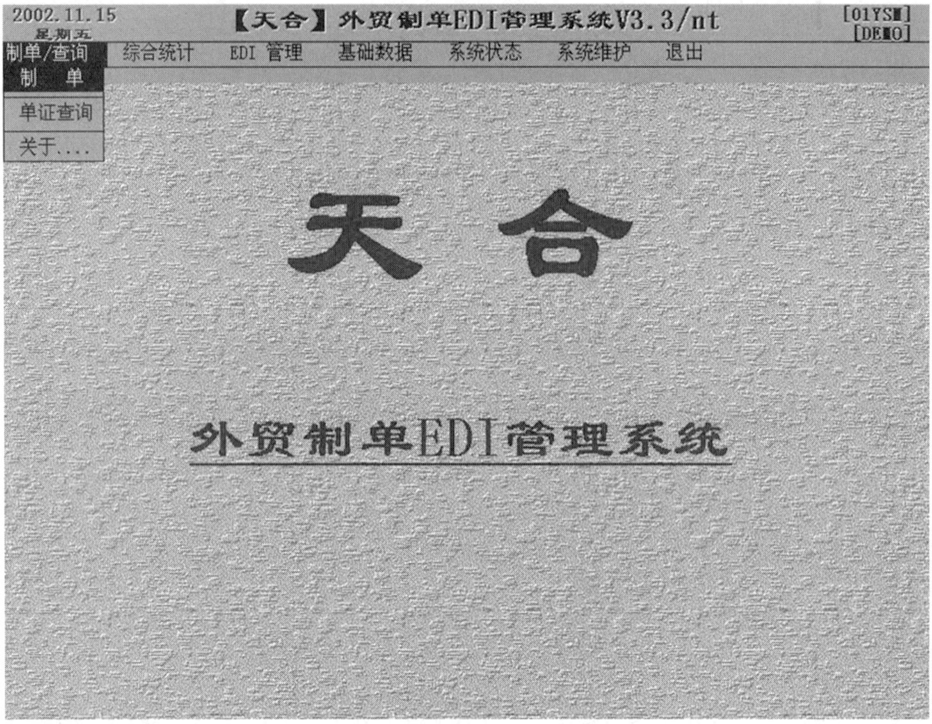
2002.11.15
星期五
【天合】外贸制单EDI管理系统V3.3/nt
[01YS■]
[DE■O]
制单/查询
综合统计
EDI 管理
基础数据
系统状态
系统维护
退出
制　单
单证查询
关于....
天 合
外贸制单EDI管理系统

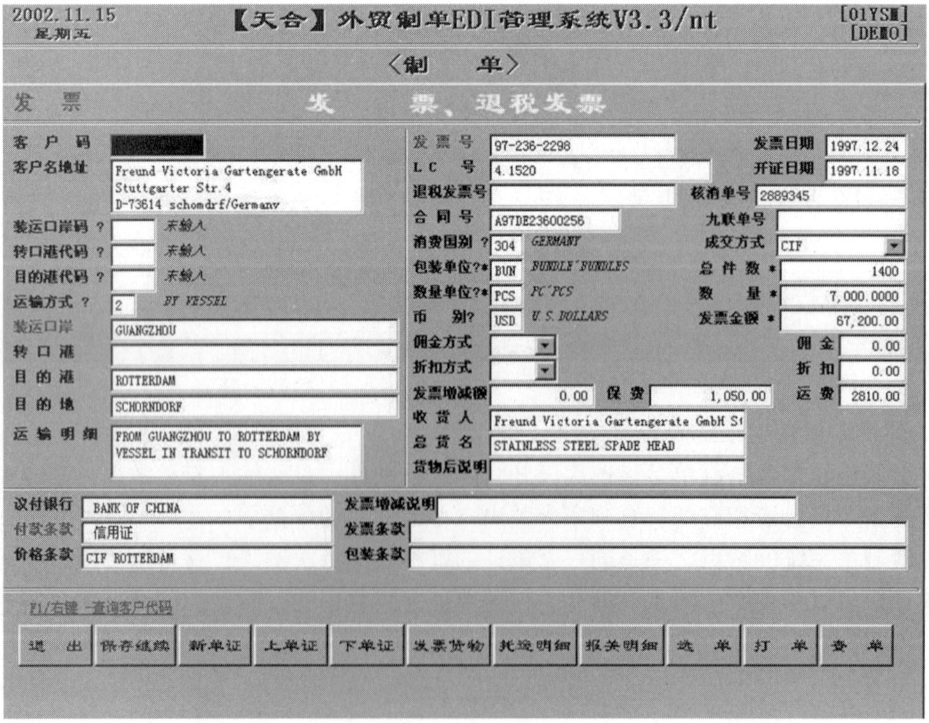
2002.11.15
星期五
【天合】外贸制单EDI管理系统V3.3/nt
[01YS■]
[DE■O]
〈制　单〉
发　票
发　票、退税发票
客 户 码
客户名地址
Freund Victoria Gartengerate GmbH
Stuttgarter Str.4
D-73614 schomdrf/Germany
装运口岸码 ？ 未输入
转口港代码 ？ 未输入
目的港代码 ？ 未输入
运输方式 ？ 2 BY VESSEL
装运口岸 GUANGZHOU
转 口 港
目 的 港 ROTTERDAM
目 的 地 SCHORNDORF
运 输 明 细
FROM GUANGZHOU TO ROTTERDAM BY
VESSEL IN TRANSIT TO SCHORNDORF
发 票 号 97-236-2298
发票日期 1997.12.24
L C 号 4.1520
开证日期 1997.11.18
退税发票号
核销单号 2889345
合 同 号 A97DE23600256
九联单号
消费国别 ？ 304 GERMANY
成交方式 CIF
包装单位?* BUN BUNDLE`BUNDLES
总 件 数 * 1400
数量单位?* PCS PC`PCS
数 量 * 7,000.0000
币 别? USD U.S.DOLLARS
发票金额 * 67,200.00
佣金方式
佣 金 0.00
折扣方式
折 扣 0.00
发票增减额 0.00
保 费 1,050.00
运 费 2810.00
收 货 人 Freund Victoria Gartengerate GmbH St
总 货 名 STAINLESS STEEL SPADE HEAD
货物后说明
议付银行 BANK OF CHINA
发票增减说明
付款条款 信用证
发票条款
价格条款 CIF ROTTERDAM
包装条款
F1/右键 -查询客户代码
退 出
保存继续
新单证
上单证
下单证
发票货物
托运明细
报关明细
选 单
打 单
查 单

四、实训内容

（一）填制海运提单

张大同12月12日将货物送至堆场，准备12月13日装船。请你替张大同填制海运提单。

1. Shipper Insert Name, Address and Phone

B/L NO.

2. Consignee Insert Name, Address and Phone

中远集装箱运输有限公司
COSCO CONTAINER LINES
TLX: 33057 COSCO CN
FAX: +86 (021) 6545 8984
ORIGINAL
Port-to Port or Combined Transport
BILL OF LADING

3. Notify Party Insert Name, Address and Phone

4. Combined Transport * Pre-carriage by	5. Combined Transport * Place of Receipt
6. Ocean Vessel Voy. No.	7. Port of Loading
8. Port of Discharge	9. Combined Transport * Place of Delivery

RECEIVED in external apparent good order and condition except as other-wise noted. The total number of packages or units stuffed in the container, the description of the foods and the weights shown in this Bill of Lading are furnished by the Merchants, and which the carrier has no reasonable means of checking and is not a part of this Bill of Lading contract. The carrier has issued the number of bills of lasing stated below, all of the tenor and date, one of the original Bills of Lading must be surrendered and endorsed or signed against the delivery of the shipment and whereupon any other original Bills of Lading shall be void. The Merchants agree to be bound by the terms and conditions of this Bill of Lading as if each had per personally signed this Bill of Lading.
SEE clause 4 on the back of thea Bill of Lading (Terms continued on the back hereof, please read carefully)
* Applicable Only When Document Used as a Combined Transport Bill of Lading.

Marks & Nos. Container / Seal No.	No. of Containers Or Packages	Description of Goods (If Dangerous Goods, See Clause 20)	Gross Weight Kgs	Measurement
		Description of Contents for Shipper's Use Only (Not part of This B/L Contract)		

10. Total Number of containers and/or packages (in words)
Subject to Clause 7 Limitation

11. Freight & Charges	Revenue Tons	Rate	Per	Prepaid	Collect
Declared Value Charge					

Ex. Rate:	Prepaid at	Payable at	Place and date of issue
	Total Prepaid	No. of Original B (s) /L	Signed for the Carrier, COSCO CONTAINER LINES

LADEN ON BOARD THE VESSEL
DATE　　　　BY
(COSCON STANDARD FORM 9801)

（二）填制装船通知

根据本笔业务信用证的要求，请你替张大同制作装船通知。

广东中山威威照明有限公司

GUANGDONG ZHONGSHAN WEIWEI LIGHTING CO.，LTD.

52，**CUIHUA ROAD，ZHONGSHAN，CHINA**

FAX：

REF. NO.：

To Messrs：

ADVICE OF SHIPMENT

（1）Name of Commodity：

（2）Quantity：

（3）Invoice Value：

（4）Name of Carrying Steamer：

（5）Date of Shipment：

（6）Credit No.：

（7）Shipping Marks：

（三）填制汇票

F14

凭
Drawn under --
信用证　　　　第　　　　号
L/C　　　　No. ----------------------------
日期　　　　年　　月　　日
dated --

1

按　　　　息　　　　付　款
Payable with interest @ ------- % per annum

号码　　　　汇票金额　　　　中国．广州　　年　　月　　日
No. ----------------- **Exchange** for 　　　　Guangzhou. China ---------- 20 ----------

见票　　　　日　后（本　汇　票　之　副　本　未　付）付
At ---------------- sight of this FIRST of Exchange (Second of exchange being unpaid)
pay to the order of -- 或其指定人
金　额
the sum of

此致
To: ---------------------------　　　　　　---------------------------

206

凭
Drawn under --
信用证　　　　第　　　　号
L/C　　　　No. ----------------------------
日期　　　　年　　月　　日
dated --

2

按　　　　息　　　　付　款
Payable with interest @ ------- % per annum

号码　　　　汇票金额　　　　中国．广州　　年　　月　　日
No. ----------------- **Exchange** for 　　　　Guangzhou. China ---------- 20 ----------

见票　　　　日　后（本　汇　票　之　副　本　未　付）付
At ---------------- sight of this SECOND of Exchange (First exchange being unpaid)
pay to the order of -- 或其指定人
金　额
the sum of

此致
To: ---------------------------　　　　　　---------------------------

（四）填制“受益人证明书”

广东中山威威照明有限公司 GUANGDONG ZHONGSHAN WEIWEI LIGHTING CO. , LTD. 52, CUIHUA ROAD, ZHONGSHAN, CHINA **BENEFICIARY'S CERTIFICATE**

（五）填制客户交单联系单

张大同填制客户交单联系单，并于2021年12月15日凭全套结汇单证向银行交单议付。请你替张大同填写客户交单联系单（通知行号为DN4008276T02）。

3053—②

客 户 交 单 联 系 单

致：中国银行

<table>
<tr><td colspan="5">兹随附下列出口单据一套，信用证业务请按国际商会现行《跟单信用证统一惯例》办理，跟单托收业务请按国际商会现行《托收统一规则》办理。</td></tr>
<tr><td rowspan="2">信用证</td><td colspan="2">开证行：</td><td colspan="2">信用证号：</td></tr>
<tr><td>通知行号：</td><td>提单日期：</td><td>效期：</td><td>交单期限　　天</td></tr>
<tr><td rowspan="3">无证托收</td><td colspan="4">付款人全名及详址：</td></tr>
<tr><td colspan="4">代收行外文名称及详址（供参考）：</td></tr>
<tr><td colspan="2">交单方式：（　）D/P　（　）D/P</td><td colspan="2">付款期限：</td></tr>
<tr><td colspan="2">发票编号：</td><td colspan="2">核销单编号：</td><td>金额：</td></tr>
</table>

单据	名称	汇票	发票	海关发票	装箱/重量单	产地证	GSP FORM A	数量/质量/重量证	检验/分析证	出口许可证	保险单	运输单据	电抄	受益人证明	船公司证明			

委办事项：（打“×”者）

（　）上述单据请按我司与贵行签订之总质押书办理押汇。

（　）上述单据系代理出口项下业务，收妥后请原币划________________

（　）开户行：____________，账号：________________

（　）若付款人拒绝付款/承兑，不必作成拒绝证书，但须以电传通知我司。

（　）附信用证及修改书共________________纸。

（　）单据中有下列不符点：（　）请向开证行寄单，我司承担一切责任。

（　）请电询开证行同意后再寄单。

（　）________________

（　）________________

（　）________________

公司联系人：　　　　联系电话：　　　　公司盖章：

<table>
<tr><td rowspan="11">银行审单记录：</td><td colspan="3">银行接单日期：</td></tr>
<tr><td colspan="2">索 汇 金 额：</td><td>BP NO.</td></tr>
<tr><td colspan="2">寄 单 日 期：</td><td>OC NO.</td></tr>
<tr><td rowspan="6">银行费用</td><td>通知/保兑：</td><td rowspan="3">索汇方式：</td></tr>
<tr><td>议/承/付：</td></tr>
<tr><td>邮　　费：</td></tr>
<tr><td>电　　传：</td><td rowspan="4">寄单方式：</td></tr>
<tr><td></td></tr>
<tr><td>小　　计：</td></tr>
<tr><td colspan="2">费用由　　　　承担</td></tr>
<tr><td colspan="3"></td></tr>
<tr><td>退单记录：</td><td colspan="2">银行经办：</td><td>银行复核：</td></tr>
</table>

五、强化提高

强化提高一

下面是一份信用证和有关资料，请认真阅读信用证并根据信用证的要求缮制全套结汇单据。

ISSUE OF A DOCUMENTARY CREDIT

ISSUING BANK : ASAHI BANK LTD. , TOKYO
SEQUENCE OF TOTAL : 1/1
FORM OF DOC. CREDIT : IRREVOCABLE
DOC. CREDIT NUMBER : ABL-AN107
DATE OF ISSUE : 20180405
EXPIRY : DATE 20180615 PLACE CHINA
APPLICANT : ABC CORPORATION, OSAKA, JAPAN.
BENEFICIARY : GUANGDONG TEXTILES IMP. AND EXP.
WOOLEN KNITWEARS COMPANY LTD.
168 XIAOBEI ROAD GUANGZHOU 510045 CHINA.
AMOUNT : USD 55 050. 00
(SAY US DOLLARS FIFTY-FIVE THOUSAND FIFTY ONLY.)
AVAILABLE WITH/BY : ASAHI BANK LTD. , NEW YORK BRANCH BY NEGOTIATION
DRAFTS AT... : DRAFTS AT SIGHT FOR FULL INVOICE VALUE
DRAWEE : ASAHI BANK LTD. , TOKYO
PARTIAL SHIPMENTS : ALLOWED
TRANSSHIPMENT : ALLOWED
LOADING IN CHARGE : GUANGZHOU PORT
FOR TRANSPORT TO... : OSAKA, JAPAN
LATEST DATE OF SHIP. : 20180531
DESCRIPT. OF GOODS : LADIES GARMENTS AS PER S/C NO. SH107 PACKING: 10 PCS/CTN

ART NO.	QUANTITY	UNIT PRICE
STYLE NO. AH -04B	1 000 PCS	USD 5. 50
STYLE NO. ROCOCO	1 000 PCS	USD 5. 10
STYLE NO. BORODAO	1 000 PCS	USD 4. 50
STYLE NO. FLORES	1 500 PCS	USD 4. 80
STYLE NO. PILAR	1 000 PCS	USD 4. 00
STYLE NO. ROMANTICO	500 PCS	USD 8. 00

PRICE TERM : CIF OSAKA
DOCUMENTS REQUIRED:

* 3/3 SET OF ORIGINAL CLEAN ON BOARD OCEAN BILLS OF LADING MADE OUT TO ORDER OF SHIPPER AND BLANK ENDORSED AND MARKED "FREIGHT PREPAID" NOTIFY APPLICANT (WITH FULL NAME AND ADDRESS).

* ORIGINAL SIGNED COMMERCIAL INVOICE IN 5 FOLD.

* INSURANCE POLICY OR CERTIFICATE IN 2 FOLD ENDORSED IN BLANK, FOR 110 PCT OF THE INVOICE VALUE COVERING THE INSTITUTE CARGO CLAUSES (A), THE INSTITUTE WAR CLAUSES, INSURANCE CLAIMS TO BE PAYABLE IN JAPAN IN THE CURRENCY OF THE DRAFTS.

* CERTIFICATE OF ORIGIN GSP FORM A IN 1 ORIGINAL AND 1 COPY.

* PACKING LIST IN 3 FOLD.

ADDITIONAL COND. : 1. T. T. REIMBURSEMENT IS PROHIBITED.

2. THE GOODS TO BE PACKED IN EXPORT STRONG COLORED CARTONS.

3. SHIPPING MARKS: ITOCHU
OSAKA
NO. 1 – 600

DETAILS OF CHARGES : ALL BANKING CHARGES OUTSIDE JAPAN INCLUDING REIMBURSEMENT COMMISSION, ARE FOR ACCOUNT OF BENEFICIARY.

PRESENTATION PERIOD : DOCUMENTS TO BE PRESENTED WITHIN 10 DAYS AFTER THE DATE OF SHIPMENT, BUT WITHIN THE VALIDITY OF THE CREDIT.

CONFIRMATION : WITHOUT

INSTRUCTIONS : THE NEGOTIATION BANK MUST FORWARD THE DRAFTS AND ALL DOCUMENTS BY REGISTERED AIRMAIL DIRECT TO US IN TWO CONSECUTIVE LOTS, UPON RECEIPT OF THE DRAFTS AND DOCUMENTS IN ORDER, WE WILL REMIT THE PROCEEDS AS INSTRUCTED BY THE NEGOTIATING BANK.

相关资料：

发票号码	SH – 25757	发票日期	APR. 20, 2018	FORM A 号码	GZ8/27685/1007
单位毛重	15.40 KGS	单位净重	13.00 KGS	单位尺码	(60×20×50) CM
船　名	DIEK335 V. 007	原材料情况	完全自产品	集装箱号码	MAKU5879524/40'
提单号码	KFT2582588	提单日期	MAY 15, 2018	保险单号码	PIC200178141

F14

凭
Drawn under ______________________

信用证　　　　第　　　　号
L/C　　　　No. ______________________

日期　　　　年　　月　　日
dated ______________________

1

按　　　　息　　　　付　款
Payable with interest @ ______ % per annum

号码　　　　汇票金额　　　　中国．广州　　年　　月　　日
No. ____________ **Exchange** for　　　　Guangzhou. China ______ 20 ______

见票　　　　日后(本汇票之副本未付)付
At ____________ sight of this FIRST of Exchange (Second of exchange being unpaid)
pay to the order of ______________________ 或其指定人

金　额
the sum of

此致
To: ______________________　　　　______________________

广东省纺织品进出口毛织品有限公司

GUANGDONG TEXTILES IMP. AND EXP. WOOLEN KNITWEARS COMPANY LTD.

168 XIAOBEI ROAD GUANGZHOU 510045 CHINA.

商　业　发　票
COMMERCIAL INVOICE

ORIGINAL

Messrs:

Invoice No. :
Invoice Date :
S/C No. :
L/C No. :
L/C Date :

Exporter:

Transport details:　　　　Terms of payment:

Marks & numbers	Descrip. of goods	Quantity	Unit price	Amount

广东省纺织品进出口毛织品有限公司

GUANGDONG TEXTILES IMP. AND EXP. WOOLEN KNITWEARS COMPANY LTD.
168 XIAOBEI ROAD GUANGZHOU 510045 CHINA.

装　箱　单
PACKING LIST

ORIGINAL

Exporter:

DATE :
Invoice No. :
B/L No. :
S/C No. :
L/C No. :

Transport details:

标记 Marks & numbers	货名 Descrip. of goods	件数 Quantity	净重 N. W.	毛重 G. W.	尺码 Measurement

BILL OF LADING

Shipper	B/L No.
	Combined Transport BILL OF LADING
Consignee	
Notify Address	For delivery of goods please apply to :

Pre-carriage by	Place of Receipt		
Ocean Vessel Voy. No.	Port of Loading		
Port of Discharge	Place of Delivery	Final Destination for the Merchant's Reference only	
Container, Seal No. & Marks & Nos.	No. of Package & Description of Goods	Gross Weight Kgs	Measurement m^3

—Particulars Furnished by Merchants—

Freight & Charges	Revenue Tons.	Rate Per	Prepaid	Collect

Ex. Rate:	Prepaid at	Payable at	Place and date of issue
	Total Prepaid	No. of Original B (s) /L	Stamp & Signature

LADEN ON BOARD THE VESSEL

Date

By································

(TERMS CONTINUED ON BACK HEREOF) (KENWA STANDARD FORM 01)

中保财产保险有限公司

PICC PROPERTY　The People's Insurance (Property) Company of China, Ltd.

发票号码　　　　　　　　　　　　　　　　　　　　　　　　保险单号次
Invoice No.　　　　　　　　　　　　　　　　　　　　　　　Policy No.

海 洋 货 物 运 输 保 险 单
MARINE CARGO TRANSPORTATION INSURANCE POLICY

被保险人:
Insured: ______________________________

中保财产保险有限公司（以下简称本公司）根据被保险人的要求，及其所缴付约定的保险费，按照本保险单承担险别和背面所载条款与下列特别条款承保下列货物运输保险，特签发本保险单。

This policy of Insurance witnesses that The People's Insurance (Property) Company of China, Ltd. (hereinafter called "The Company"), at the request of the Insured and in consideration of the agreed premium paid by the Insured, undertakes to insure the undermentioned goods in transportation subject to the conditions of this Policy as per the Clauses printed overleaf and other special clauses attached hereon.

保险货物项目 Descriptions of Goods	包装 单位 数量 Packing Unit Quantity	保险金额 Amount Insured

承 保 险 别　　　　　　　　　　　　　　　　　　　　　　　　货 物 标 记
Conditions　　　　　　　　　　　　　　　　　　　　　　　　Marks of Goods

总 保 险 金 额:
Total Amount Insured: ______________________________

保费　　　　　　　　载运输工具　　　　　　　　　　开航日期
Premium As arranged . Per conveyance S. S ________ Slg. on or abt ________

起运港　　　　　　　　　　　　　　　　　　　　　　目的港
From ______________________ To ______________________

所保货物，如发生本保险单项下可能引起索赔的损失或损坏，应立即通知本公司下述代理人查勘。如有索赔，应向本公司提交保险单正本（本保险单共有　份正本）及有关文件。如一份正本已用于索赔，其余正本则自动失效。

In the event of loss or damage which may result in a claim under this Policy, immediate notice must be given to the Company's Agent as mentioned hereunder. Claims, if any, one of the Original Policy which has been issued in　Original (s) together with the relevant documents shall be surrendered to the Company. If one of the Original Policy has been accomplished, the others to be void.

中保财产保险有限公司
THE PEOPLE'S INSURANCE (PROPERTY) COMPANY OF CHINA, LTD.

赔款偿付地点
Claim payable at ______________________________

日期　　　　　　　　　　　　在
Date ______________________ at ______________________

地址:
Address: ______________________________

Original

<table>
<tr><td colspan="3">1. Goods consigned from (Exporter's business name, address, county)</td><td colspan="3" rowspan="2">Reference No.

GENERALIZED SYSTEM OF PREFERENCES
CERTIFICATE OF ORIGIN
(Combined declaration and certificate)
FORM A
issued in THE PEOPLE'S REPUBLIC OF CHINA
(COUNTRY)
See Notes overleaf</td></tr>
<tr><td colspan="3">2. Goods consigned to (Consignee's name, address, country)</td></tr>
<tr><td colspan="3">3. Means of transport and route (as far as known)</td><td colspan="3">4. For official use</td></tr>
<tr><td>5. Item number</td><td>6. Marks and numbers of packages</td><td>7. Number and kind of packages; description of goods</td><td>8. Origin criterion (see Notes overleaf)</td><td>9. Gross weight or other quantity</td><td>10. Number and date of invoices</td></tr>
<tr><td colspan="3">11. Certification
It is hereby certified, on the basis of control carried out, that the declaration by the exporter is correct.

Place and date, signature and stamp of certifying authority</td><td colspan="3">12. Declaration by the exporter
The undersigned hereby declares that the above details and statements are correct; that all the goods were produced in
----
(country)
and that they comply with the origin requirements specified for those goods in the Generalized System of Preferences for goods exported to
----
(importing country)

Place and date, signature of authorized signatory</td></tr>
</table>

强化提高二

下面是一份信用证和有关资料，请认真阅读信用证并根据信用证的要求缮制如下单据。

有关资料：

发票号码	97 - 236 - 2298	发票日期	1997 年 12 月 24 日
提单号码	CANE103014	提单日期	1997 年 12 月 30 日
船名	PUSAN SENATOR	出口口岸	广州新风（5101）
装运港	广州港	商品编码	8201. 1000
外汇核销单号码	3445679	FORM A 号码	GZ8/80060/0010
保单号码	8897524	保险费	350 美元
运费	2 200 美元	杂费	150 美元
生产厂家	广东中山金辉农具厂	货物装箱情况	5 件/捆
净重	7. 20 千克/捆	毛重	7. 60 千克/捆
尺码	（64 × 18 × 11）厘米/捆	唛头	F. V. ART NO. 29099 F. V. ART NO. 22199
集装箱号码	1 × 20’ FCL HJCU874765 - 4 SEAL 05328		

Volksbank**Sc**… **rndorf**

MEMBER OF THE
GENO GROUP GERMANY

FAX MESSAGE

From:	Volksbank Schorndorf, Joh.-Phil.-Palm-Str. 39, D-73614 Schorndorf/Germany
To:	DG-Bank, Hong Kong/Hong Kong
Test:	[redacted] / USD 67.200.-- / 19.11.1997

Issue of a Documentary Credit

Kindly note that we hereby establish our **irrevocable** documentary Credit No. **4.1520**

Date of Issue	: November 18, 1997
Expiry Date	: January 18, 1998, Place: China
Applicant	: Freund Victoria Gartengeräte GmbH Stuttgarter Str. 4 D-73614 Schorndorf/Germany
Beneficiary	: Guangdong Machinery Import & Export Corporation (Group) 720 Dong Feng Road East Guangzhou / P.R. China
Amount	: USD 67.200,00 Say: US Dollars sixtyseventhousandtwohundred exactly
Available with/by	: Any bank by negotiation against the documents detailed herein and beneficiary's drafts at sight drawn on us under L/C-No. 4.1520 for 100 p.c. of the invoice value.
Partial Shipments	: Allowed
Transshipment	: Allowed
Loading in Charge	: China ports
For Transport to	: Rotterdam port by seafreight
Latest Date of Shipment	: January 3, 1998
Descript. of Goods	: 4.500 pcs. of Stainless Steel Spade Head S821/29099 USD 9,60 per pcs. 2.500 pcs. of Stainless Steel Spade Head F807/22199 USD 9,60 per pcs. according to Sales Contract No. A97DE23600256 dd. Nov. 12, 1997 and Fax Order dd. Oct.9, 1997/knr-sche. CIF Rotterdam (Incoterms 1990).
Documents required	: 1. Signed commercial invoice 3-fold 2. Full Set of Clean on board marine Bills of Lading, made out to order of Wim Bosman BV, P.O.Box 54064, NL-3008 JB Rotterdam, Netherlands. Marked: 'Freight Prepaid' Notify: Applicant (as indicated above)

1997年11月24日 上午

WE HEREBY CERTIFY THAT THIS IS THE TRUE PHOTOSTATIC COPY
For and on behalf of
DG BANK Deutsche Genossenschaftsbank
Hong Kong Branch

Authorized Signatures

印鉴核符

H:\AMIPR… DKUM… F… NDB.SAM

VolksbankSchorndorf

MEMBER OF THE
GENO GROUP GERMANY

L/C 4.1520
Page 2

LA05/15 7668

3. GSP Certificate of Origin, Form A, certifying goods of origin in China, issued by competent authorities
4. Packing-List, 3-fold
5. Insurance Policy/Certificate, issued to the applicant (as indicated above), covering risks as per 'Institute Cargo Clauses (A)', and 'Institute War Clauses (Cargo)' including Warehouse to Warehause Clause up to final destination at Schorndorf, for at least 110 pct of CIF-Value, marked: 'Premium Paid', showing claims if any payable in Germany, naming settling agent in Germany.

Additional Conditions	: If an amendment to that credit is not accepted by the beneficary the beneficiary's signed statement to that effect is required.
Details of Charges	: All banking charges outside the issuing bank are for account of beneficiary. USD 60,00 being our handling charges for documents not in conf. with L/C terms are also for account of beneficiary. The advising charges for the first Advising Bank for USD 80,-- will be deducted from proceeds upon payment.
Presentation Period	: Documents must be presented within 21 days after shipping date shown on B/L, but within the validity of the L/C.
Confirmation	: Without.
Instructions	: On receipt of complete set of documents in conformity with the terms and conditions of this credit, we will remit the proceeds following the instructions of the documents accompanying letter.
Additonal instructions	: Documents must be forwarded direct to us by courier service in one lot addressed to Volksbank Schorndorf, Joh.-Phil.-Palm-Str.39, D-73614 Schorndorf/Germany.

This message is the only operative instrument and no mail confirmation will follow.
Please acknowledge receipt.
This credit is subject to the Uniform Customs and Practice for Documentary Credits (1993 Revision), International Chamber of Commerce, Paris, Publication No. 500.

Regards
Volksbank Schorndorf
International Department
D-73614 Schorndorf

WE HEREBY CERTIFY THAT THIS IS THE TRUE PHOTOSTATIC COPY
For and on behalf of
DG BANK Deutsche Genossenschaftsbank
Hong Kong Branch

Authorized Signatures

印鉴核符 M

H:\A\ S\DKU\MAKK\FREUND8.SAM

F14

凭
Drawn under ....
信用证　　第　　号
L/C　　No. ....
日期　　年　　月　　日
dated ....

1

按　　息　　付　款
Payable with interest @ .... % per annum

号码　　汇票金额　　中国．广州　　年　　月　　日
No. .... **Exchange** for .... Guangzhou. China .... 19 ....

见票　　日后（本汇票之副本未付）付
At .... sight of this FIRST of Exchange (Second of exchange being unpaid)
pay to the order of .... 或其指定人

金　额
the sum of

此致
To: ....　　................................

广东省机械进出口（集团）公司

GUANGDONG MACHINERY IMPORT AND EXPORT CORP. (GROUP)

726 DONGFENG ROAD EAST, GUANGZHOU, CHINA

商 业 发 票

ORIGINAL

COMMERCIAL INVOICE

Messrs:

Invoice No. :
Invoice Date :
S/C No. :
L/C No. :
L/C Date :

Exporter:

Transport details:

Terms of payment:

Marks & numbers	Descrip. of goods	Quantity	Unit price	Amount

广东省机械进出口（集团）公司

GUANGDONG MACHINERY IMPORT AND EXPORT CORP. (GROUP)
726 DONGFENG ROAD EAST, GUANGZHOU, CHINA

装　箱　单
PACKING LIST

ORIGINAL

Exporter:

Date :
Invoice No. :
B/L No. :
S/C No. :
L/C No. :

Transport details:

标记 Marks & numbers	货名 Descrip. of goods	件数 Quantity	净重 N. W.	毛重 G. W.	尺码 Measurement

BILL OF LADING

Shipper

B/L No.

Combined Transport BILL OF LADING

Consignee

Notify Address

For delivery of goods please apply to :

Pre-carriage by

Place of Receipt

Ocean Vessel　Voy. No.

Port of Loading

Port of Discharge

Place of Delivery

Final Destination for the Merchant's Reference only

—Particulars Furnished by Merchants—

Container, Seal No. & Marks & Nos.	No. of Package & Description of Goods	Gross Weight Kgs	Measurement m^3

Freight & Charges	Revenue Tons.	Rate	Per	Prepaid	Collect

Ex. Rate:	Prepaid at	Payable at	Place and date of issue
	Total Prepaid	No. of Original B (s) /L	Stamp & Signature

LADEN ON BOARD THE VESSEL
Date
By································

(TERMS CONTINUED ON BACK HEREOF)

(KENWA STANDARD FORM 01)

Original

<table>
<tr><td colspan="3">1. Goods consigned from (Exporter's business name, address, county)</td><td colspan="3" rowspan="2">Reference No.

GENERALIZED SYSTEM OF PREFERENCES
CERTIFICATE OF ORIGIN
(Combined declaration and certificate)
FORM A
issued in THE PEOPLE'S REPUBLIC OF CHINA
(COUNTRY)
See Notes overleaf</td></tr>
<tr><td colspan="3">2. Goods consigned to (Consignee's name, address, country)</td></tr>
<tr><td colspan="3">3. Means of transport and route (as far as known)</td><td colspan="3">4. For official use</td></tr>
<tr><td>5. Item number</td><td>6. Marks and numbers of packages</td><td>7. Number and kind of packages; description of goods</td><td>8. Origin criterion (see Notes overleaf)</td><td>9. Gross weight or other quantity</td><td>10. Number and date of invoices</td></tr>
<tr><td colspan="3">11. Certification
It is hereby certified, on the basis of control carried out, that the declaration by the exporter is correct.

Place and date, signature and stamp of certifying authority</td><td colspan="3">12. Declaration by the exporter
The undersigned hereby declares that the above details and statements are correct; that all the goods were produced in
----
(country)
and that they comply with the origin requirements specified for those goods in the Generalized System of Preferences for goods exported to
----
(importing country)

Place and date, signature of authorized signatory</td></tr>
</table>

中保财产保险有限公司

PICC PROPERTY　The people's insurance (Property) Company of China, Ltd.

发票号码　　保险单号次
Invoice No.　　Policy No.

海 洋 货 物 运 输 保 险 单
MARINE CARGO TRANSPORTATION INSURANCE POLICY

被保险人：
Insured: ______________________________

中保财产保险有限公司（以下简称本公司）根据被保险人的要求，及其所缴付约定的保险费，按照本保险单承担险别和背面所载条款与下列特别条款承保下列货物运输保险，特签发本保险单。

This policy of Insurance witnesses that The People's Insurance (Property) Company of China, Ltd. (hereinafter called "The Company"), at the request of the Insured and in consideration of the agreed premium paid by the Insured, undertakes to insure the undermentioned goods in transportation subject to the conditions of this Policy as per the Clauses printed overleaf and other special clauses attached hereon.

保险货物项目 Descriptions of Goods	包装 单位 数量 Packing Unit Quantity	保险金额 Amount Insured

承 保 险 别　　　　货 物 标 记
Conditions　　　　Marks of Goods

总 保 险 金 额：
Total Amount Insured: ______________________________

保费　　载运输工具　　开航日期
Premium As arranged . Per conveyance S. S ________ Slg. on or abt ________

起运港　　目的港
From ________________ To ________________

所保货物，如发生本保险单项下可能引起索赔的损失或损坏，应立即通知本公司下述代理人查勘。如有索赔，应向本公司提交保险单正本（本保险单共有　份正本）及有关文件。如一份正本已用于索赔，其余正本则自动失效。

In the event of loss or damage which may result in a claim under this Policy, immediate notice must be given to the Company's Agent as mentioned hereunder. Claims, if any, one of the Original Policy which has been issued in　Original (s) together with the relevant documents shall be surrendered to the Company. If one of the Original Policy has been accomplished, the others to be void.

中保财产保险有限公司
THE PEOPLE'S INSURANCE (PROPERTY) COMPANY OF CHINA, LTD.

赔款偿付地点
Claim payable at ______________________________

日期　　在
Date ________________ at ________________

地址：
Address: ______________________________

强化提高三

下面是一份信用证和有关资料，请认真阅读信用证并根据信用证的要求缮制如下单据。

```
98OCT22  17:15:23                                      Logical Terminal P5A7
MT S700                 Issue of a Documentary Credit              Page 00001
                                                                   Func GZPRQ
MSGACK  DWS765I Auth OK, key B1980419F862E4A3, BKCHCNBJ SAIBJPJT record652333
Basic Header          F  01 BKCHCNBJA400 8954 778732
Application Header    O 700 1624 981022 SAIBJPJTCXXX 4970 776422 981022 1524 N
                                     *ASAHI BANK LTD, THE (FORMERLY THE
                                     *KYOWA SAITAMA BANK, LTD.)
                                     *TOKYO
User Header           Service Code     103:
                      Bank. Priority   113:
                      Msg User Ref.    108:
                      Info. from CI    115:
Sequence of Total     *27    : 1 / 1
Form of Doc. Credit   *40 A  : IRREVOCABLE
Doc. Credit Number    *20    : LC-410-046405
Date of Issue          31 C  : 981022
Expiry                *31 D  : Date 990115 Place CHINA
Applicant             *50    : SUMITOMO CORPORATION OSAKA.
Beneficiary           *59    : GUANGDONG YUE FENG TRADING CO.
                               NO.31 ZH .N AN ROAD GUANGZHOU,
                               CHINA.
Amount                *32 B  :            Currency USD Amount 98.000,00
Pos. / Neg. Tol.(%)    39 A  : 5  / 5
Available with/by     *41 D  : ANY BANK
                               BY NEGOTIATION
Drafts at ...          42 C  : DRAFTS AT SIGHT FOR FULL INVOICE
                               VALUE
Drawee                 42 A  : SAIBJPJT
                              *ASAHI BANK LTD, THE (FORMERLY THE
                              *KYOWA SAITAMA BANK, LTD.)
                              *TOKYO
Partial Shipments      43 P  : ALLOWED
Transshipment          43 T  : ALLOWED
Loading in Charge      44 A  :
                SHIPMENT FROM CHINESE MAIN PORT
For Transport to       44 B  :
                TO OSAKA, JAPAN
Latest Date of Ship.   44 C  : 981231
Descript. of Goods     45 A  :
                HALF DRIED PRUNE 1998CROP
                GRADE    SPEC                  QNTY  UNIT PRICE            SHIPMENT
                                              (CASE) (USD/CASE)
                  B    L:700CASE  M:700CASE  1,400     21.0  C AND F OSAKA  NOV.,1998
                  A    L:700CASE  M:700CASE  1,400     26.0  C AND F OSAKA  DEC.,1998
                  B    L:700CASE  M:700CASE  1,400     21.0  C AND F OSAKA  DEC.,1998
                PACKING:IN WOODEN CASE, 12KGS PER CASE
                TRADE TERMS: C AND F OSAKA
Documents required     46 A  :
                +2/3 SET OF CLEAN ON BOARD OCEAN BILLS OF LADING MADE OUT TO
                ORDER OF SHIPPER AND BLANK ENDORSED AND MARKED ''FREIGHT
                PREPAID'' AND ''NOTIFY SUMITOMO CORPORATION OSAKA.''
                +MANUALLY SIGNED COMMERCIAL INVOICE IN TRIPLICATE(3) INDICATING
                APPLICANT'S REF. NO. SCLI-98-0474.
                +PACKING LIST IN TRIPLICATE(3).
                +MANUALLY SIGNED CERTIFICATE OF ORIGIN IN TRIPLICATE(3).
                +BENEFICIARY'S CERTIFICATE STATING THAT CERTIFICATE OF
                MANUFACTURING PROCESS AND OF THE INGREDIENTS ISSUED BY GUANGDONG
                YUE FENG TRADING CO., SHOULD BE SENT TO SUMITOMO CORP ESCLZ
                SECTION.
                +CERTIFICATE OF WEIGHT AND QUALITY IN TRIPLICATE.
Additional Cond.       47 A  :
                1. INSURANCE TO BE EFFECTED BY BUYER.
                2. TELEGRAPHIC REIMBURSEMENT CLAIM PROHIBITED.
```

```
98OCT22   17:15:44                                     Logical Terminal P5A7
MT S700                Issue of a Documentary Credit              Page 00002
                                                                  Func GZPRQ
                   3. 1/3 ORIGINAL B/L AND OTHER SHIPPING DOCUMENTS MUST BE SENT
                      DIRECTRY TO APPLICANT SUMITOMO CORP ESCLZ SECTION IN 3DAYS
                      AFTER B/L DATE. AND SENT BY FAX.
                   4. AMOUNT AND QNTY 5PCT MORE OR LESS ALLOWED.
                   5. THIS COMMODITY FREE FROM RESIN.
Details of Charges    71 B : ALL BANKING CHARGES OUTSIDE JAPAN
                             ARE FOR ACCOUNT OF BENEFICIARY.
Presentation Pariod   48   : DOCUMENTS TO BE PRESENTED WITHIN 15
                             DAYS AFTER THE DATE OF SHIPMENT,
                             BUT WITHIN THE VALIDITY OF THE
                             CREDIT.
Confirmation         *49   : WITHOUT
Instructions          78   :
                  THE NEGOTIATING BANK MUST FORWARD THE DRAFTS AND ALL DOCUMENTS BY
                  REGISTERED AIRMAIL DIRECT TO US (INT'L OPERATIONS OFFICE MAIL
                  ADDRESS: C.P.O.BOX NO.800 TOKYO 100-8691 JAPAN) IN TWO
                  CONSECUTIVE LOTS. UPON RECEIPT OF THE DRAFTS AND DOCUMENTS IN
                  ORDER, WE WILL REMIT THE PROCEEDS AS INSTRUCTED BY THE
                  NEGOTIATING BANK.
Trailer                      Order is <MAC:> <FAC:> <ENC:> <CHK:> <TNG:> <PDE
                             MAC:9E9080D4
                             CHK:AEFC879BF339
```

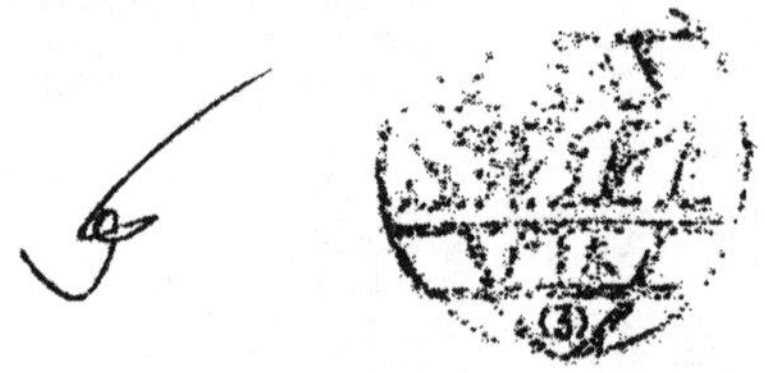

有关资料：（1998 年 12 月装运）

发票号码	98IN－C314	发票日期	1998 年 11 月 18 日
提单号码	GSOK30088	提单日期	1998 年 12 月 1 日
船名	CHANG GANG V. 98097H	托运日期	1998 年 11 月 18 日
装运港	广州港	出口报检日期	1998 年 11 月 22 日
出口核销单位代码	25112AB88－1	出口报关日期	1998 年 11 月 28 日
外汇核销单号码	4548056	FORM A 号码	GZ9/80070/0012
合同号码	YF98－29876	商品编码	0813.2000
运费	1 700 美元	杂费	120 美元
生产厂家	广州农垦丰华食品厂	出口口岸	广州海关（5100）
净重	12.00 千克/箱	毛重	14.00 千克/箱
尺码	（35×25×20）厘米/箱	唛头	GA NOS1－2800 OSAKA MADE IN CHINA
集装箱号码	2×20’ FCL TRIU1567537 SEAL 08133 KHLU6206867 SEAL 08134		

F14

凭
Drawn under ______________________
信用证　第　号
L/C　No. ______________
日期　年　月　日
dated ______________________

1

按　息　付　款
Payable with interest @ ____ % per annum

号码　汇票金额　中国．广州　年　月　日
No. ____________ **Exchange** for　Guangzhou. China ______ 19 ______

见票　日后（本汇票之副本未付）付
At __________ sight of this FIRST of Exchange (Second of exchange being unpaid)
pay to the order of ______________________________ 或其指定人

金　额
the sum of

此致
To: ______________　______________

广东省粤丰贸易公司

GUANGDONG YUEFENG TRADING CO.

NO. 31 ZHENAN ROAD GUANGZHOU, CHINA

商　业　发　票

ORIGINAL

COMMERCIAL INVOICE

Messrs:

Invoice No.　:
Invoice Date　:
L/C　No.　:

Exporter:

Transport details:

Terms of payment:

Marks & numbers	Descrip. of goods	Quantity	Unit price	Amount

广东省粤丰贸易公司

GUANGDONG YUEFENG TRADING CO.

NO. 31 ZHENAN ROAD GUANGZHOU, CHINA

装　箱　单

PACKING LIST

ORIGINAL

Exporter:

Invoice Date :

Invoice No. :

Transport details:

标记 Marks & numbers	货名 Descrip. of goods	件数 Quantity	净重 N. W.	毛重 G. W.	尺码 Measurement

BILL OF LADING

Shipper	B/L No.
	Combined Transport BILL OF LADING
Consignee	
Notify Address	For delivery of goods please apply to :

Pre-carriage by	Place of Receipt	
Ocean Vessel　Voy. No.	Port of Loading	
Port of Discharge	Place of Delivery	Final Destination for the Merchant's Reference only

—Particulars Furnished by Merchants—

Container, Seal No. & Marks & Nos.	No. of Package & Description of Goods	Gross Weight Kgs	Measurement m^3

Freight & Charges	Revenue Tons.	Rate	Per	Prepaid	Collect

Ex. Rate:	Prepaid at	Payable at	Place and date of issue
	Total Prepaid	No. of Original B (s) /L	Stamp & Signature

LADEN ON BOARD THE VESSEL
Date
By································

(TERMS CONTINUED ON BACK HEREOF)　　(KENWA STANDARD FORM 01)

Original

<table>
<tr><td colspan="2">1. Exporter</td><td colspan="3" rowspan="2">Certificate No.

CERTIFICATE OF ORIGIN
OF
THE PEOPLE'S REPUBLIC OF CHINA</td></tr>
<tr><td colspan="2">2. Consignee</td></tr>
<tr><td colspan="2">3. Means of transport and route</td><td colspan="3" rowspan="2">5. For certifying authority use only</td></tr>
<tr><td colspan="2">4. Country/region of destination</td></tr>
<tr><td>6. Marks and numbers</td><td>7. Number and kind of packages; description of goods</td><td>8. H. S. Code</td><td>9. Quantity</td><td>10. Number and date of invoices</td></tr>
<tr><td colspan="2">11. Declaration by the exporter
The undersigned hereby declares that the above details and statements are correct, that all the goods were produced in China and that they comply with the Rules of Origin of the People's Republic of China.

Place and date, signature and stamp of authorized signatory</td><td colspan="3">12. Certification
It is hereby certified that the declaration by the export is correct.

Place and date, signature of authorized signatory</td></tr>
</table>

广东省粤丰贸易公司

GUANGDONG YUEFENG TRADING CO.

NO. 31 ZHENAN ROAD GUANGZHOU, CHINA

CERTIFICATE OF MANUFACTURING PROCESS AND OF THE INGREDIENTS

ORIGINAL

To Messrs.

RE: Date :

Invoice No. :

L/C No. :

3053—②

客户交单联系单

致：中国银行

兹随附下列出口单据一套，信用证业务请按国际商会现行《跟单信用证统一惯例》办理，跟单托收业务请按国际商会现行《托收统一规则》办理。

信用证	开证行：		信用证号：	
	通知行号：	提单日期：	效期：	交单期限　　天
无证托收	付款人全名及详址：			
	代收行外文名称及详址（供参考）：			
	交单方式：（　）D/P　（　）D/P		付款期限：	
发票编号：		核销单编号：		金额：

单据	名称	汇票	发票	海关发票	装箱/重量单	产地证	GSP FORM A	数量/质量/重量证	检验/分析证	出口许可证	保险单	运输单据	电抄	受益人证明	船公司证明			

委办事项：（打“×”者）

（　）上述单据请按我司与贵行签订之总质押书办理押汇。

（　）上述单据系代理出口项下业务，收妥后请原币划____________________

（　）开户行：__________，账号：____________________

（　）若付款人拒绝付款/承兑，不必作成拒绝证书，但须以电传通知我司。

（　）附信用证及修改书共____________________纸。

（　）单据中有下列不符点：（　）请向开证行寄单，我司承担一切责任。

（　）请电询开证行同意后再寄单。

（　）____________________

（　）____________________

（　）____________________

公司联系人：　　　　联系电话：　　　　公司盖章：

银行审单记录：	银行接单日期：		
	索汇金额：		BP NO.
	寄单日期：		OC NO.
	银行费用	通知/保兑：	索汇方式：
		议/承/付：	
		邮　　费：	
		电　　传：	寄单方式：
		小　　计：	
	费用由　　　　承担		
退单记录：	银行经办：		银行复核：

中 国 外 运 广 东 公 司
出口货物托运单

提单编号________　托运日期________　托运单位编号________

合约编号________

船　名________　船期________　运往地点________

托 运 人________

收 货 人________

通　知________

标记及号码	件　数	货　名	重量（公斤）		容积吨
			净	毛	
合计			共重		

特约事项		

可否转船			（托运人盖章）		
可否分批		需要提单正本　份副本　份			
货物堆存地点		装船期限		结汇期限	
运费缴付方式		运费账单开送			
信用证号码		货价	F. O. B.	C. I. F.	
运往香港船名		实际装船日期			

运费吨：　运费率：　运费金额：

中华人民共和国海关
出境货物检验检疫申请

电子底账数据号：

申请单位（加盖公章）：　　　　　　　　　　　　　　　　＊编号：__________

申请单位登记号：　　　联系人：　　　电话：　　　申请日期：　　年　　月　　日

发货人	（中文）	
	（外文）	
收货人	（中文）	
	（外文）	

货物名称（中/外文）	H. S. 编码	产地	数/重量	货物总值	包装种类及数量

运输工具名称号码		贸易方式		货物存放地点	
合同号		信用证号		用途	
发货日期		输往国家（地区）		许可证/审批号	
启运地		到达口岸		生产单位注册号	
集装箱规格、数量及号码					

合同、信用证订立的检验检疫条款或特殊要求	标记及号码	随附单据（画“√”或补填）	
		□合同	□包装性能结果单
		□信用证	□许可/审批文件
		□发票	□
		□换证凭单	□
		□装箱单	□
		□厂检单	□

需要证单名称（画“√”或补填）		＊检验检疫费	
□品质证书　__正__副	□植物检疫证书　__正__副	总金额（元人民币）	
□重量证书　__正__副	□熏蒸/消毒证书　__正__副		
□数量证书　__正__副	□出境货物换证凭单　__正__副		
□兽医卫生证书　__正__副	□	计费人	
□健康证书　__正__副	□		
□卫生证书　__正__副	□	收费人	
□动物卫生证书　__正__副	□		

申请人郑重声明：	领取证单	
1. 本人被授权申请检验检疫。	日期	
2. 上列填写内容正确属实、货物无伪造或冒用他人的厂名、标志、认证标志，承担货物质量责任。		
签名：________	签名	

注：有“＊”号栏由海关填写。

中华人民共和国海关出口货物报关单

预录人编号：　　　　　　　　海关编号：

<table>
<tr><td>境内发货人</td><td colspan="2">出境关别</td><td colspan="2">出口日期</td><td colspan="2">申报日期</td><td>备案号</td></tr>
<tr><td>境外收货人</td><td colspan="2">运输方式</td><td colspan="2">运输工具名称及航次号</td><td colspan="3">提运单号</td></tr>
<tr><td>生产销售单位</td><td colspan="2">监管方式</td><td colspan="2">征免性质</td><td colspan="3">许可证号</td></tr>
<tr><td>合同协议号</td><td colspan="2">贸易国（地区）</td><td colspan="2">运抵国（地区）</td><td>指运港</td><td colspan="2">离境口岸</td></tr>
<tr><td>包装种类</td><td>件数</td><td>毛重（千克）</td><td>净重（千克）</td><td>成交方式</td><td>运费</td><td>保费</td><td>杂费</td></tr>
<tr><td colspan="8">随附单证及编号</td></tr>
<tr><td colspan="8">标记唛码及备注</td></tr>
<tr><td colspan="8">项号　商品编号　商品名称及规格型号　数量及单位　单价/总价/币制　原产国（地区）　最终目的国（地区）　境内货源地　征免</td></tr>
<tr><td colspan="8"></td></tr>
<tr><td colspan="8"></td></tr>
<tr><td colspan="8"></td></tr>
<tr><td colspan="8"></td></tr>
<tr><td colspan="8"></td></tr>
<tr><td colspan="8"></td></tr>
<tr><td colspan="8">特殊关系确认：　价格影响确认：　支付特许权使用费确认：　自报自缴：</td></tr>
<tr><td colspan="7">报关人员　报关人员证号　电话　兹申明对以上内容承担如实申报、依法纳税之法律责任
申报单位　　申报单位（签章）</td><td>海关批注及签章</td></tr>
</table>

实训模块十一　审　单

一、实训目的

本模块的实训，使学生了解审单的重要性及审单的主要内容。能依据合同、信用证和《UCP600》等国际惯例审核单据，并对单据的不符点进行修改。

二、实训任务

（1）根据合同、信用证和《UCP600》等国际惯例审核单据。
（2）根据信用证填写本笔业务需提交议付银行议付的各种单据份数。

三、实训提示

（一）结汇单据审核应考虑的主要问题

1. 商业发票

（1）单据名称是否与信用证的表述一致（如“商业发票”或“发票”）？
（2）商业发票的抬头人是否为信用证的开证人？
（3）商业发票的出票日期和号码是否漏填？出票日期是否迟于信用证规定的到期日？
（4）商业发票中货物的描述是否与信用证的要求相一致？
（5）商业发票是否列明合同或信用证规定的贸易术语？
（6）商业发票的总值大小写是否一致？含佣金或折扣是否按要求列明？
（7）商业发票的总值是否超过信用证规定的最高金额？
（8）信用证要求在商业发票内加列如船名、原产地等的声明文句，是否按要求一一详列？
（9）信用证要求商业发票手签时，是否按要求处理？
（10）商业发票的出票人是否为信用证的受益人？

2. 汇票

（1）采用信用证付款方式时，是否按信用证规定的出票条款填写？
（2）汇票的金额是否与商业发票的金额一致？
（3）汇票的金额是否超过信用证规定的金额？

（4）汇票的付款人是否误填为进口商？

（5）付款人的名称、地址是否填写齐备？

（6）出票人的名称、地址、签章是否齐备？

（7）汇票须背书时是否按合同或信用证的要求处理？

（8）汇票的出票日期是否在信用证规定的有效期内？

（9）采用托收付款方式时，是否填写该笔交易的商品名称和数量？

（10）采用托收付款方式时，是否填写该笔交易的合同号码？

3. 提单

（1）提单的类型是否符合信用证的要求（如要求提供已装船提单、直运提单或集装箱提单等）？

（2）提单的收货人、被通知人是否按信用证的要求填制？

（3）提单中的船名、航次是否具体完整？

（4）提单中的装运港、目的港及转运港是否填写正确？是否出现逻辑错误？

（5）提单中的运输包装数量是否错填为计价数量？包装数量是否与装箱单一致？计价数量是否与商业发票一致？

（6）提单是否有不良批注？

（7）FOB 出口成交时，提单是否错填为“运费预付”（FREIGHT PREPAID）？CFR 或 CIF 出口成交时，提单是否错填为“运费待付”（FREIGHT COLLECT）？

（8）提单日期是否迟于投保日期及信用证规定的最迟装运日期？

（9）提单是否需要背书？背书的类型是否符合信用证的要求？

（10）当出现提单内容更改时，更改处是否有提单签发人的签章？

4. 保险单

（1）被保险人是否按信用证的要求填写？

（2）保险金额是否已包含信用证或合同要求的投保加成部分？

（3）保险金额的大小写是否一致？

（4）保险金额货币单位是否与信用证一致？

（5）保险条款是否按信用证的要求填写？

（6）对舱面提单，保险单是否加保抛弃和浪击落海附加险？

（7）保险单中的船名、航次、装运港、目的港是否与提单相一致？

（8）保险单的份数是否与信用证或合同的要求一致？

（9）赔款偿付地点和投保地点是否混淆？

（10）保险单是否按要求背书？

5. 原产地证明书

（1）原产地证明书的类型是否按信用证或合同的要求出具（如一般原产地证明书或普惠制原产地证明书 FORM A）？

（2）签证机构是否符合信用证或合同的要求？

（3）一般原产地证明书或普惠制原产地证明书 FORM A 的第一项是否漏填了出口国的名称？

（4）一般原产地证明书或普惠制原产地证明书 FORM A 的第二项是否漏填了进口国的名称？

（5）原产地证明书第三项的填制规范是否符合要求？

（6）原产地证明书第七项的填制规范是否符合要求？

（7）一般原产地证明书第七项的包装数量和第九项的计价数量是否混淆？

（8）一般原产地证明书第八项商品编码的位数是否正确？

（9）普惠制原产地证明书 FORM A 第十二项的出口国和进口国是否错填为装运港和目的港？

（10）一般原产地证明书或普惠制原产地证明书 FORM A 的签发日期和申请日期是否出现逻辑错误（如签发日期早于申请日期）？

（二）《UCP600》对单据的部分要求

（1）除非信用证另有规定，只要单据注明为正本，如必要时，已加签字，银行也将接受下列方法制作或看来是按该方法制作的单据作为正本单据：①影印、自动或电脑处理；②复写。

（2）单据签字可以手签，也可用签样印制、穿孔签字、盖章、符号表示或其他任何机械或电子证实的方法处理。

（3）除非信用证另有规定，银行将接受标明副本字样或没有标明正本字样的单据作为副本单据，副本单据无须签字。

（4）如信用证要求多份单据，诸如“一式两份”“两张”“两份”等，可以提交一份正本，其余份数以副本来满足，但单据本身另有显示者除外。

（5）当要求提供运输单据、保险单据和商业发票以外的单据时，信用证中应规定该单据的出单人及其措辞或内容。如信用证对此未做规定，只要所提交单据的内容与提交的其他规定单据不矛盾，银行将接受此类单据。

（6）除非信用证另有规定，银行将接受出单日期早于信用证日期的单据，但该单据必须在信用证和本惯例规定的期限内提交。

四、实训内容

根据前面的实训模块，你已经帮张大同缮制好全套结汇单据，请你依据前面的合同、信用证和《UCP600》审核全套结汇单据，并填写本笔业务需提交议付银行议付的各种单据份数。

单据	名称	汇票	发票	海关发票	装箱/重量单	产地证	GSP FORM A	数量/质量/重量证	检验/分析证	出口许可证	保险单	运输单据	电抄	受益人证明	船公司证明			

五、强化提高

强化提高一

广东省外贸开发公司拟出口货物一批，并已按期装运，公司单证员制好全套单据，请你根据下面的信用证和给定的资料审核该套结汇单据，找出单据的不符点并进行修改。

Issue of a Documentary Credit

Sequence of Total	*27	: 1 / 1
Form of Doc. Credit	*40 A:	IRREVOCABLE TRANSFERABLE
Doc. Credit Number	*20	: 4785. 28
Date of Issue	31 C:	190710
Expiry	*31 D:	Date190926 Place CHINA
Applicant	*50	: BRUSSELS LACES AND GIFTS SERV. SA. RUE DE LUSAMBO. 21/23. 1190 BRUXELLES. BELGIUM
Beneficiary	*59	: GUANGDONG FOREIGN TRADE IMPORT AND EXPORT CORPERATION. 351 TIANHE ROAD GUANGZHOU, CHINA.
Amount	*32 B:	Currency USD Amount 21 200. 00
Pos. / Neg. Tol. (%)	39 A:	05 / 05
Available with/by	*41 D:	ANY BANK IN　CHINA BY NEGOTIATION
Drawee	42 A:	MMM COMMERCIAL　BANK 197RUE DE LUSAMBO, BELGIUM
Partial Shipments	43 P:	ALLOWED
Transshipment	43 T:	ALLOWED
Loading in Charge	44 A:	GUANGZHOU, CHINA
For Transport to...	44 B:	ANTWERP
Latest Date of Ship.	44 C:	190911
Descript. of Goods	45 A:	

HUCK FASTENING PRODUCTS

BOM – T20 – 12GA　4 000 PCS　@ USD 2. 80

BOM – F20 – 12GA　4 000 PCS　@ USD 2. 50

AS PER S/C NO. : GD – 98 – 23757 CFR ANTWERP,

FIVE PERCENT MORE OR LESS IN QUANTITY ALLOWED

Documents Required 46 A:

* MANUALLY SIGNED COMMERCIAL INVOICE IN TRIPLICATE. INDICATING THE B/L NO. AND THE CONTAINER NO.

* PACKING LIST IN TRIPLICATE, INDICATING THE NAME OF S. S.

* FULL SET CLEAN MULTIMODAL (COMBINED) TRANSPORT BILLS OF LADING PLUS 2 NON-NEGOTIABLE COPIES CONSIGNED TO ORDER OF MMM COMMERCIAL BANK MARKED NOTIFY APPLICANT. AND FREIGHT PREPAID, INDICATING THE L/C NO.

Additional Cond. 47 A:

AN ADDITIONAL FEE OF USD 30.00 OR EQUIVALENT WILL BE DEDUCTED FROM THE PROCEEDS PAID UNDER ANY DRAWING WHERE DOCUMENTS PRESENTED ARE FOUND NOT TO BE IN8888

STRICT CONFORMITY WITH THE TERMS OF THIS CREDIT.

DOCUMENTS MUST BE PRESENTED NOT LATER THAN 15 DAYS AFTER THE DATE OF SHIPMENT, BUT WITHIN THE VALIDITY OF THE CREDIT.

THIS TELETRANSMISSION IS THE OPERATIVE INSTRUMENT AND SUBJECT TO U. C. P. 1993 REVISION ICC PUBLICATION NO. 600 AND ENGAGES US IN ACCORDANCE WITH THE TERMS THEREOF.

Details of Charges 71 B: ALL FOREIGN BANK CHARGES ARE FOR THE ACCOUNT OF THE BENEFICIARY

Confirmation *49 : WITHOUT

Instructions 78 :

PLEASE FORWARD ALL DOCUMENTS TO MMM COMMERCIAL BANK

197RUE DE LUSAMBO, BELGIUM

UPON RECEIPT OF DOCUMENTS IN ORDER WE WILL REMIT IN ACCORDANCE WITH NEGOTIATING BANKS INSTRUCTIONS.

Send. To Rec. Info. 72 B 49 : MAIL ACKNOWLEDGEMENT OF THIS LETTER OF CREDIT AND/OR ANY SUBSEQUENT AMENDMENTS NOT REQUIRED.

Trailer Order is <MAC: > <PAC: > <ENC: > <CHK: > <TNG: > <PDE: >

MAC: B3DEFB51

CHK: 3D4F84D99341

发票日期	2019 年 9 月 5 日	发票号码	983057
提单日期	2019 年 9 月 15 日	提单号码	INTG432906
船名	KFTE / COSOT V. 0023C	转运港	香港
集装箱号码	1×40' FCL　INTU3889645	包装	50 PCS/ CTN
型号	毛重	净重	尺码
BOM－T20－12GA	5. 00 KGS/CTN	4. 00 KGS/CTN	(42×23×25) CM/CTN
BOM－F20－12GA	10. 00 KGS/CTN	8. 50 KGS/CTN	(55×30×34) CM/CTN
唛头	GDFT/ GD－98－23757/ ANTWERP		

Issuer

GUANGDONG FOREIGN TRADE IMPORT AND EXPORT CORPERATION.
351 TIANHE ROAD GUANGZHOU, CHINA.

COMMERCIAL　INVOICE

To
BRUSSELS LACES AND GIFTS SERV. SA.
RUE DE LUSAMBO. 21/23.
1190 BRUXELLES. BELGIUM

No.
983057

Date
SEP. 5, 2019

Transport details

FROM:　GUANGZHOU
W/T:　HONGKONG
TO:　ANTWERP
VESSEL:　KFTE / COSOT V. 0023C

S/C No.
GD－98－23757

L/C No.
4785. 28

Terms of payment
BY L/C

Marks and numbers	Number and kind of packages; Description of goods	Quantity	Unit price	Amount
GDFT GD－98－23757 ANTWERP	HUCK FASTENING PRODUCTS BOM－T20－12GA	4 000 PCS	@ USD 2. 80	USD 11 228. 00
	BOM-F20－12GB	4 000 PCS	@ USD 2. 50	USD 10 025. 00
		8 000 PCS	CFR ANTWERP	USD 21 253. 00

TOTAL QUANTITY: 8 000 PCS　　PACKING: 160 CARTONS
TOTAL WEIGHT : NET　WT. : 1 000. 00 KGS　　GROSS　WT. : 1 200. 00 KGS
TOTAL:　U. S. DOLLARS　TWENTY-TWO THOUSAND AND TWO HUNDRED ONLY.

GUANGDONG FOREIGN TRADE IMPORT AND EXPORT CORPERATION.
351 TIANHE ROAD GUANGZHOU, CHINA.
(签章)

Issuer GUANGDONG FOREIGN TRADE IMPORT AND EXPORT CORPERATION. 351 TIANHE ROAD GUANGZHOU, CHINA.	PACKING LIST	
To BRUSSELS LACES AND GIFTS SERV. SA. RUE DE LUSAMBO. 21/23. 1190 BRUXELLES. BELGIUM	No. 983057	Date SEP. 5, 2019

Marks and numbers　Description of goods　Number and kind of packages

GDFT	HUCK FASTENING PRODUCTS				
GD－98－23757	BOM－T20－12GA	81 CTNS	@4.00 KGS	@5.00 KGS	@(42×23×25) CM×80
ANTWERP			320.00 KGS	400.00 KGS	=1.932 CBMS
	HUCK FASTENING PRODUCTS				
	BOM－F20－12GA	81 CTNS	@8.50 KGS	@10.00 KGS	@(55×30×34) CM×80
			680.00 KGS	800.00 KGS	=4.420 CBMS
		162 CTNS	1 000.00 KGS	1 200.00 KGS	6.42 CBMS

TOTAL QUANTITY: 8 000 PCS　PACKING: 162 CARTONS

TOTAL: ONE HUNDRED AND SIXTY CARTONS ONLY.

GUANGDONG FOREIGN TRADE IMPORT AND
EXPORT CORPERATION.
351 TIANHE ROAD GUANGZHOU, CHINA.
（签章）

Consignor

GUANGDONG FOREIGN TRADE IMPORT AND EXPORT CORPERATION.
351 TIANHE ROAD GUANGZHOU, CHINA.

FBL

No. INTG432906	Countr Code. HK

NEGOTIABLE FIATA
MULTIMODAL TRANSPORT
BILL OF LADING
Issued subject to UNCTAD/ICC Rules for Multimodal Transport Documents (ICC publication 481).

Consigned to order of
BRUSSELS LACES AND GIFTS SERV. SA.
RUE DE LUSAMBO. 21/23.
1190 BRUXELLES. BELGIUM

INTERGROUP
SHIPPING (ASIA) LTD.

Notify address

BRUSSELS LACES AND GIFTS SERV. SA.
RUE DE LUSAMBO. 21/23.
1190 BRUXELLES. BELGIUM

3 Floor, Block 2 Tien Chu Centre.
1E Mok Cheong Street,
Tokwawan, KowLoon, Hong Kong.
Tel: (852) 2760 8872
P. O. Box 20445
Hennessy Road Post Office
Fax: (852) 2760 8442
Telex: 43429 INGRO HX
Cable Address: HKINGROUP

	Place of receipt
Ocean vessel KFTE / COSOT V. 0023C	Port of loading ANTWERP
Port of discharge GUANGZHOU	Place of delivery

LICENCE NO.

Marks and numbers	Number and kind of packages	Description of goods	Gross weight	Measurement
GDFT GD－98－23757 ANTWERP	160 CARTONS	HUCK FASTENING PRODUCTS	1 200. 00 KGS	6. 42 CBM

1 * 40' FCL
INTU3889645

TOTAL: ONE HUNDRED AND SIXTY CARTONS ONLY.

FREIGHT COLLECT

ORIGINAL

according to the declaration of the consignor

Declaration of Interest the consignor In timely delivery (Clause 6. 2.)	Declared value for ad valorem rate according to The declaration of the consignor (Clauses 7 and 8).

The goods and instructions are accepted and dealt with subject to the Standard Conditions printed overleaf.
Taken in charge in apparent good order and condition, unless otherwise noted herein, at the place of receipt for transport and delivery as mentioned above.
One of these Multimodal Transport Bills of Lading must be surrendered duly endorsed in exchange for the goods. In Witness whereof the original Multimodal
Transport Bills of Lading all of this tenor and date have been signed in the number stated below, one of which being accomplished the other (s) to be void.

Freight amount	Freight payable at	Place and date of issue ANTWERP, SEPT. 15, 2019
Cargo Insurance through the undersigned ☐ not covered ☐ Covered according to attached Policy	Number of Original FBL's THREE	Stamp and signature

强化提高二

（一）商业发票审核

广东省轻工家电有限公司与香港 ABC 公司达成一笔出口交易。卖方按期开来即期不可撤销跟单信用证，买方也于 2018 年 2 月 8 日开出商业发票。请根据下面信用证提供的内容审核并修改商业发票。

香港南洋商业银行

致：广东省轻工家电有限公司

日期：2018 年 2 月 4 日
信用证号：472/818
金额：USD 155 000.00
通知行：广州中国银行

敬启者：

兹开立不可撤销之信用证以贵公司为受益人，开证人为香港 ABC 贸易公司，总金额为壹拾伍万伍千美元整，由受益人开具即期汇票以香港南洋商业银行为付款人，支取 100% 发票金额之货款并随附下列单据：

1. 手签商业发票一式二份
2. 保险单包括平安险及战争险按 110% 发票金额投保
3. 全套洁净“已装船”提单，作成“凭指定”（to order）并“空白背书”（endorsed in bank）列明货物自贵埠运至新加坡，注明“运费付讫”通知开证人船名、数量及装运日期之电报副本证明装运下列货物：

50 台灯架（Lamp Holder）型号为 W1052/55874 每台美元 3 100（按销货确认书 JT126 号）CIF 新加坡

分批装运：允许分批装运　转运：不允许转运

装运日期不得迟于　2018 - 3 - 28

交单日期：2018 - 4 - 15　广州

特别条款：金额及数量可增减 5%

凡根据本信用证并按照其所列条款开出之汇票，如及时提出敝行同意对其出票人、背书人及善意持有人履行付款责任。

本证受国际商会 1994 年修订之跟单信用证统一惯例 600 号出版物约束。

香港南洋商业银行

广东省轻工家电有限公司

GUANGDONG LIGHT ELECTRICAL APPLIANCES COMPANY LIMITED

52, DEZHENG ROAD SOUTH GUANGZHOU, CHINA

商业发票
COMMERCIAL　INVOICE

MESSRS:

ABC TRADE CO.,
NO. 80, MOSQUE ROAD, HONGKONG.

INVOICE NO.　: 98DSP3298

INVOICE DATE　: FEB. 8, 2018

L/C　NO.　: 002/9803

EXPORTER:

GUANGDONG　LIGHT ELECTRICAL
APPLIANCES COMPANY LIMITED.

TRANSPORT DETAILS:

FROM　GUANGZHOU TO SINGAPORE
W/T　HONG KONG　BY VESSEL

TERMS　OF　PAYMENT:

BY　L/C

MARKS	DESCRIPTION OF GOODS	QUANTITY	UNIT PRICE	AMOUNT
N/M	LAMP HOLDERS	500 PCS	@ USD 3 100.00	USD 155 000.00
		500 PCS		USD 155 000.00

TOTAL QUANTITY: 50 PCS PACKING: 50 CTNS

TOTAL : U. S. Dollars ONE HUNDRED AND FIFTY FIVE THOUSAND ONLY.

GUANGDONG LIGHT ELECTRICAL
APPLIANCES COMPANY LIMITED

（二）FORM A 审核

广东省东风进出口公司（GUANGDONG DONGFENG IMPORT AND EXPORT CORP. 122 DONGFENG ROAD EAST, GUANGZHOU.）与 SANYEI HONG KONG 14/F., KAISER ESTATE 1, MAN YUE STREET, HUNG HOM, SYDNEY, AUSTRALIA 达成一笔交易，内容主要有：2 400 件不锈钢铲头（STAINLESS STEEL SPADE HEAD），每 12 件扎成 1 捆，2019 年 12 月 1 日出运，该公司填制好如下 FORM A，请审核并修改。

Original

<table>
<tr><td colspan="3">1. Goods consigned from (Exporter's business name, address, county)

GUANGDONG MACHINERY IMPORT AND
EXPORT CORP.
122 DONGFENG ROAD EAST, GUANGZHOU</td><td colspan="3" rowspan="2">Reference No. GZ9/12078/6311

GENERALIZED SYSTEM OF PREFERENCES
CERTIFICATE OF ORIGIN
(Combined declaration and certificate)

FORM A

issued in THE PEOPLE'S REPUBLIC OF CHINA
(COUNTRY)
See notes overleaf</td></tr>
<tr><td colspan="3">2. Goods consigned to (Consignee's name, address, country)

SANYEI HONG KONG
14/F., KAISER ESTATE 1, MAN YUE STREET,
HUNG HOM, SYDNEY</td></tr>
<tr><td colspan="3">3. Means of transport and route (as far as known)

ON/AFTER DEC. 01, 2020
FROM GUANGZHOU TO SYDNEY BY VESSEL</td><td colspan="3">4. For official use</td></tr>
<tr><td>5. Item number</td><td>6. Marks and numbers of packages</td><td>7. Number and kind of packages; description of goods</td><td>8. Origin criterion (see notes overleaf)</td><td>9. Gross weight or other quantity</td><td>10. Number and date of invoices</td></tr>
<tr><td>1</td><td>KMART
SYDNEY
NO. 1 - 200</td><td>TWO THOUSAND FOUR HUNDRED (2400) PCS OF
STAINLESS STEEL SPADE HEAD
***</td><td>"P"</td><td>2 400 PCS</td><td>YSM199901
NOV. 11,
2019</td></tr>
<tr><td colspan="3">11. Certification
It is hereby certified, on the basis of control carried out, that the declaration by the exporter is correct.

GUANGZHOU NOV. 21, 2019
Place and date, signature and stamp of certifying authority</td><td colspan="3">12. Declaration by the exporter
The undersigned hereby declares that the above details and statements are correct; that all the goods were produced in
GUANGZHOU
(country)
and that they comply with the origin requirements specified for those goods in the Generalized System of Preferences for goods exported to
SYDNEY
(importing country)
GUANGZHOU NOV. 20, 2019
Place and date, signature of authorized signatory</td></tr>
</table>

（三）海运提单审核

广东省荣华贸易有限公司与法国巴黎 ABC 公司成交一笔出口交易。ABC 公司按期开来信用证，荣华公司按期出运，并填制好海运提单，请根据下面信用证提供的内容审核及修改海运提单。

ISSUING BANK	:	METITA BANK LTD. FIN-00020 METITA
Term of Doc. Credit	:	IRREVOCABLE
Credit Number	:	LRT9802457
Date of Issue	:	190505
Expiry	:	Date 190716 Place CHINA
Applicant	:	A. B. C. CORP. AKEKSANTERINK AUTO P. O. BOX 9, FINLAND
Beneficiary	:	GUANGDONG RONGHUA TRADE CO. LTD. 168, DEZHENG ROAD SOUTH, GUANGZHOU, CHINA
Amount	:	Currency USD Amount 36 480. 00 (SAY U. S. DOLLARS THIRTY SIX THOUSAND FOUR HUNDRED AND EIGHTY ONLY)
Pos. / Neg. Tol. (%)	:	5/5
Available with/by	:	ANY BANK IN ADVISING COUNTRY BY NEGOTIATION
Partial Shipments	:	NOT ALLOWED
Transhipment	:	ALLOWED
Loading in Charge	:	GUANGZHOU
For Transport to	:	HELSINKI
Shipment Period	:	AT THE LATEST JULY 16, 2019
Descrip. of Goods	:	9 600 PCS OF WOMEN'S SWEATERS
UNIT PRICE	:	USD 3. 80/PC, PACKING: 12 PCS/CTN OTHER DETAILS AS PER S/C NO. 98 SGQ468001 CFR HELSINKI
Documents Required	:	* FULL SET OF CLEAN ON BOARD MARINE BILLS OF LADING, MADE OUT TO ORDER OF METITA BANK LTD, FINLAND, MARKED "FREIGHT PREPAID" AND NOTIFY APPLICANT (AS INDICATE ABOVE)
Additional Cond.	:	1. T. T. REIMBURSEMENT IS PROHIBITED. 2. ALL DOCUMENTS MUST BE MARKED THE S/C NO. AND L/C NO. 3. SHIPPING MARKS: ABC/HELSINKI/NO. 1 - 800

……

相关资料：

出运日期：2019 年 5 月 20 日　　总毛重：13 600. 00 千克　　总尺码：15 立方米

BILL OF LADING

Shipper
GUANGDONG RONGHUA TRADE CO., LTD.
168, DEZHENG ROAD SOUTH, GUANGZHOU, CHINA.

B/L No. KEN－98－25401

Combined Transport BILL OF LADING
RECEIVED in apparent good order and condition except as otherwise noted the total number of containers or other packages or units enumerated below for transportation from the place of receipt to the place of delivery subject to the terms and conditions hereof. One of the Bills of Lading must be surrendered duly endorsed to the Carrier by or on behalf of the Holder of the Bill of Lading, the rights and liabilities arising in accordance with the terms and conditions hereof shall, without prejudice to any rule of common law or statute rendering them binding on the Merchant, become binding in all respects between the Carrier and the Holder of the Bill of Lading as though the contract evidenced hereby had been made between them. IN WITNESS whereof the number of original Bills of Lading stated under have been signed. All of this tenor and date, one of which being accomplished, the other (s) to be void.

Consignee
A. B. C. CORP.
AKEKSANTERINK AUTO
P. O. BOX 9, FINLAND

Notify Address
METITA BANK LTD.
FIN－00020 METITA, FINLAND

For delivery of goods please apply to:

Pre-carriage by	Place of Receipt
Ocean Vessel　Voy. No DONGFANGHONG/SUISUN 103	Port of Loading GUANGZHOU

Port of Discharge	Place of Delivery	Final Destination for the Merchant's Reference only
HELSINKI VIA HONG KONG		

—Particulars Furnished by Merchants—

Container, Seal No. & Marks & Nos.	No. of Package & Description of Goods	Gross Weight Kgs	Measurement m^3
N/M	800 CTNS WOMENS SWEATERS TOTAL: EIGHT HUNDRED CARTONS ONLY.	13 600.00 KGS FREIGHT COLLECT	15M³

FREIGHT & CHARGES	Revenue Tons.	Rate	Per	Prepaid	Collect

Ex. Rate:	Prepaid at	Payable at	Place and date of issue GUANGZHOU MAY. 20, 2019
	Total Prepaid	No. of Original B (s) /L THREE (3)	Stamp & Signature

LADEN ON BOARD THE VESSEL
Date

By ________________

强化提高三

请你根据下面的信用证审核该套结汇单据，指出单据中的不符点并进行修改。

GUANGZHOU INT'L FINANCIAL BUILDING.
197 DengFengXi Road, Guangzhou,
P. R. China

中国银行 广东省分行
BANK OF CHINA
GUANGDONG BRANCH
GUANGZHOU, CHINA

ORIGINAL

信 用 证 通 知 书

通知日：JULY 23, 2018
我行号码：DN4007896T02

致：省茶叶
CHINA TUHSU GUANGDONG
TEA IMP. & EXP. CORP.

开 证 行：
DEUTDEHH DEUTSCHE BANK
AG HANBURG

转 递 行：

信用证号：6005729745H3
开证日期：180722
本证页数（不包面函）：
我行费用负担：Beneficiary Account

金额：DEM 31 428.00
来证方式：Full SWIFT/Telex
我行是否加保：Unnecessary

敬启者：

兹通知贵司，我行收自上述银行的信用证一份，现随附通知，并请注意下列打“X”条文：

( ) 该行首次来证，请慎重处理。
( ) 此证如需加保，请与我行联系。
( ) 此证尚未生效，请切勿出货。
( ) 此证印押未符，请切勿出货。

注意事项：

1. 贵司交单时，请将信用证及通知书一并提示；
2. 我行保兑信用证，限向我行交单议付，否则保兑无效；
3. 非我行保兑信用证，不构成我行任何责任；
4. 费用由受益人负担时，对我行客户，我行会主动借记其账，收取我行费用；
5. 请注意我行对信用证中有关条款的提示。

贵司负担费用：
通知费：CNY 200.00
保兑费：CNY
预先通知费：CNY
电报费：CNY

备注：

中 国 银 行 广 东 省 分 行 具
FOR BANK OF CHINA GUANGDONG BRANCH

下列项目仅供我行使用：
ADV-CHG：USD
CONFIRM：USD
PRE-ADV：USD
TLS-CHG：USD
($)

2018JUL22　　　　　　　　　　　　　　　　　　　Logical Terminal　GDPF
MT S700　　　　Issue of a Documentary Credit　　　　Page　00001
　　　　　　　　　　　　　　　　　　　　　　　　　Func　JSRVPR1

User Header	Service Code			103:
	Bank Priority			113:
	Msg User Ref.			108:
	Info. From CI			115:
Sequence of Total	*27		:	1 / 1
Form of Doc. Credit	*40	A	:	IRREVOCABLE
Doc. Credit Number	*20		:	6005729745H3
Date of Issue	31	C	:	180722
Expiry	*31	D	:	970915 PLACE CHINA
Applicant	*50		:	TEA COMPANY LIMITED, HAMBURG 345 GREEN TREE STREET, HAMBURG
Beneficiary	*59		:	CHINA TUHSU GUANGDONG TEA IMP. & EXP. CORP. 351 TIANHE ROAD, GUANGZHOU, CHINA
Amount	*32	B	:	EUR 31 428. 00 (DEUTSCHE MARK THIRTY ONE THOUSAND FOUR HUNDRED AND TWENTY EIGHT ONLY.)
Pos. / Neg. Tol. (%)	39	A	:	03 / 03
Available with/by	*41	D	:	ANY BANK BY NEGOTIATION AGAINST THE DOCUMENTS DETAILED HEREIN AND BENEFICIARY´S DRAFT AT 30 DAYS SIGHT DRAWN ON US UNDER L/C NO. 60057 + 9745H3 FOR 100 P. C. OF THE INVOICE VALUE.
Drawee	42	D	:	DEUTDEHH DEUTSCHE BANK AG HANBURG
Partial Shipments	43	P	:	Not Allowed
Transhipment	43	T	:	Allowed
Loading in Charge	44	A	:	CHINA PORTS
For Transport to…	44	B	:	HAMBURG
Shipment Period	44	C	:	AT THE LATEST AUG. 31, 2018
Descript. of Goods	45	A	:	

4439 CHINA BLACK TEA ABT. 8000KGS @ EUR 4. 05/KG CIFC3% HAMBURG
(1 × 20' FCL/200 PAPERSACKS)
PACKED IN PAPERSACKS, PALLETIZED AND CONTAINERIZED AS PER THE
SALES CONFIRMATION NO. BT7095
THE PRICE IS TO BE UNDERSTOOD PER KILO NET SHIPPED WEIGHT
CIF HAMBURG LESS 3 PERCENT COMISSION.

Documents required	46	A	:	

+ SIGNED COMMERCIAL INVOICE IN 4 – FOLD.

+CERTIFICATE OF WEIGHT IN 4－FOLD.
+FULL SET OF CLEAN ON BOARD MARINE BILLS OF LADING, MADE OUT TO ORDER, MARKED "FREIGHT PREPAID" AND NOTIFY APPLICANT.
+GSP CERTIFICATE OF ORIGIN FORM A, CERTIFYING GOODS OF ORIGIN IN CHINA, ISSUED BY COMPETENT AUTHORITIES.
+INSURANCE POLICY/CERTIFICATE COVERING ALL RISKS AND WAR RISK, INCLUDING WAREHOUSE TO WAREHOUSE CLAUSE, ISSUED FOR AT LEAST 110 PCT OF CIF－VALUE.

2018JUL22　　Issue of a Documentary Credit　　Logical Terminal　GDPF
MT S700　　Page　00002
Func　JSRVPR1

Addition Cond.　47 A :
IF BILLS OF LADIGN ARE REQUIRED ABOVE, PLEASE FORWARD DOCUMENTS IN TWO MAILS, ORIGINALS SEND BY COURIER AND DUPLICATES BY REGISTERED AIRMAIL.

Details of Charges　71 B :　BANK CHARGES EXCLUDING ISSUING BANKS ARE FOR ACCOUNT OF BENEFICIARY.

Presentation Period　48 :　DOCUMENTS TO BE PRESENTED WITHIN 15 DAYS FROM SHIPMENT DATE

Confirmation　*49 :　WITHOUT

Instructions　78 :
DISCREPANT DOCUMENTS, IF ACCEPTABLE, WILL BE SUBJECT TO A CISCREPANCY HANDLING FEE OF USD 50.00 OR EQUIVALENT WHICH WILL BE FOR ACCOUNT OF BENEFICIARY.
SPECIAL NOTE: ISSUING BANK WILL DISCOUNT ACCEPTANCES ON REQUEST, FOR A/C OF BENEFICIARY (UNLESS OTHERWISE STATED) AT APPROPRIATE LIBOR RATE PLUS 1.00 PER CENT MARGIN.

Send. To Rec. Info.　72 :　THIS CREDIT IS ISSUED SUBJECT TO 1993 REVISION, I. C. C. PUBLICATIONS NO. 600

Trailer　　Order is <MAC:><PAC:><ENC:><CHK:><TNG:><PDE:>
MAC: ID20750E
CHK: 5034662F74BC

相关资料：

发票号码	GDT－03Y2988	发票日期	2018.08.11	FORM A 号码	GZ7/80067/0159
船　名	SUISU/SENTOR V. 001	产品原材料情况	完全自产品	集装箱号码	TEXU3730336/20'
装运港	GUAGNZHOU	转运港	香港	总尺码	24 CBM
提单号码	GSG03－723858	提单日期	2018.08.23	保险单号码	PC200178141
单位毛重	40.7 KGS/PAPERSACK		单位净重	40.00 KGS/PAPERSACK	
唛头	H&L/HAMBURG/NO.1－200		包装	200 PAPERSACK	

F14

凭
Drawn under DEULDEHH DEUTSCHE BANK AG. , HAMBURG
信用证 第 号
L/C No. 6005729745H3
日期 年 月 日
dated 22 JULY, 2018

按 息 付 款
Payable with interest @ % per annum

号码 汇票金额 中国. 广州 年 月 日
No. **Exchange** *for* EUR 31 428. 00 Guangzhou. China 20

见票 日 后(本 汇 票 之 副 本 未 付) 付
At * * * * * * sight of this FIRST of Exchange (Second of exchange being unpaid)
pay to the order of BANK OF CHINA, GUANGZHOU 或其指定人

金 额
the sum of EUROPEAN DOLLARS THIRTY ONE THOUSAND FOUR HUNDRED AND TWENTY EIGHT ONLY.

此致
To DEULDEHH DEUTSCHE BANK AG. HAMBURG

CHINA TUHSU GUANGDONG TEA IMP. & EXP. CORP.
351 TIANHE ROAD, GUANGZHOU, CHINA
(签章)

中国土畜广东茶叶进出口公司

China Tuchu Guangdong Tea Imp. & Exp. Corp.

351 TianHe Road, Guangzhou, China

商业发票

COMMERCIAL INVOICE

ORIGINAL

Messrs:

HAALSSEN & LYON GMBH
PICKHUBEN
20447 HAMBURG

INVOICE NO. : GDT－03Y2988
INVOICE DATE : AUG. 11, 2018
L/C NO. : 6005729745H3
S/C NO. : BT7095

Transport details:

FROM GUANGZHOU TO HAMBURG
VIA HONGKONGBY SEA

Terms of payment:

L/C AT SIGHT

Marks & Numbers	Description Of Goods	Quantity	Unit Price	Amount
H&L HAMBURG NO. 1－200	4439 CHINA BLACK TEA	8 000 KGS	@ EUR 4. 05	EUR 32 400. 00
				CIF HAMBRUG EUR 31 428. 00

TOTAL QUANTITY: 8 000 KGS PACKING: 200 PAPERSACKS
TOTAL WEIGHT: N. W. : 8 000 KGS G. W. : 8 140 KGS
TOTALEUROPEAN DOLLARS THIRTY ONE THOUSAND FOUR HUNDRED AND TWENTY EIGHT ONLY.
PACKING: IN PAPERSACKS, PALLETIZED AND CONTAINERIZED INTO 1 ×20' FCL.

CHINA TUSHU GUANGDONG TEA
IMP. & EXP. CORP.
（签章）

中国土畜广东茶叶进出口公司

China Tuchu Guangdong Tea Imp. & Exp. Corp.

351 TianHe Road, Guangzhou, China

CERTIFICATE OF WEIGHT

ORIGINAL

No.: GDT－03Y2988

Date: AUG. 11, 2018

L/C No.: 6005729745H3

Shipping Marks	Quantities & Descriptions of Goods	Net Weight	Gross Weight
H&L	4439 CHINA BLACK TEA		
HAMBURG	200 PAPERSACKS	40 KGS/PAPERSACK	40.7 KGS/PAPERSACK
NO. 1－200		8 000 KGS	8 140 KGS
	TOTAL	8 000 KGS	8 140 KGS

TOTAL　EIGHT THOUSAND KGS ONLY.

CHINA TUSHU GUANGDONG TEA
IMP. & EXP. CORP.

Original

1. Goods consigned from (Exporter's business name, address, country) CHINA TUSHU GUANGDONG TEA IMP. & EXP. CORP. 351 TIANHE ROAD, GUANGZHOU, CHINA	Reference No. GZ7/80067/0159 GENERALIZED SYSTEM OF PREFERENCES CERTIFICATE OF ORIGIN (Combined declaration and certificate) FORM A issued in THE PEOPLE'S REPUBLIC OF CHINA (COUNTRY) See notes overleaf
2. Goods consigned to (Consignee's name, address, country) HALSSEN & LYON GMBH PICKHUBEN 20447 HAMBURG	
3. Means of transport and route (as far as known) ON/AFTER AUGUST 11, 2018 FROM GUANGZHOU TO HAMBURG BY VESSEL	4. For official use

5. Item num-ber	6. Marks and numbers of packages	7. Number and kind of packages; description of goods	8. Origin criterion (see notes overleaf)	9. Gross weight or other quantity	10. Number and date of invoices
01	H&L HAMBURG NO. 1 – 200	(8000) EIGHT THOUSAND KGS OF 4439 CHINA BLACK TEA **********************************	"P"	8 140 KGS	TA7149 AUG. 11, 2018

11. Certification	12. Declaration by the export
It is hereby certified, on the basis of control carried out, that the declaration by the exporter is correct. GUANGZHOU, AUG. 14, 2018 Place and date, signature and stamp of certifying authority	The undersigned hereby declares that the above details and statements are correct; that all the goods were produced in CHINA (country) and that they comply with the origin requirements specified for those goods in the Generalized System of Preferences for goods exported to GERMANY (importing country) GUANGZHOU, AUG. 13, 2018 Place and date, signature of authorized signatory

BILL OF LADING

Shipper CHINA TUSHU GUANGDONG TEA IMP. & EXP. CORP. 351 TIANHE ROAD, GUANGZHOU, CHINA	B/L No. GSG03 – 723858
Consignee TO ORDER	Combined Transport BILL OF LADING RECEIVED in apparent good order and condition except as otherwise noted the total number of containers or other packages or units enumerated below for transportation from the place of receipt to the place of delivery subject to the terms and conditions hereof. One of the Bills of Lading must be surrendered duly endorsed to the Carrier by or on behalf of the Holder of the Bill of Lading, the rights and liabilities arising in accordance with the terms and conditions hereof shall, without prejudice to any rule of common law or statute rendering them binding on the Merchant, become binding in all respects between the Carrier and the Holder of the Bill of Lading as though the contract evidenced hereby had been made between them. IN WITNESS whereof the number of original Bills of Lading stated under have been signed. All of this tenor and date, one of which being accomplished, the other (s) to be void.
Notify Address TEA COMPANY LIMITED, HAMBURG 345 GREEN TREE STREET, HAMBURG.	For delivery of goods please apply to:

Pre-carriage by	Place of receipt	
Ocean Vessel Voy. No SUISU/ SENTOR V. 001	Port of Loading GUANGZHOU	
Port of Discharge HAMBURG	Place of Delivery	Final Destination for the Merchant's Reference only

—Particulars Furnished by Merchants—

Container, Seal No. & Marks & Nos.	No. of Package & Description of Goods	Gross Weight Kgs	Measurement m^3
H&L HAMBURG NO. 1 – 200 TEXU3730336/20′	200 PAPERSACKS 4439 CHINA BLACK TEA FREIGHT PREPAID TOTAL TWO HUNDRED PAPERSACKS ONLY.	8 140 KGS	24

FREIGHT & CHARGES	Revenue Tons.	Rate	Per	Prepaid	Collect

Ex. Rate:	Prepaid at	Payable at	Place and date of issue GUANGZHOU, AUG. 23, 2018
	Total Prepaid	No. of Original B (s) /L TWO	Stamp & Signature

LADEN ON BOARD THE VESSEL
Date
By……………………………

(TERMS CONTINUED ON BACK HEREOF) (KENWA STANDARD FORM 01)

实训模块十二　出口核算

一、实训目的

通过本模块的实训，提高学生的出口核算能力，学生能进行成本核算、盈亏核算、价格换算、运费核算和保险费核算。

二、实训任务

（1）根据有关资料计算出口进货价款（含增值税）、出口退税额、办公费用、其他费用、出口总成本。

（2）根据有关资料计算保险费、出口外汇净收入、出口人民币净收入、出口商品换汇成本、盈亏率。

三、实训提示

（一）成本核算

1. 出口总成本

出口总成本是指出口商品的进货成本加上出口前的一切费用和税金。出口总成本所包含的费用是在出口前所产生的，包括公司办公费、运杂费、银行费（包括议付费、通知费和寄单费等）、报关费、报检费、单证费等。如果出口进货价款已包含增值税，国家对该产品的出口有退税的，出口总成本还应减去出口退税额。

$$\text{出口总成本}=\text{出口进货价款（含增值税）}+\text{出口前费用}-\text{出口退税额}$$

2. 出口商品换汇成本

出口商品换汇成本是指以某种商品的出口总成本与出口销售外汇净收入之比，得出用多少元人民币换回一美元。出口商品换汇成本如高于银行的外汇牌价，则出口为亏损，反之，则出口有盈利。其计算公式如下：

$$\text{出口商品换汇成本}=\frac{\text{出口总成本（元人民币）}}{\text{出口销售外汇净收入（美元）}}$$

3. 出口退税额

对有进出口经营权的外贸企业收购货物直接出口或委托其他外贸企业代理出口货物

的，应依据购进出口货物所取得的增值税专用发票上列明的销售额和该货物使用的退税率计算退税。其公式是：

$$出口退税额 = \frac{出口进货价款（含增值税）}{1 + 增值税率} \times 出口退税率$$

（二）盈亏核算

1. 出口销售外汇净收入

出口销售外汇净收入和出口销售人民币净收入都与 FOB 价有密切联系。

2. 出口商品盈亏率

出口商品盈亏率是指出口商品盈亏额与出口总成本的比率。出口商品盈亏额是指出口销售人民币净收入与出口总成本的差额，前者大于后者为盈利；反之，为亏损。其计算公式如下：

$$出口商品盈亏率 = \frac{出口销售人民币净收入 - 出口总成本}{出口总成本} \times 100\%$$

（三）价格换算

1. FOB、CFR 和 CIF 的换算

$$CIF = \frac{FOB + 海运运费}{1 - 投保加成 \times 保险费率}$$

该公式已包括了 FOB、CFR 和 CIF 的换算。注意投保加成与保险加成率的区别。

2. 佣金（折扣）换算

$$净价 = 含佣价 \times （1 - 佣金率）$$

$$净价 = 含折扣价 \times （1 - 折扣率）$$

（四）运费核算

1. 杂货班轮运费的计算

班轮运费由基本运费和附加运费两部分组成。基本运费是指货物从装运港到目的港所应收取的费用，其中包括货物在港口的装卸费用，它是构成全程运费的主要组成部分。其计算标准主要有以下六种：

（1）按货物的毛重计收，即以重量吨收取。重量吨为公吨、长吨或短吨，视船公司采用公制、英制或美制而定。按此方法计费者，在班轮运价表中商品名称后面注有“W”字样。

（2）按货物的体积计收，即以尺码吨收取。尺码吨为立方米或立方英尺。前者为公制，后者为英制，视船公司采用何种度量衡制度而定。按此方法计费者，在班轮运价表中商品名称后面注有“M”字样。

（3）按货物的价格计收，即以有关货物的 FOB 总价值按一定的百分比收取。按此方法计费者，在班轮运价表中商品名称后面注有“A. V.”或“Ad. Val”字样，也称从价运费。

（4）按收费较高者计收，即以重量吨、尺码吨（W/M）两者或以重量吨、尺码吨、

货物的价格（W/M or A. V.）三者中，选择较高者收费。此外，还有以重量吨、尺码吨两者中，选择较高者收费后，另加收一定百分比的从价运费。

（5）按货物的件数计收。

（6）大宗商品交易下，由船、货双方议定。

附加费是指针对某些特定情况或需要作特殊处理的货物而在基本运费之外加收的费用。附加费名目繁多，主要有超重附加费、超长附加费、直航附加费、转船附加费、港口拥挤附加费、选港附加费等。

班轮运费 = 商品数量 × 计费标准 × 基本运费 ×（1 + 各种附加费率之和）

2. 集装箱班轮运费的计算

集装箱班轮运费可分为基本运费和附加运费。其基本运费的计算方法有：

（1）对具体的航线按货物的等级和不同的计费标准来计算基本运费。

（2）对具体航线按货物等级及巷型、尺寸的包箱费率，或仅按箱型、尺寸的包箱费率而不考虑货物种类和级别计算基本运费。采用包箱费率计算集装箱基本运费时，只需要根据具体航线、货物等级以及箱型、尺寸所规定的费率乘以箱数即可。

集装箱班轮运输中的附加费与杂货班轮运输中的情况相似。但实践中有时会将基本运费和附加费合并在一起，以包干费（all in freight）的形式计收运费。此时称为包干费率，又称“全包价”（all in rate，A. I. R.）。

（五）保险费核算

保险金额是保险公司赔偿的最高金额，即当承保货物在运输途中发生了承保范围的风险时，保险公司给予的最高金额的赔偿。保险费则是投保人在向保险公司办埋手续时，保险公司根据其承保范围的大小按一定的保险费率，向投保人收取的费用。保险金额和保险费的计算公式是：

保险金额 = CIF（或 CIP）总值 × 110%

保险费 = CIF（或 CIP）总值 × 110% × 保险费率

四、实训内容

（一）整理跟单流程表

张大同以时间为顺序登记本笔业务的各个环节，请你替张大同填写如下的跟单流程表。

业务环节	日期
签订合同	
催证	
申请开证	
开证行开证	
通知行通知	
要求改证	
开证行改证	
办理托运	
出口报检	
出口报关	
投保	
装运	
制单，交单结汇	

（二）业务核算

张大同根据该笔业务，列出如下有关成本和费用数据，请你代张大同核算有关项目。

业务数据汇总表

编号：001

单位或部门	广东中山威威照明有限公司	合同号码	98SGQ468001
业务员	张大同	签约日期	2021. 11. 15
买方	法国巴黎 Le Vernet 贸易有限公司	信用证号码	LRT9802457
商品进货价	威威牌节能灯 LY－5W－A50　110V 5W　E27/B22　RMB 2. 00/只 LY－5W－A60　110V 7W　E27/B22　RMB 2. 50/只 （商品进货价包含 17% 增值税）		
出口成交价	威威牌节能灯 LY－5W－A50　110V 5W　E27/B22　29 000 只　每只 0. 45 美元 LY－7W－A60　110V 7W　E27/B22　29 000 只　每只 0. 55 美元 贸易术语：CIF 勒阿弗尔		
装箱情况	包装：箱包装，每箱 100 只 纸箱规格：63 厘米×32 厘米×24 厘米 纸箱净重：每箱 2. 4 千克 纸箱毛重：每箱 4. 5 千克		
运费	每 40 英尺集装箱 3 850 美元（CY/CY，不含码头费和拖车至仓库费用）		
保费率	平安险：0. 25%		
拖车费、报关费、码头费	中山工厂至广州港：2 500 元人民币		
公司办公费用	每出口创汇 1 美元扣 0. 30 元人民币计算		
开证通知费	200 元人民币		
改证通知费	100 元人民币		
议付费率	0. 125%（元人民币）		
退税率	13%		
汇率	100 美元＝687. 78～689. 88 元人民币		

1．出口进货价款（含增值税）

2．出口退税额

3．保险费

4．出口外汇净收入

5．出口人民币净收入

6．办公费用

7．其他费用

8．出口总成本

9．出口商品换汇成本

10．盈亏率

五、强化提高

强化提高一

广州浪声贸易有限公司与日本 BBF 有限公司达成一笔出口交易，出口 4 680 双“健康”牌运动鞋，型号 JK－42－XL，22.5 美元/双 CFR 东京即期不可撤销信用证付款。其他条件如下：

1. 国内购货价（含 17% 增值税）：

商品货名	型号、规格	数量（双）	单价（元人民币/双）
“健康”牌运动鞋	JK－42－XL	4 680	120.00

2. 包装：12 双/箱，全部货物装一个 20’集装箱。
3. 净重：20 千克/箱　毛重：25 千克/箱　尺码：(90×50×35) 厘米/箱
4. 保险费率：0.50%
5. 办公费：按外汇净收入中每 1 美元扣 0.30 元人民币计算
6. 出口退税率：15%
7. 汇率：1 美元＝6.877 8～6.898 8 元人民币
8. 开证通知费：200 元人民币
9. 议付费率：0.125%
10. 拖车费，报关费和码头费合计：2 000 元人民币
11. 运费：880 美元/20’集装箱

请根据以上条件，核算如下内容：
1. 出口进货价款（含增值税）
2. 出口退税额
3. 出口外汇净收入
4. 出口人民币净收入
5. 议付费
6. 办公费用
7. 出口前其他费用
8. 出口总成本
9. 出口商品换汇成本
10. 盈亏率
11. 若买方要求将价格改报为 CIFRC 5% 东京，广州浪声贸易有限公司应报何价？

强化提高二

广州金果贸易有限公司与英国 ABC 有限公司达成一笔出口交易，出口 8 000 件电子节能灯架，其中，型号 22W/B22 共 4 000 件，2.5 美元/件 CIF 伦敦，型号 32W/B22 共 4 000 件，3.0 美元/件 CIF 伦敦，即期不可撤销信用证付款。其他条件如下：

1. 国内购货价（含 17% 增值税）：

商品货名	型号、规格	数量（件）	单价（元人民币/件）
电子节能灯架	22W/B22	4 000	16.00
	32W/B22	4 000	20.00

2. 包装：10 件/箱，全部货物装一个 20’ 集装箱。
3. 净重：24 千克/箱　毛重：30 千克/箱　尺码：(75 × 30 × 30) 厘米/箱
4. 保险费率：一切险：0.50%，战争险、罢工险：0.30%
5. 办公费：按外汇净收入中每 1 美元扣 0.30 元人民币计算
6. 出口退税率：13%
7. 汇率：1 美元 = 6.877 8 ~ 6.898 8 元人民币
8. 开证通知费：200 元人民币
9. 议付费率：0.125%
10. 拖车费，报关费和码头费合计：2 500 元人民币
11. 运费：2 680 美元/20’ 集装箱

请根据以上条件，核算如下内容：

1. 出口进货价款（含增值税）
2. 出口退税额
3. 保险费
4. 出口外汇净收入
5. 出口人民币净收入
6. 议付费
7. 办公费用
8. 出口前其他费用
9. 出口总成本
10. 出口商品换汇成本
11. 盈亏率
12. 若买方要求将价格改报为 FOBC 3% 广州，广州金果贸易有限公司应报何价？

强化提高三

广东粮油食品进出口公司与加拿大枫叶有限公司达成一笔出口交易，出口200公吨中国丝苗大米，规格 Moisture：1% max. Impurities：1% max. Breakage Rate：5% max. 316.6 欧元/公吨 FOBC 3%广州，即期不可撤销信用证付款。其他条件如下：

1. 国内购货价（含9%增值税）：

商品货名	型号、规格	数量（公吨）	单价（元人民币/公吨）
中国丝苗大米	Moisture：1% max. Impurities：1% max. Breakage Rate：5% max.	200	2 800.00

2. 包装：100千克/麻布袋
3. 保险费率：平安险：0.50%，战争险、罢工险：0.35%，大米保险加费费率：0.35%
4. 办公费：按外汇净收入中每1美元扣0.15元人民币计算
5. 出口退税率：7%
6. 汇率：1欧元＝10.152 8～10.171 4元人民币；1美元＝0.811 4欧元（中间价）
7. 开证通知费：200元人民币
8. 议付费率：0.125%
9. 拖车费，报关费和码头费合计：20 000元人民币
10. 运费：按“W”计费，每运费吨80美元

请根据以上条件，核算如下内容：
1. 出口进货价款（含增值税）
2. 出口退税额
3. 保险费
4. 出口外汇净收入
5. 出口人民币净收入
6. 议付费
7. 办公费用
8. 出口前其他费用
9. 出口总成本
10. 出口商品换汇成本
11. 盈亏率
12. 若买方要求将价格改报为CIFC 5%蒙特雷尔，广东粮油食品进出口公司应报何价？

参考文献

1. 黎孝先. 国际贸易实务［M］. 北京：对外经济贸易大学出版社，1994.

2. 全国国际商务专业人员职业资格考试指定用书编委会. 国际商务基础理论与实务［M］. 北京：中国对外经济贸易出版社，2003.

3. 余世明. 国际商务单证实务［M］. 8 版. 广州：暨南大学出版社，2020.

4. 余世明. 国际贸易实务及案例［M］. 广州：暨南大学出版社，2020.

5. 余世明，等. 国际商务模拟实习教程［M］. 4 版. 广州：暨南大学出版社，2013.

6. 全国外贸中等专业学校教材编写组. 对外经贸英语函电［M］. 北京：对外经济贸易大学出版社，2000.

7. 王乃彦. 外贸英语口语［M］. 北京：对外经济贸易大学出版社，2000.

8. 刘洪，陈祥国. 商务英语听说［M］. 北京：对外经济贸易大学出版社，2002.